TRANSGENDER IN THE POST-YUGOSLAV SPACE

Lives, Activisms, Culture

Edited by
Bojan Bilić, Iwo Nord, and Aleksa Milanović

With a foreword by
Agatha Milan Đurić

First published in Great Britain in 2022 by

Policy Press, an imprint of
Bristol University Press
University of Bristol
1–9 Old Park Hill
Bristol
BS2 8BB
UK
t: +44 (0)117 374 6645
e: bup-info@bristol.ac.uk

Details of international sales and distribution partners are available at bristoluniversitypress.co.uk

© Bristol University Press 2022

British Library Cataloguing in Publication Data
A catalogue record for this book is available from the British Library

ISBN 978-1-4473-6761-1 hardcover
ISBN 978-1-4473-6762-8 ePub
ISBN 978-1-4473-6763-5 ePdf

The right of Bojan Bilić, Iwo Nord, and Aleksa Milanović to be identified as editors of this work has been asserted by them in accordance with the Copyright, Designs and Patents Act 1988.

Cover design: Andrew Corbet
Front cover image: Performance *Masks* by Asocijacija Spektra; Kolašin, Montenegro, September 2019; Courtesy of Miloš Vujović
Bristol University Press use environmentally responsible print partners.
Printed and bound in Great Britain by CPI Group (UK) Ltd, Croydon, CR0 4YY

FSC
www.fsc.org
MIX
Paper from
responsible sources
FSC® C013604

Contents

Notes on contributors   v
Acknowledgements   viii
Foreword by Agatha Milan Đurić   ix

Introduction: In post-Yugoslav trans worlds   1
    Bojan Bilić, Iwo Nord, and Aleksa Milanović

PART I **Lives**
1   Transgender lives in North Macedonia: citizenship, violence,   23
    and networks of support
    Slavcho Dimitrov

2   The resilience of trans existence through solidarity in   40
    Montenegro: (non)pathologising narratives of transgender lives
    Jovan Ulićević and Čarna Brković

3   Transgender and non-binary persons, mental health, and   59
    gender binarism in Serbia
    Jelena Vidić and Bojan Bilić

PART II **Activisms**
4   From survival to activism: tracing trans history in Kosovo   97
    from the 1970s onwards
    Lura Limani

5   Tortuous paths towards trans futures: the trans movement in   133
    Slovenia
    Martin Gramc

6   (Post)socialist gender troubles: transphobia in Serbian leftist   155
    activism
    Bojan Bilić

PART III **Culture**
7   Trans artivism in the post-Yugoslav space: resistance and   179
    inclusion strategies in action
    Aleksa Milanović

8   'The truth is what is in the body': an interview with Aleks Zain   196
     Slađana Branković

9   Queering sevdah: gender-nonconformity in the traditional   208
     music of Bosnia and Herzegovina
     Tea Hadžiristić

Index   227

Notes on contributors

Bojan Bilić is a psychologist and political sociologist doing research on feminist and LGBTQ activisms, the anthropology of non-heterosexual sexualities and gender variance as well as the initiatives for democratising psychiatry in the post-Yugoslav space. He is Lise Meitner Fellow at the Research Unit Gender Studies, Faculty of Philosophy and Education, University of Vienna, Adjunct Professor of Gender and Social Movements in South East Europe at the School of Political Sciences, University of Bologna, and a visiting lecturer at the University of Sarajevo Center for Interdisciplinary Studies. Bojan is the founder of the *Queering YU Network*, an informal collective of scholars and activists which explores the history and politics of (post-)Yugoslav queer engagement.

Slađana Branković holds an MA degree in Theory of Culture and Gender Studies from the University of Belgrade. Branković is currently a PhD candidate in the Sociology Department, Justus Liebig University, in Giessen, Germany, and a scholarship holder of the Hans Böckler Foundation. They engage with subjects of naturalisation of Western sex/gender regimes, discursive strategies in intersex advocacy, and intersex representation in visual arts.

Čarna Brković is Lecturer at the Institute for Cultural Anthropology and European Ethnology at the University of Göttingen. She holds a PhD in Social Anthropology from the University of Manchester and a graduate degree in Ethnology and Anthropology from the University of Belgrade. She has won a Wenner Gren Engaged Research grant to study gender and moral reasoning together with trans people in Montenegro.

Slavcho Dimitrov is a PhD candidate at the Department for Multidisciplinary Studies of Contemporary Arts and Media at Singidunum University in Belgrade. He holds an MA in Multidisciplinary Gender Studies from Cambridge University and an MA in Philosophy and Gender at the Euro-Balkan Institute, Skopje, North Macedonia. He is the founder of the international Summer School for Sexualities, Cultures, and Politics and one of the founders of the Research Center for Cultures, Politics, and Identities (IPAK.Center) in Belgrade. He is also a year-long curator of the Skopje Pride Weekend, a festival of queer arts, culture, and theory. In his theoretical and research practice his focus is set on political philosophy, cultural, gender and queer theory, embodiment and affects, aesthetics, social choreography, and performance studies. In 2020 he received the Igor Zabel Award grant.

Agatha Milan Đurić is an activist from Belgrade, Serbia. After graduating from the University of Belgrade Faculty of Drama Arts, she became active in Arkadija, the first Serbian organisation for gay and lesbian rights as well as in other peace activist groups. She worked at the School for Children with Blindness or Visual Impairment and the Roma Cultural Centre. She is the founder of Geten (formerly Gayten-LGBT) and the LGBTIQ Helpline, which were the first organisations to support trans people and LGBTIQ Roma in Serbia. She was one of the organisers of the 2001 Belgrade Pride and a co-author of the first Serbian LGBTIQ radio show Gayming. She is recognised as the first Serbian drag queen trans queer performer known as Viva la Diva.

Martin Gramc is a PhD candidate at the Institute of Biomedical Ethics and the History of Medicine at the University of Zürich. They are researching the collaboration and ethics of multidisciplinary healthcare teams working in the field of intersex care. They hold a master's degree in sociology from the Faculty of Social Sciences, University of Ljubljana, and are affiliated with the Ljubljana-based Peace Institute. They have been involved in activist initiatives against injustice in the post-socialist Yugoslav space.

Tea Hadžiristić is a researcher and policy analyst who has written on world politics, history, and gender in Southeastern Europe. She holds an MSc in International Relations Theory from the London School of Economics, and an HBA in International Relations and Political Science from the University of Toronto. She lives and works in Toronto.

Lura Limani is a researcher, editor, and activist. She worked as the editor-in-chief of *Prishtina Insight*, an online magazine produced by BIRN Kosovo. She holds an MA in cultural studies from the University of Freiburg and studied sociology and philosophy at the University of Prishtina and New York University. Previously, she was a fellow at the Institute for the Study of Human Rights at Columbia University in New York. Limani's work has been published in *Prishtina Insight*, *Balkan Insight*, *Osservatorio Balcani e Caucaso*, *Fabrikzeitung*, and so on. Limani is one of the founders of the Kosovo Oral History Initiative, an archive of life stories of people of Kosovo, and the independent literary magazine *Lirindja*.

Aleksa Milanović is Assistant Professor at the Faculty of Media and Communications in Belgrade and the author of *Representation of Transgender Identities in Visual Arts* (2015, in Serbian) and *Media Construction of Other Body* (2019, in Serbian). He holds a PhD in Transdisciplinary Studies of Contemporary Arts and Media from Singidunum University in Belgrade and an MA degree in Theory of Arts and Media from the University of Arts in Belgrade. He is engaged in scientific research work in which he mainly deals with body studies and gender studies in the field of transgender and queer studies, theorising the discourse of different, non-normative genders by analysing representations of transgender and other gender bodies within mass media, visual arts, and popular culture. He has been involved in activism since 2008, when he volunteered for numerous activist organisations and informal activist groups working to promote LGBTI rights. He participated in the founding of the Trans Network Balkan in 2014, as well as the Kolektiv Talas TIRV (Collective Wave TIGV) in 2020. He is currently an Arts and Culture Coordinator in the Trans Network Balkan.

Iwo Nord is based in Stockholm as Lecturer in Gender and Transgender Studies at DIS Study Abroad in Scandinavia. He is also a PhD candidate and teacher in Gender Studies at Södertörn University, with affiliation to the Center for Baltic and East European Studies. His doctoral project ethnographically explores Belgrade as a transnational destination for gender-affirming surgery. He has participated in strengthening Transgender Studies in the Nordic region and was one of the founders of Trans Fest Stockholm, an activist organisation that creates cultural and community events. He is committed to working transnationally and transregionally and is involved in trans academic and activist collaborations both in the Nordic and the former Yugoslav space.

Jovan Ulićević is a biologist and trans activist from Montenegro. He is one of the founders of Association Spektra, an organisation working on the advancement of human rights of trans, gender diverse, and intersex persons in Montenegro, where he is working as a director, as well as Trans Network Balkan, a regional trans and intersex organisation, where he is a coordinator for regional capacity building. Jovan is a member of the Organisational Board of Montenegro Pride. His work is focused on equality and social justice, using feminist, intersectional, and community-based perspective.

Jelena Vidić is a psychologist and psychotherapist. She holds a PhD in Psychology from the Faculty of Philosophy, University of Belgrade. She is a coordinator for psychological support, research, and training within Geten, a Belgrade-based centre for LGBTIQA human rights. She also works as an individual and group psychotherapist in private practice. In the past 15 years she has worked on various projects in the domain of psychosocial support and mental health, mainly with different marginalised groups, and as a teacher. Her work is grounded in feminism and gender-affirmative approach.

Acknowledgements

While working on this volume, we were occasionally surprised by how much could be accomplished with practically no other resources than the strength of our commitment to each other and to our common vision of a more inclusive world. With this in mind, we were inspired by and grateful for the perseverance with which our authors stuck to our book as we rode the emotional roller coaster of the protracted and all-embracing corona times. Our desire for this volume to see the light of the day and the strength of our belief in the importance of writing ultimately prevailed over the innumerable – and sometimes particularly taxing – vicissitudes that we lived in the course of the last three years.

We would also like to thank our reviewers for supporting our proposal, as well as Shannon Kneis and Anna Richardson, our editors at Bristol University Press/Policy Press, and Annie Rose of Newgen Publishing UK, for accompanying us with patience and generosity through the production process.

Foreword:
The Yellow Brick Road of trans queer survival in Yugoslavia and after

Agatha Milan Đurić

> It's always best to start at the beginning –
> and all you do is follow the Yellow Brick Road.
>> Glinda, the Good Witch of Oz

The editors of this pioneering volume asked me to provide a text in which I would reflect upon my life. So here I offer a few contours of its developmental trajectory: I start with my childhood years, which I spent living like Dorothy in a world without a name, a language, or a possibility for understanding myself and the feeling of being 'trapped in permanent trauma'. I then move towards my activist engagement throughout the war-torn 1990s and the dissolution of Yugoslavia, and end by going around that sense of isolation and multiple oppressions in contemporary Serbia and the wider region that are still, to a great extent, marked by an authoritarian political culture.

I write this text with the aim of giving voice to my unquenchable desire for a trans queer life, one that I have been living in spite of the potent matrix of cis-heteronormative hegemony that forced me to explore and connect sexual and gender subcultures, immerse myself in gender-related studies, and unyieldingly look for those with whom I could share my political commitments and concerns. This has meant opening up the space for those – trans, intersex, queer – whose intricate and painful lives were almost completely unknown because their existence disturbed the entrenched binary categories of gender identity upon which social life has rested for a lot of time.

Ever since my earliest childhood I felt that I was 'different' from the majority of children who surrounded me, that something about me was not 'right' but could not be easily captured by words. It was not only the question of whether I was attracted to dolls (which I indeed was, mostly using them for my tiny puppetry that helped me to transform and circumvent the reality of perpetual family violence) rather than to balls or plastic pistols that were then considered typical boys' toys. Years would pass before I realised that the feeling of 'being the only one in the world' afflicted many children and not only those belonging to the LGBTIQ+ spectrum. Growing up in the 1980s in socialist Yugoslavia was for me little more than a dense sequence of traumatic episodes, which I normalised by saying to myself: 'I deserve it all for being something totally wrong.'

As I failed to adapt to the expected gender roles, violence was an omnipresent element of my life – it was there in my family and at school colouring all forms of social interaction. To leave home meant encountering physical and psychological oppression, but staying at home also supplied me with its proper share of cruelty. Going to school equalled exposing myself to threats and harassment inevitably accompanied by guilt, shame, and fear that paralysed me strengthening my idea that I was solely responsible for bringing that calamity upon myself. The power of destructive messages that are so deeply inscribed in our bodies and psyche is devastating and can be condensed in one crucial, reverberating statement: 'I must not and should not exist!' I was overwhelmed by the conviction that everything I was, did, or expressed was deeply wrong – every movement, look, word, or thought …

Nevertheless, in spite of the violent surroundings, there was a resilient force within me that continued to thrive and look for ways to show itself to the world. With a few school mates I set up a theatre where we performed shows and concerts (we had, for example, our own Eurovision contest) and in which I always sang, acted, or impersonated female characters. When I think about this now, after so many years, one question keeps imposing itself on my mind – how could I even think of something like that given all the bullying that I had been subjected to, which our performances only stimulated and multiplied. Throughout the Yugoslav 1980s it was virtually impossible to see or even to believe that people like me existed, so it was enormously important to come across the very first identification models. As I became more familiar with Western popular culture, figures like David Bowie, Boy George, Annie Lennox, punk bands, certain filmmakers, writers, and books played such an important role in encouraging me to accept myself and go on living regardless of patriarchal dichotomies and oppressions.

Once in high school I started discovering literature about queer subculture and stumbled upon *Second Serve*, a book and a film about a trans woman, which was a fundamental element in the process of my self-awareness expansion (Richards and Ames, 1983). This was followed by the stories of Christine Jorgensen, Lili Elbe, and others who helped me access the worlds which I had not known existed. In the later years of this period, I was influenced by my Psychology teacher Maja Kandido-Jakšić (1995) and her doctoral thesis *Androginy as a Mental Health Model* in which she explored the historical and socio-psychological aspects of the culturally prescribed and rigidly enforced binary gender roles and convincingly argued about their negative impact on mental health.

Activism and *trans*formation

During my studies at the Faculty of Dramatic Arts and Faculty of Philosophy in Belgrade I read the journal *Potkulture*, which brought some of the first texts about homosexuality as well as about the work of Magnus Hirschfeld and thus represented another island of meaning in what looked like a widespread conspiracy of silence about sexual and gender non-normativity. In the beginning of the 1990s, Maja Kandido-Jakšić introduced me to the well-known surgeon Sava Perović and his team, which had been already working on gender affirmation surgeries (or – as they used to call them – sex change surgeries). On one occasion on which Dr Perović was receiving an award, Maja publicly spoke about compulsory cis-heteronormativity, the failure to acknowledge gender as a spectrum, and the constraining of trans people to undergo surgical interventions even if they did not want to do so (see Vidić and Bilić, this volume). It is striking that this famous surgeon openly spoke about his homophobia and I myself, albeit in the later stages of my activist engagement, frequently wrote about his exploitative work and his team's abuse of trans people.

The dissolution of Yugoslavia and the wars on the territory of our common country, accompanied by a strong rise of nationalism and militarism, were disastrous experiences. The thought of serving in the army and being potentially drafted was unbearable, so I decided to join peace organisations with which I participated in many protests against the Milošević regime (Bilić, 2012). At that time I also worked at a school for blind and visually impaired children and at the Romani cultural centre and I often wondered about whether I would have had access to children and refugees if I had been open about my gender identity. Such dilemmas started creating a painful fissure in me: mechanisms of exhaustion, giving up on myself and my own feelings for the sake of being accepted into the predominantly cis-heterosexual settings. Sara Ahmed's (2014) idea of 'sweaty concepts' nicely captures that kind of difficulty that for the most part remains invisible to those belonging to the dominant group.

During the years marked by an armed conflict that was tearing apart the Yugoslav space, Vjeran Miladinović Merlinka, who identified as both gay and crossdresser, became more publicly visible, especially through Želimir Žilnik's 1995 film *Marble Ass*. In a documentary manner, that film, in which Merlinka plays the lead role, portrays homosexual and trans existence in Serbia at the time pointing to the problems of violence, marginalisation, rejection, and lack of choice. In such circumstances, sex work was often the only option for survival and a source of income, but it also, as the film underlines, led to new cycles of stigmatisation and violence. It should not be forgotten that Merlinka was one of the participants in the first public debate about homosexuality which took place at the Belgrade Youth Centre (Dom omladine) in 1986 (Živković, 2005).

One of the watershed moments in my activist life was a discovery of the interview with Dejan Nebrigić, which was published in the early 1990s. There Dejan spoke openly about himself as a gay man as well as about his activist work in various spheres, especially in *Arkadija*, the first Serbian organisation dedicated to the affirmation of gay and lesbian culture. In 1993 I met some members of that group and timidly joined them while at the same time attending the programme of the Centre for Women's Studies. *Arkadija*'s goals, debates, and publications were primarily oriented towards gay and lesbian rights, decriminalisation, and depathologisation of homosexuality. It was clear that the organisation's focus had to do with non-heterosexuality; however, I felt a strong need for more inclusivity of people who do not see themselves in the gender binary matrix and do not have sexuality as the primary focus. That meant, sometimes, unfortunately a new series of challenging and painful moments, microaggressions, and conflicts of values and political views that surfaced when I brought up the question about the inclusion of trans people in our work. To one such enquiry, a well-known lesbian activist asked me when I expressed the need for trans inclusion: "And what would we need them for?" Upon stating that I identified as a gender queer person, I would sometimes be told: "What is that even supposed to mean? You cannot have an identity of an ant!" Many of us felt on our skin the heavy burdens of LGBTIQ+ 'otherism', of that complex dynamic that often guides the operation of the 'community' traversed by numerous lines of distinction and differentiation (Gramc, this volume).

Although not formally extinguished, Arkadija withered away in 2000, but it served as a platform for further activist engagement by generating two organisations: Labris, devoted to the advancement of lesbian rights, and Gayten-LGBT, today known as Geten. The name of the organisation was inspired by Gethen, a planet that appears in Ursula K. Le Guin's (1969) feminist science fiction novel *The Left Hand of Darkness*. Gethen residents are ambisexual beings who adopt sexual attributes only once a month and can become sexually male or female. As there are no fixed gender roles, there is no gender-related inequality, discrimination, or violence and Gethen is presented as a society that has never witnessed wars. In 2019, with Le Guin's permission, we officially renamed our organisation Geten. It was founded as the first all-inclusive organisation of LGBTIQ+ people in Serbia endeavouring to appreciate the uniqueness of every individual and believing in the idea that diversity and solidarity enrich us, enable us to learn, and open new platforms upon which to be together, especially keeping in mind that many of our identities intersect.

One of the first actions of Geten, done in cooperation with Labris, was the organisation of the first Belgrade Pride march in 2001. Led by the enthusiasm unleashed in the wake of political changes, we thought that the moment was ripe for us to show that we were there, living in the society that stubbornly refused to see us. A lot has been already written about that event, but along with the brutal violence that took place on that day, I would like to stress that some lesbian activist organisers thought that bisexual and transgender identities should not be represented either in the programme of the Pride itself or in any published material that accompanied its organisation. The same thing happened also in 2005 when there was a celebration of the 15th anniversary of Serbian LGBTIQ+ activism, but some of us reacted against that politics that negated our identities and our values.

For me as an activist, it was a great challenge when in 2001, Dušan Maljković and I were invited by the Radio 202 editor to produce and conduct a programme dedicated to LGBTIQ+ people, which we called *Gejming*. That was an exclusive opportunity to reach non-heterosexual and transgender people across Serbia, including those in rural areas, who lived in fear, isolation, and oppression. Our voices could finally be heard in the public sphere including those of transgender sex workers whose status used to be then and still is today quite a controversial question in the wider legal and political frame but also among feminist circles, more specifically. I find this text the right venue to recall how I have argued in favour of solidarity, destigmatisation, and decriminalisation of sex work, and insisted that that question had to be discussed primarily by those who did sex work themselves, and that sex workers need to be fully included in the whole scope of political activism, especially keeping in mind the intersection of our identities (many of my trans women friends found sex work as their only source of survival).

Further gender troubles

Towards the end of the 1990s I started working as a drag queen probably because I tried to come to terms with those early traumatic experiences in which both children and adults reacted with disgust and aggression to my performances. My first 'official' show took place in the framework of the Women's Studies programme led, among others, by Žarana Papić, the well-known activist and professor of anthropology, who said at that event that stepping out of the prescribed gender roles was one of the most serious cultural 'misdemeanours' and encouraged us to think about why such an act would be considered threatening to the social order. *Viva la Diva* – my drag name – has been a way of engaging with that dilemma through the means of art ... The appearance of the Belgrade Queer Collective immensely enriched both my artistic and activist work because we innovatively strived towards a convergence of artistic, activist, and political engagement, and considered such a synthesis the most adequate framework for exploring the entanglements between homo–bi–trans–phobia, sexual work, classism, racism, clericalism, nationalism, and the related questions of belonging and difference that the intensifying neoliberal capitalism was sharpening to unbearable levels.

Moreover, the launching of the LGBTIQ+ helpline and the Geten self-support group for trans people in 2006 were important moments in my personal and activist development (Vidić and Bilić, this volume). Working at the helpline made it possible for me to talk to people across Serbia and often be the first person to which they would confide their most intimate experiences related to their identities, which sometimes also included suicidal thoughts. The most important dimension of that work was the possibility to offer psychological and legal help to those living outside of major urban centres where strands of homo–bi–transphobic oppression are denser.

Ever since the foundation of Geten, the absence of trans people from the usual 'meeting points' (including virtual) of the 'community' was conspicuous, so there was a clear need for creating a platform that would enable us to come and act together. I considered this an even more urgent task after receiving openly transphobic and racist remarks from those in charge of gay and lesbian clubs who invited me to perform as a drag queen. Our self-help group came into being with the idea of offering a safe haven within which we could network, empower each other exchange information, and plan our future political, legal, institutional, and other actions. The group also provided an opportunity for doing research on the basis of which we could improve the quality of our lives in different spheres. The challenges that we faced there have been numerous – including work on trauma that has marked our lives, to the medical team which long operated with practically no legal regulation and monopolised and exploited trans people, to dehumanising legislative and administrative procedures, to poverty, unemployment, and intersectional discrimination and violence. It has been so important for many of us to register and discuss various topics of great personal and social significance such as internalised homophobia and transphobia, patriarchy, gender binarism, and conformity, and all the other values and challenges that the White cis–hetero–patriarchal system imbued us with.

In lieu of a conclusion

The Yellow Brick Road that I have co-built over the last four decades still has not taken us to the Emerald City of acceptance and love, but it has certainly improved legal solutions, increased the visibility and inclusion of trans-intersex-queer existence and culture, and put under control – at least partially – the urge of the medical discourse to have the final word on our bodies. Through our joint engagement we have made the public more familiar with the heterogeneity and the richness of the trans community, helped educate trade unions and employers about non-discriminatory practices in the workplace, and initiated legal and institutional (including within the medical sphere) changes, the latest one being our model law about gender identity and the rights of intersex people, which is entirely based upon the principle of self-identification and depathologisation of trans identities (Đurić, 2012; Đurić, Jeremić, and Vidić, 2016).

Nevertheless, after all these years, like so many of us, I am still not recognised by the current Serbian legal system and I continue to be – to use Kate Bornstein's (2016) words – a 'gender outlaw' occupying that liminal status that is also reflected by my name. I (and many other people from the trans and queer spectrum) also do not exist for, or rather, I am unacknowledged by a group of radical feminists known as trans-exclusionary radical feminists (TERFs) as well as by some right-wing and left-wing individuals and collectives (see Bilić, this volume) ... Because of this I think that every trans life, every effort we make to live in the world that is telling us we should not be there – is a revolution. I understand it is hard, confusing, and perhaps at moments even horrifying for many people to begin to unpack the nature of the normative postulates that have guided the mankind through history – the imposed gender dichotomy and a whole system of structures and hierarchies that have been so solidly built upon it. But even if it is not really possible to rationally *understand* all of that which appears to question and 'transgress' our gender 'status quo', there is still, or at least I hope, that capacity immanent to all human beings, namely – empathy, which enables us to *feel* how it may be for the other person to inhabit that complex intersection of stigmatised identities.

This precious volume manages to combine empathy with knowledge, and by doing so promises to augment our possibilities to freely experience and express ourselves in our region that has gone through such harsh times ... We need books like this to empower us to live a life without aggression, violence, pathologisation ... to encourage us to go beyond those suffocating frames that want to determine who we are and what it is that we can be ...

References

Ahmed, S. (2014) *The willful subjects*. Durham and London: Duke University Press.

Bilić, B. (2021) *We were gasping for air: (Post-)Yugoslav anti-war activism and its legacy*. Baden-Baden: Nomos.

Bornstein, K. (2016) *Gender outlaw: On men, women and the rest of us*. New York: Vintage Books.

Đurić, M. (2012) Od nevidljivog do vidljivog T. In S. Gajin (ed) *Model zakona o priznavanju pravnih posledica promene pola i utvrđivanja transseksualizma: Prava trans osoba – od nepostojanja do stvaranja zakonskog okvira* (pp 9–26). Belgrade: CUPS and Gayten-LGBT.

Đurić, M., Jeremić, M. and Vidić, J. (eds) (2016) *Trans, interseks, kvir: Osvrti i novi horizonti*. Belgrade: Gayten-LGBT.

Kandido-Jakšić, M. (1995) Polne uloge i zdravlje. *Psihologija*, 3–4, 315–38.

Le Guin, U.K. (1969) *The left hand of darkness*. New York: Ace Books.

Richards, R. and Ames, J. (1983) *Second serve: The Renee Richards story*. New York: Stein and Day.

Živković, Lj. (2005) *Prvo je stiglo jedno pismo: Petnaest godina lezbejskog i gej aktivizma u Srbiji i Crnoj Gori*. Belgrade: Labris.

Introduction:
In post-Yugoslav trans worlds

Bojan Bilić, Iwo Nord, and Aleksa Milanović

Towards the end of December 2020, as we were entering the most intense phase of our work on this volume, the three of us joined many of our friends, colleagues, and co-authors in signing a statement with which a group of Belgrade-based organisations and activists condemned transphobia and sent a message of support to trans people across the region.[1] This document was a response to the letter[2] that another set of activist initiatives published to show solidarity with the Zagreb Centre for Women's Studies. They felt compelled to do so given that the Centre came under fire once it was revealed that its newly elected executive director had reposted some of the controversial comments with which J.K. Rowling disputed trans women's right to identify as women. Trans hostility, which was (also) uncritically imported from middle class-oriented fractions of British feminism, quickly merged with the more radical and conservative currents within the field of regional activist politics to form a particularly regressive hybrid (Bilić, this volume). All of a sudden wombs, chromosomes, hormones, and genes came to be tossed around in endless angry debates similar to those one might imagine taking place at a biology symposium (Bakić, 2020). Not only did such an incursion of essentialising attitudes, accompanied by spirals of cynicism, inflict a great deal of personal damage, but it also offered us an opportunity to witness how our feminist and leftist arenas, already reduced to the point of almost complete political irrelevance, became fractured yet again, this time along a new – trans – line.

When the three of us met in the spring of 2019 for an initial brainstorming on how a volume about trans lives, activisms, and culture in the post-Yugoslav space should look, hardly could anyone have imagined that *we*[3] would find ourselves in the midst of a 'TERF war' (Pearce et al, 2020) by the time of its completion. Although we came together prompted by the need for an anthology that would start documenting the still rather dispersed threads of trans existence and activist engagement in our region, little did we expect that the importance of our joint endeavour would increase at such a pace. Perhaps we should have seen it coming. On closer inspection, this latest reconfiguration is little more than yet another symptom of the process through which fragments of the regional feminist 'scene' have distanced themselves from the emancipatory potential of their socialist past and become increasingly entangled with the authoritarian and patriarchal matrices that have been governing social life over the last few decades.

Sadly though, that reactionary anti-trans tsunami that has travelled across national borders over the last few years has not spared some of our most prominent feminist teachers. Much to our regret, the letter of support to the Zagreb Centre included activists of the internationally renowned Women in Black who were throughout the 1990s determined to stand in the way of the nationalistically and religiously driven movement that tried to yet again relegate women to the sphere of domesticity and reproduction (Bilić, 2012a, 2012b). If there is one feminist lesson that has traversed our turbulent turn of the century, it is this collective's founding principle that 'we should not let ourselves be deceived by our own'. Many of us matured politically as we struggled to embrace this powerful message that invited us as a matter of urgency to raise our voice against oppressive family arrangements, renounce spurious but potentially lethal national allegiances, and demonstrate courage of thought and action by rejecting what the hypertrophied patriarchal 'tradition' had in store for our futures. Nowhere else is that critical charge to become worthy of its feminist name than in its capacity to reinvigorate the calcified positions of *our own* feminist pioneers and commit itself to loosening their definitional grip on our gender embodiments when they start holding on a bit too tightly.

However, if the time was ripe for us to stand up to and perhaps also part ways with some of our acclaimed feminist predecessors in order to create a space for new genders and gender terminologies, this is not to say that we could easily and unambiguously take refuge in the opposite camp. Like in so many other instances in which the burdens of oppression painfully press the body calling for a resolute counteroffensive, it seemed that the task of steering regional feminism away from its discriminatory course could not afford more sophisticated verbal calibrations. We thought that this political rupture might have perhaps announced the emergence of a new language, one that would try to step out of unending loops of erasure and help suture the wounds inflicted by decades of racist, misogynous, homophobic, and transphobic denigration. We hoped that new affective horizons of togetherness would have been suggested as an alternative to our perpetual political suffocation, which often occurs also within our own circles, those ever-shrinking territories of inclusive feeling and knowing.

Alas, in alarming circumstances in which ways of life and potentially life itself may be at stake, fragile imaginaries of emancipation are even more likely to retreat in front of authoritarian structures that weave the tissue of regional sociality and extend their resilient threads deep into the pores of (supposedly) liberatory mobilisations. Such moments of particularly high tension reveal the extent to which the counterrevolutionary force of Yugoslavia's dissolution has shackled vocabularies of freedom pervading also the fields of (declaratively) progressive organising.[4] In this regard, as three activist scholars dedicated to critically strengthening both the regional and more widely transnational cause of gender and sexual diversity, we were disheartened by the view of the LGBTI Equal Rights Association for the Western Balkans and Turkey that the statement of the Centre for Women's Studies' new director was 'yet another example of the dangerous influence that academia has in igniting trans exclusionary narratives in broader public which further endangers the lives of trans people' (ERA, 2020, online).

These two positions, trans-hostile conservative feminism, on the one hand, and trans-affirming activist anti-academism, on the other, constitute the eye of a needle through which we want to pass with this volume. As a group of activist scholars and research-appreciative activists, we have come together led by our interest in the dynamics through which the transnational intensification of trans-related engagement has played out in the post-Yugoslav space, a geopolitical semi-periphery characterised by the wounds of armed conflicts and transition from socialism to variegated neoliberal capitalisms. With this introduction we do not intend to offer an exhaustive historical account of the (post-)Yugoslav 'transgender phenomenon' that could serve as a background for the ensuing chapters – it is yet to be written and may hopefully be inspired and buttressed by this book. Rather, we would here like to cast into relief some of our major political concerns that act as a force of cohesion for all of our authors' contributions.

In the first introductory section we take a look at the increased visibility of trans-related issues in post-Yugoslav public spheres and social science scholarship (Milanović, 2015, 2019; Vidić, 2021) examining the implications of its coincidence with both the erasure of progressive socialist legacies, on the one hand, and the expansion of the European Union as the major neocolonial political actor in the region, on the other. We then expand on the reasons why our research encompasses the entire Yugoslav space perceiving it as a political formation that offered a vision of modernity different from the ones usually associated with contemporary capitalist globalisations. With both this and previous collections (Bilić and Janković, 2012; Bilić, 2016a; Bilić and Kajinić, 2016; Bilić and Radoman, 2019), we approach non-normative genders and sexualities as a particularly revealing prism through which to look at how the Yugoslav socialist project was imagined and put into practice, why it is that it came crashing down in such a destructive, traumatising fashion, and how some of its most emancipatory elements could be resurrected in novel, queer/trans ways. We then consider a range of epistemological challenges that such an endeavour entails and focus on the ways in which trans people and the post-Yugoslav semi-periphery – as well as the two of them *together* – may address the world on their own terms and in their own rapidly evolving narratives.

Challenges of the trans turn

When sociological and anthropological research about 'non-normative' sexualities in Eastern Europe started intensifying, especially in the wake of Kulpa and Mizielińska's (2011) ground-breaking volume *De-Centring Western Sexualities*, many of us were concerned about what 'LGBT' might mean in our non-Western geo-political environments. Disclaimers were sometimes needed to warn against the potentially misleading nature of the fast-spreading acronym. Not only did that string of identity letters (growing longer over the years) place together gays and lesbians who, both in the post-Yugoslav space and transnationally, have often opted for separate liberatory trajectories, but it also included two groups of people, namely bisexual-[5] and transgender-identified persons, that at the time, were hardly visible, especially in terms of activist representation.

In other words, the T began circulating within Eastern European activist networks before becoming more firmly anchored in a corpus of political, social, legal,[6] and economic claims. Mizielińska and Kulpa account for this 'inclusion before coming into being' (p 14) by arguing that there was a 'temporal disjuncture', a fissure that has opened up between Western, Anglo-American (or, as they also say, perhaps *only* American) lexicons forged in long-term activist struggles, on the one hand, and Eastern European non-heterosexual and gender-transformative mobilisations, on the other. While the history of trans emancipation in the West indeed justified the broadening of non-cis-heteronormative politics into 'LGBT'[7], in Eastern European contexts, the T was in the beginning not only a 'purely discursive invocation' (p 14) but also an example of the process through which Western categories lose some of their political content as they are removed from their places of origin and transferred/translated into new social settings.

In the post-Yugoslav space, more specifically, the LGBT activist shell also started acquiring its T substance around 2005 even though the acronym had been used already from the beginning of the century as it 'felt like "the right thing to do"' (Hodžić, Poštić, and Kajtezović, 2016, p 37) in anticipation of more visible trans activists.[8] The 2005 conference *Transgressing Gender: Two is not Enough for Gender (E)quality*, which took place in Zagreb, Croatia, was particularly relevant for initiating regional debates about gender diversity and inaugurating a period of dynamic activist engagement.[9] This development has been also reflected in our series of interlocking books about post-Yugoslav feminist anti-war and LGBT activisms: the necessity and the wish to pay more attention to trans-related topics rather than subsume them under the wider 'LGBT' label first led to a footnote (Bilić, 2016b), then to a chapter (Hodžić, Poštić, and Kajtezović, 2016), and steadily grew to such an extent to require an entire volume.[10]

This counterhegemonic process of 'footnote expansion', which reflects the uneven and contentious transnational intensification of 'non-normative' sexual and gender politics over the last three decades, has to a great extent run parallel with the East-bound enlargement of the European Union and the painful neocolonial peripheralisation and ethnic fragmentation of the Yugoslav space. A lot of homophobic and transphobic violence that has taken place over that period could be traced back to the distinctly ambivalent character of the regional 'transition' to capitalism: while it has, on the one hand, foreclosed economic possibilities and rapidly impoverished and depopulated the Yugoslav successor states, it provided the background against which various LGBT-related grievances found their way into the public sphere more assertively than ever before (Sears, 2005). This coincidence is particularly relevant for the category of *transgender*, which has experienced dramatic transnational dissemination while neoliberal capitalism consolidated itself around the world at the expense of dispossession, environmental devastation, and death (Stryker, 2006; Kancler, 2016; Stryker and Aizura, 2013; Gržinić, Kancler, and Rexhepi, 2020). Such simultaneity may imply a misleading conceptual symbiosis between gender diversity and capitalist predatory pursuits of surplus value on a global scale.

To counter the risks of this conceptual pairing we have striven to continuously politicise gender and sexuality and carve out a niche for our volume(s) within that often subdued tradition of decolonial scholarship, which approaches them as a site of resistance that interacts with other operators of power, most notably race and class. In doing so, we have found some breathing space in the intellectual feat of Black feminists and feminists of colour with which they struggled to protect themselves from a social structure immersed in centuries of racist oppression. Combining Quijano's (2000, 2007) foundational insight that Western modernity has an inextricable colonial undercurrent[11] characterised by racialisation and violence, with work on intersectionality (for example, Crenshaw, 1989, 1991), Lugones (2008) arrived at the analysis of what she called 'the modern/colonial gender system'. According to her, Quijano uncritically embraced the (Western) Eurocentred, capitalist understanding of gender through biological dimorphism, and the patriarchal and heterosexual organisation of social relations. In other words, Lugones argued that the gender binary system, in the way in which it was imposed on colonised populations, along with various forms of exploitation, slavery, and servitude, was itself infused with racist Eurocentrism. Binary sexual difference was a colonial invention with a distinctly racialising function: it negated the humanity of the colonised peoples by leaving them out of the Western understanding of (proper) 'man' and 'woman'[12] while also working towards the erasure of alternative gender systems or forms of social organisation, which did not afford primary importance to sexual difference. Given that from the cognitive perspective of Eurocentred hegemony all human relations were articulated 'fictionally, in biological terms' (Lugones, 2008, p 2), social class ended up resting on the idea that gender and race were inseparable categories (gender/race).

With this in mind, transgender lives and non-normative gender embodiments can hardly be recovered without engaging not only with the ways in which gender has been historically embedded in binary-patriarchal-colonial matrices but also with today's rapid diffusion of *transgender* as a notion stemming from White Eurocentred modernity. While long-term activist efforts have recently led to a formal (albeit still not equally applied) depathologisation of trans identities in the International Classification of Diseases (ICD-11) and the visibility of trans people has been steadily increasing, this is far from suggesting that the powerful colonial/racialising mechanisms of (trans) liveability differentiation have been dismantled. Continual reconfigurations of global neoliberal capitalisms enable the appearance of new forms of subjectivity affording them/us access to the public sphere only if they/we can be exploited as a market niche and associated with the profit-oriented modes of production and consumption (Valentine, 2007). In this regard, transnational circulations of the Western category of *transgender* continuously supply conceptual vocabularies for articulating gender diversity beyond the borders of the Western world while at the same time perpetuating engines of differentiation that operate along racial/ethnic, class, ability, and other intersecting lines (Kancler, 2016).

Things get even more complicated when we add the semi-periphery, socialism, and post-socialism to the violent colonial equation. Located between the 'centre' and the 'periphery', the semi-periphery is a sphere of social hybridity with its own logic that at once embraces and resists Western/Anglo-Saxon explanatory paradigms. Reworking and going beyond Wallerstein's world-systems analysis on the basis of her academic experience in the post-Yugoslav space, Blagojević (2009, see also Blagojević and Yair, 2010) argued that the semi-periphery is constituted by a crossroads of oppositions, which may look like a 'location of a discursive void': it is at the same time 'white/non-white, European/noneuropean, postcolonial/nonpostcolonial, citizen/noncitizen, and gender/nongender'. Consistently presented as Europe's unruly homophobic Other, Eastern Europe/'the Balkans'/the post-Yugoslav space is a site of geo-political ambiguity: it is close enough to the Western 'core' to deserve 'being taken care of', but still way too far to be considered eligible for admission to the 'First World' (Kulpa, 2014).

Having experienced socialism as an interruption of and a dam to the Western capitalist temporality, Eastern Europe after 1989 – and the post-Yugoslav space after the 1990s – had to be (re)set on the course of Western modernity. It has thus been pushed into a didactical, hegemonic relation with its Western counterpart, which sees it as a region locked in a 'post-communist' transition that is supposed to asymptotically run towards (while never really achieving) the Western European liberal model of rights (Kulpa, 2014). Western activist struggles (which have largely departed from their leftist, revolutionary origins in our homonationalist and homonormative times; Puar, 2007) have transformed non-normative sexualities and non-binary gender embodiments – exactly those that (mostly) used to be suppressed through Western colonial domination – to such an extent that they can nowadays figure as a tool of this neoliberal pedagogy (Akintola, 2017). Along with the already familiar colonial methods of resource extraction and labour exploitation, 'LGBT' communities have been added to the panoply of *neo*colonial instruments with which the Western 'core' conditions, teaches, and effectively colonises 'its' semi-peripheral East. These new gender and sexual subjectivities that are (ab)used as agents of colonisation operate in parallel with a potent suppression of socialist legacies. They create a major challenge for grassroots intersectionally sensitive and anti-racist mobilisations by moulding LGBT activist imaginaries in specifically identitarian terms and making it hard for them to build upon locally-grounded emancipatory achievements.

Trans Yugoslavias: towards the future that already was

In his widely celebrated *The Wretched of the Earth*, Frantz Fanon (1961/2004) argues that colonialism's major ambition is to become omnipresent: it is not content solely with the force of physical coercion, but it aims at taking possession of the native's past in order to master, disfigure, and eventually destroy it. In this regard, the aggressive post-socialist evacuations of socialist pasts are among the most conspicuous evidence of colonial operationality in Fanon's terms. Ever since the 1990s, the Yugoslav socialist past has been subjected to overwhelming attacks of amnesia. Along one of its axes, the so-called 'Western Balkans'[13] functions as an artificial formation that should fill the void left in the wake of Yugoslavia's disappearance. This neologism, arising from the unstable politics of European Union expansion, announces a technocratic subdivision of the Balkans that fragments our cultural space, unravels historical affinities among the Yugoslav peoples, and works towards distancing them/us from their/our own non-capitalist traditions.[14] On the other hand, the multinational Yugoslav socialist state vanishes under the 1990s' nationalist avalanche that it was supposed to keep in check: strong currents of revisionism invade its anti-fascist foundations and erase the socialist federation because it can not be rendered compatible with the lucrative narratives of ethnic exclusivity (Milekić, 2021).

Like our previous volumes, with this one too we are determined to swim against the current of such profound forgetting. As a matter of fact, the critically approached Yugoslavia constitutes an indispensable ingredient of our decolonial and anti-nationalist commitment.[15] This is not only due to the fact that its geographical frame contains our shared, intimate memories and institutional structures, but Yugoslavia – the one that emerged out of the People's Liberation Struggle against Nazism and Fascism – enabled our up to now closest encounter with modernity that was detached from the colonising impulse. A socialist experiment and a modernising project of unprecedented proportions in the history of the Yugoslav peoples, Yugoslavia could, from our today's vantage point, be regarded as a fragile *queer* entity: a state in constant flux, it struggled (certainly declaratively and to a certain extent also in practice) to cut through class hierarchies, emancipate women, suture deeply entrenched racial/ethnic and religious divisions, attenuate poverty, promote education, strengthen peace and international cooperation, and help undo the consequences of decade-long colonial domination across the non-Western world (Bilić, 2019). If we push this logic further, in the context of our current volume, we could even discern some of its metaphorically *trans* dimensions. The erasures of Yugoslavia as a socialist idea have occluded the fact that it was a state strongly committed to problematising – together with others – binary oppositions in world politics. Yugoslavia's complexity often slips through the binary-oriented Cold War vocabularies in the same way in which the gender dichotomy obscures a multiplicity of gender embodiments and non-binary gender (hi)stories.

It is, therefore, perhaps not entirely accidental that our work coincides with the increasing interest in recovering the Non-Aligned Movement of which Yugoslavia was one of the founding and most important members (Stubbs, 2020; Videkanić, 2020). That monumental project of international cooperation, which unfolded across diverse political, social, economic, and cultural scales, expanded Yugoslav horizons towards Africa, Asia, and Latin America drawing the contours of alternative, non-colonial globalisations and endeavouring to give the world more than two relevant actors. Yugoslavia was, thus, essential for our experience of decolonial political hybridity and non-binarity and with this volume we would like to add it as a precedent to the disintegration of the Soviet Union, the hegemonic rise of the United States, the development of the European Union, and new configurations of global capitalism, all of which, according to Stryker (2006), have led to a re-examination of conceptual binaries paving the way for the appearance of trans studies.

Surely, however, the visions of socialist modernity are imbued with ambivalence: to engage with the Yugoslav state intellectually (and) emotionally means to enter into a realm of contradictions and position oneself in the vicinity of disappointment. As queers we know all too well that 'any history of actualized utopian communities would be replete with failures' (Muñoz, 2009, p 27). In spite of its progressive legislation and the enthusiasm of many of its people, socialist Yugoslavia did not manage to dismantle oppressive matrices that it inherited from its political antecedents. Quite early on it became clear not only that equality and the elimination of class distinction were a chimera but also that the socialist revolution probably would not be 'able to cross the threshold of the family' (Morokvašić, 1986, p 127) and organise intimate lives on a non-patriarchal and non-heteronormative basis. More than anything, streams of racism continued to flow along its North–South axis (Bakic-Hayden and Hayden, 1992; Baker, 2018) and the nationalist sentiment within the constitutive republics often went counter to the Party's programmatic slogan of 'brotherhood and unity'. These strands of dehumanisation would converge towards the end of the 1980s and in the early 1990s turning the socialist state into an abyss that devoured thousands of lives and stripped generations of more promising futures.

We keep this painful heritage of Yugoslavia's cis-, heteronormative, and nationalist patriarchy[16] in mind so that we can temper its captivating call at our time of pronounced dispossession, capitalist crisis, and insecurity. Even though its socialist appeal may mislead us into uncritical idealisations or even push us into politically unproductive romanticism, our invocations of Yugoslavia should not be dismissed as merely nostalgic: they go along the sobering lines of three recent region-wide grassroots declarations: on a common, polycentric language spoken in Bosnia and Herzegovina, Croatia, Montenegro, and Serbia, on the necessity for a historical science resistant to revisionism, and on solidarity in dealing with common social and economic challenges.[17] As we, equipped with these elementary values and premises, rummage through Yugoslavia's ruins, we do not turn a blind eye to its numerous shadows, but we strive to rescue the most politically vital elements that have been trapped beneath the layers of vitriolic nationalisms and patriarchal authoritarianisms. We look for that indestructible core of decolonial, anti-racist, and anti-fascist *togetherness* because we urgently need it an ideological compass for navigating the murky waters of today's politics: we would like to eventually turn it into a legacy that may be mobilised as a response to the stultifying toxicity of the present (Muñoz, 2009) and creatively (re)employed for generating new paradigms of inclusion.

As this is our fourth collective LGBT-related book with a Yugoslav/regional coverage, there is for us little doubt that 'non-normative' genders and sexualities have the potential (and perhaps also the responsibility) to replenish exhausted post-socialist imaginaries with new political content. Yugoslavia, even though it may not explicitly figure in them, serves as a backdrop for the ensuing chapters because it allows us to rely upon our own positionalities when (re)staging an encounter between gender diversity and socialism (Sernatinger and Echeverria, 2013). We separate emancipatory gestures from unfulfilled promises and revamped racisms by drawing the (post)socialist Yugoslav space through a queer–trans lens. In the course of this re-reading, which affords it feminist–queer–trans dimensions (largely missing from both its life and numerous fractured afterlives), Yugoslavia, an erased state, violently forgotten, is being resuscitated by many of its own erased: it thus acquires a new political charge and becomes legitimised as a political project on novel grounds. Such queer rearticulations of (post)socialist experience make it possible for us to challenge the silence that envelops socialist gender trajectories (Kancler, 2013) so that dissident gender practices of the past start living new lives.[18] This does not only (re)connect us with the most progressive strands of transnational gender and sexual liberation[19], but it also stimulates us to think about and act towards forging transformative alliances here and now.

Making books, making ourselves

Like with our previous volumes, with this one too we set out to rekindle the rebellious roar of feminism and help restore that mode of being in and with the world that celebrates belonging-in-difference (Muñoz, 2009, p 20), struggles to expand our possibilities, and revives our hopes depleted by long years of violence and destruction. As we have, over the last decade, moved across the alphabet of sexual and gender diversity arriving to the T with this book, we have also gone down a slope of political and material marginalisation addressing issues that directly concern an ever smaller number of people. While doing so, we have mobilised our feminist and queer shields to protect us from thinking that a quantitative descent may translate into a decrease of social relevance. On the contrary, we have enjoyed coming closer to an appreciation of the singularity of human experience and its capacity to persevere in spite of the funnelling function of authoritarian social structures. We have engaged with what still to a great extent are 'non-normative' gender embodiments and sexual desires, approaching them not primarily as 'identities' in need of legal recognition/regulation but rather as spaces of disobedient feeling-thinking – repositories of disruptive *knowledges* of resistance and survival.

Throughout this process we have often stumbled upon epistemological concerns about how that knowledge – that we produce and that produces us – is to be accumulated within and disseminated from our semi-peripheral space. When tackling this question we set out from the premise that in the context of global (academic) coloniality, the semi-periphery is not perceived (and consequently has a hard time perceiving itself) as a site of knowledge production; rather, if anything, in the global knowledge market its insights are treated as partial, limited, inferior, and perhaps even irrelevant (Blagojević, 2009). Such 'cognitive irrelevance' arises from the gaze of Western modernity pointed towards the semi-periphery as 'its non-absolute other [with the task of] homogenizing its multiplicity and diversity following the well-known logic of either neglecting the other or misinterpreting it as the same' (Tlostanova, 2014, p 1).

The tendency of the core to shy away from and flatten the complexity of the semi-periphery instead of embracing the insights that it has to offer has had devastating consequences in our region in the period of transition from socialism to neoliberal capitalism: it prioritised fast implementations of external policy solutions inflating technical 'expertise' (rather than 'knowledge') of the local liberal cadres of translation at the expense of critical scholarship and activist research-based policies (Blagojević, 2009). While in the core countries knowledge production normally precedes policy making, in the semi-periphery, half-implemented, hybrid, and not entirely fitting policies run fast ahead of knowledge production because of the strong marginalisation of academia in general, and the critical social sciences in particular, and its frequent auto-colonial distance from its own social context (Blagojević, 2009). In other words, supposedly emancipatory impulses seep from the Western 'centre' into semi-peripheral publics and popular cultures ending up in routine revisions of legislation while only superficially penetrating the layers of social values reproducing along the way semi-periphery's 'semi-ness' as a space that is simultaneously progressive and conservative.

Within such hierarchised configurations, both social science scholars and activists from the semi-periphery are chained to the carousel of repetition, replication, and reproduction of the Western original (Blagojević, 2009). As they are rarely perceived as 'creators' of knowledge – a role reserved mostly for academics coming from the core – semi-peripheral scientists' central function is that of translation/transmission of the knowledge that arrives from the centre (Blagojević, 2009; Clarke et al, 2015). Especially in the sphere of gender studies, which is in the focus of Blagojević's interest, knowledge has been mostly imported from the West through an enormous amount of translation/transmission done by locally based scholars. This, as she claims, more mechanical and less creative way of knowledge communication from the core towards the semi-periphery, was a particularly rewarding activity for semi-peripheral scientists because it enabled direct contact with Western authors and power networks that could be approached in intelligible Western idioms to provide funding and assure reception and recognition.

Bearing in mind that the post-Yugoslav space is an *ambiguous* part/non-part of the Western world – its abovementioned non-absolute Other – national and regional strategies of trans resistance are inspired by and draw upon larger transnational mobilisations stemming from the core while also taking specific local shapes. Therefore, our volume cannot purport to perform a radical departure from Western perspectives: an expectation that it could offer an 'authentic' trans or any 'non-normative' experience that would be free of Western vocabularies would probably constitute the highest form of its exoticisation. Accordingly, our book engages with Western knowledge production by paying attention to how global relationships of power shape the way in which trans discourses, practices, and knowledges travel, are translated, and materialise locally. We surely cannot escape colonial arrangements, but we have tried to come closer to the role of 'creators' by operating as 'counter-transmitters' and opening up a route along which knowledge would also flow in a reverse direction – from the semi-periphery to the core. A transgender studies perspective that both acknowledges the Anglo-American bias in much trans scholarship and unpacks the processes of knowledge and policy translation can shed a new light upon how gender difference is understood and practised in our region (Nord, 2013).

In this regard, our book arises from a collaboration of both trans- and cis-identified researchers and activists who share the conviction that trans people *are* the primary carriers of knowledge about trans lives. In the local milieus in which strong patriarchal/hetero- and cis-normative currents traverse formal academic institutions, this embodied knowledge – as legitimate as any other – has consistently accrued within trans activist organisations, but it has been disseminated from them through still insufficiently acknowledged channels. Our collection approaches such groups, in which many of us participate, as epistemic communities and communities of praxis recognising that they have travelled far ahead of their official academic counterparts in terms of garnering trans-related knowledge. They have moved beyond mere 'trans testimonies' (Ashley, 2019) and engaged in developing a critical and analytical perspective vis-à-vis the dominant norms of medicine and entrenched social ideas about gender as a binary category. Thus, our book aims to start building an academic platform upon which such community-generated knowledge can be more systematically shaped to enter into and transform dominant academic discourses and mainstream gender-related policies and perceptions. Synchronised with the transnational movement for gender and sexual liberation, the ensuing chapters uncover alternative gender-related epistemologies seeking to put them to the service of social justice and enhance our collective sensitivity to the needs and demands of trans and non-binary people.

Moreover, our own engagement over the years has embodied an effort to bring academia and activism into a politically productive symbiosis within which these two spheres – two nourishing vessels of feminism – can enrich each other and by doing so maximise the probability of taking our lives and our communities in more promising directions. When putting together this book, we repeatedly tried to weld the rage and passion of the activist with the composure and intellectual acuity of the scholar as we strove to increase the intelligibility of trans bodies by triggering and sustaining what Foucault (2003, p 7) called 'the insurrection of subjugated knowledges'.[20] According to him, the excavation of what has been historically occluded and pushed to the margins of social legitimisation proceeds along two intertwined axes: the first one draws upon the traditional tools of scholarship and meticulous technical expertise to bring into the light of the day what has stayed hidden in the archives and other repositories of historical content; the second, on the other hand, delves into 'singular local knowledges' to recover 'the raw memory of fights' inscribed in the stamps that the power of disciplinary institutions has left on the minds and the bodies of those who have been silenced, discarded, and humiliated. Such genealogical pairing which breathes new life into both 'the buried and the disqualified', does not only begin to undo the discriminatory 'hierarchy of erudition' drawing the contours of a new, more just and inclusive academia, but it also helps us to devise activist strategies with which to articulate and respond to the pressing issues we face today.

Our purpose, thus, is to contribute to transnational currents of trans-related knowledge through a series of experientially/empirically based, conjuncturally sensitive analyses about how trans liberation has been unfolding in the post-Yugoslav/post-socialist semi-periphery in three major intertwined domains: lives, activisms, and culture. The first part (*Lives*) brings four contributions based either on authors' personal trans experiences or on long-term ethnographic work in trans communities. This section explores the challenges that trans people have encountered through the process of becoming more visible in public arenas across the post-Yugoslav space. The second part (*Activisms*) examines histories and politics of trans activist organising emphasising the strategies through which the T has increasingly come to assume its proper place within LGBT initiatives. Contributions to this section operate both diachronically and synchronically positioning trans engagement in the history of regional feminist and non-heterosexual activist endeavours while also critically engaging with contemporary tensions and conflicts within leftist activist groups. The third part (*Culture*) brings innovative contributions about the ways in which gender non-normativity has been represented in (post-)Yugoslav popular culture as well as about how artistic endeavours have been employed as activist instruments. These three sections taken together offer a unique entry point into the post-Yugoslav and Eastern European trans landscape and constitute a solid basis for further research in this underexplored area.

Finally, we believe that it is high time that our space, which has been for so long subjected to the oppressive canon of nationalist politics, broke that stranglehold and embraced a heteroglossic diversity of gender embodiments and experiences. Therefore, this book, like its predecessors within our collective, is not supposed to constitute only a gathering point of already established authors: more broadly and more ambitiously, it purports to shape disparate strands of both existing and potential trans-related scholarship into a new field of regional queer- and trans-led queer/trans studies that can exist alongside and hybridise with global threads of activist engagement and scholarly production on an equal footing. We hope that our piece in the transnational mosaic of trans emancipation will sharpen the tools we use to celebrate trans vitality and bring about life-affirming social change.

Notes

1   The petition *Against Transphobia*, published on 21 December 2020, is available here: https://transserbia.org/vesti/1781-protiv-transfobije

2   This letter is available here: https://marks21.info/pismo-podrske-centru-za-zenske-studije-u-zagrebu/

3   This polysemic 'we' refers primarily to us as three co-editors with our different positions within the field of Yugoslav studies and LGBT activist scholarship. All three of us – Bojan is a sociologist of the (post-)Yugoslav anti-war, feminist, and LGBT movement(s) while Iwo and Aleksa are trans scholars and activists – have been committed both to bridging the gap between academia and activism as well as to reigniting the queer dimension of regional activist endeavours by expanding their intersectional (and especially class-related) sensitivity. Throughout the introduction, this 'we' also often encompasses our authors and stretches towards those who would still today identify as Yugoslavs: 'This "we" does not speak to a merely identitarian logic but instead to a logic of futurity. The "we" speaks to a "we" that is "not yet conscious", the future society that is being invoked and addressed at the same moment. The "we" is not content to describe who the collective is but more nearly describes what the collective and the larger social order could be, what it should be' (Muñoz, 2009, p 20).

4   For example, the petition that the three of us signed mentions a 'handful' (šačica) of transphobic activists. Not only is this word imbued with negative connotations associated with the 1990s when the regime of Slobodan Milošević used it to discredit its opponents (for example, Istinomer, 2011) and belittle their resistance, but it also draws upon the right-wing idea, frequently mobilised against the LGBT population, that numerical figures directly translate into political relevance. In this regard, one of the crucial questions within our wider political project of queering the post-Yugoslav space is how to liberate progressive threads of thought (and) action from the reactionary discourses with which they have become entangled.

5   For a chapter about bisexual life and activism that appeared within our collective, see Hura (2016).

6   Marija Draškić, professor at the University of Belgrade Law School, was a forerunner of legal analysis of the relationship between transsexuality and marriage in Serbia. See Draškić (1994).

7   Nevertheless, according to Binnie and Klesse (2012, p 445) 'the term LGBTQ signifies a coalitional practice between different collectivities of actors. The term is controversial because it insinuates a quasi-natural confluence of interests around certain gender and/or sexual subjectivities'.

8   Agatha Milan Đurić states that there was an initiative to give more space to transgender people at the first Belgrade Pride in 2001. However, this idea was not favourably received by other activist currents, especially lesbian ones, that took part in the organisation of the event (Transserbia.org, 2022). See also Đurić, this volume.

9   In the late 1980s, the Croatian philosopher Milan Polić (1988) published a text in the women's magazine *Žena* discussing the potential of transsexuality to transform gender binaries and destabilise patriarchal gender regimes. See also Krznar (2021) and Rogoznica (2011).

10 Trans is not the only issue that has gone through this process in our collective work over the last ten years. Lesbian activist engagement, for example, had a similar footnote

(Bilić, 2012b) to chapter (Mlađenović, 2012; Mlađenović, 2016) to volume (Bilić and Radoman, 2019) to monograph (Bilić, 2020) trajectory. The 'trans path' is continued by Nord's doctoral research, which explores Belgrade as an important but insufficiently visible node in the web of transnational migrations organised around gender confirmation surgeries (see also Rakić et al, 1993; Nord, 2019).

[11] Quijano (2000, 2007) claimed that Eurocentred capitalist power functions on the global scale along two main axes: 'the coloniality of power' and 'modernity'.

[12] The entanglement between race and gender comes to the fore in a particularly poignant manner in the speech of Sojourner Truth, a former slave turned abolitionist and women's rights activist, subsequently entitled 'Ain't I a Woman?'

[13] 'Western Balkans' refers to the former Yugoslav space while excluding Slovenia and including Albania.

[14] Rexhepi (2018) argues that some critical attempts to question these configurations, underscore Europe's orientalising of the Balkans while claiming that it is 'predominantly Christian' and without any 'colonial legacies'.

[15] Muñoz (2009, p 29) argues that 'the transregional or the global as modes of spatial organization potentially displace the hegemony of an unnamed here that is always dominated by the shadow of the nation-state and its mutable and multiple corporate interests'. In his text on queer regionality, Binnie (2016) also claims that a critical regional lens on LGBT politics may uncover sub-national and transnational political formations that can be occluded by a focus on the national scale.

[16] See in this regard how Milan Agatha Đurić writes about their experience of growing up in the 1980s' Yugoslavia (Đurić, this volume).

[17] The Declaration on the Common Language (Deklaracija o zajedničkom jeziku) was issued in 2017, the declaration *Defend History* (Odbranimo istoriju) in 2020, and the Declaration on Regional Solidarity (Deklaracija o regionalnoj solidarnosti) also in 2020.

[18] Within this framework we can understand how today's Slovenian transgender movement recovers Ljuba Prenner, a Yugoslav/Slovenian lawyer assigned female at birth, who stated that it was thanks to socialist advances in the sphere of gender that he could start donning men's clothes in the wake of the Second World War (Pirnar, 2006).

[19] Here, for example, we think about Leslie Feinberg, a US American radical activist, a member of the Workers World Party, and the author of *Transgender Liberation: A Movement Whose Time Has Come*, who stated: "Remember me as a revolutionary communist" (Childs, 2014).

[20] In the context of his non-heteronormative sexuality research, Plummer (2010) talks about 'subterranean traditions' that are at odds with those publicly known. He argues that in everyday community life there are subterranean worlds that have been largely ignored by mainstream sociology. Whereas what is on the surface may be hegemonic, 'beneath there is a seething world of resistance, alternatives – of all kinds' (Plummer, 2010, online).

References

Akintola, H.E. (2017) Britain can't just reverse the homophobia it exported during the empire. *The Guardian*. Retrieved on 28 September 2021 from www.theguardian.com/commentisfree/2017/jul/28/britain-reverse-homophobia-empire-criminlisation-homosexuality-colonies

Ashley, F. (2020) We must respect trans people's expertise beyond their personal experience. *Huffington Post*. Retrieved on 28 September 2021 from https://www.huffingtonpost.ca/florence-ashley/we-must-respect-trans-peoples-expertise-beyond-their-personal-experience_a_23703871/

Baker, C. (2018) *Race and the Yugoslav region: Postsocialist, post-conflict, postcolonial?* Manchester: Manchester University Press.

Bakić, A. (2020) TERF: Radikalna desnica u feminističkom ruhu. Retrieved on 28 September 2021 from https://voxfeminae.net/pravednost/terf-radika lna-desnica-u-feministickom-ruhu/

Bakic-Hayden, M. and Hayden, R. (1992) Orientalist variations on the theme 'Balkans': Symbolic geography in recent Yugoslav cultural politics. *Slavic Review, 51*(1), 1–15.

Bilić, B. (2012a) Not in our name: Collective identity of the Serbian Women in Black. *Nationalities Papers: The Journal of Nationalism and Ethnicity, 40*(4), 607–23.

Bilić, B. (2012b) *We were gasping for air: (Post-)Yugoslav anti-war activism and its legacy.* Baden-Baden: Nomos.

Bilić, B. (ed) (2016a) *LGBT activism and Europeanisation in the post-Yugoslav space: On the rainbow way to Europe.* London: Palgrave Macmillan.

Bilić, B. (2016b) Whose pride? The 'LGBT community' and the organisation of Pride Parades in Serbia. In K. Slootmaeckers, H. Touquet, and P. Vermeersch (eds) *The EU enlargement and gay politics: The impact of eastern enlargement on rights, activism and prejudice* (pp 203–20). London: Palgrave Macmillan.

Bilić, B. (2019) Introduction: Recovering/rethinking (post-)Yugoslav lesbian activisms. In B. Bilić and M. Radoman (eds) *Lesbian activism in the (post-)Yugoslav space: Sisterhood and unity* (pp 1–26). London: Palgrave Macmillan.

Bilić, B. and Janković, V. (eds) (2012) *Resisting the evil: (Post-)Yugoslav anti-war contention.* Baden-Baden: Nomos.

Bilić, B. and Kajinić, S. (eds) (2016a) *Intersectionality and LGBT activist politics: Multiple others in Croatia and Serbia* (pp 1–29). London: Palgrave Macmillan.

Bilić, B. and Radoman, M. (eds) (2019) *Lesbian activism in the (post-)Yugoslav space: Sisterhood and unity.* London: Palgrave Macmillan.

Binnie, J. (2016) Critical queer regionality and LGBTQ politics in Europe. Gender, Place & Culture: *A Journal of Feminist Geography, 23*(11), 1631–42.

Binnie, J. and Klesse, C. (2012) Solidarities and tensions: Feminism and transnational LGBTQ politics in Poland. *European Journal of Women's Studies, 19*(4), 444–59.

Blagojević, M. (2009) *Knowledge production at the semiperiphery: A gender perspective.* Belgrade: Institut za kriminološka i sociološka istraživanja.

Blagojević, M. and Yair, G. (2010) The catch 22 syndrome of social scientists in the semiperiphery: Exploratory sociological observations. *Sociologija, 52*(4), 337–464.

Childs, E. (2014) "Remember me as a revolutionary communist": An interview with Leslie Feinberg. Retrieved on 7 June 2022 from https://jacobin.com/2014/12/leslie-feinberg-as-a-revolutionary-communist

Clarke, J., Bainton, D., Lendvai, N., and Stubbs, P. (2015) *Making policy move: Towards a politics of translation and assemblage.* Bristol: Policy Press.

Crenshaw, K.W. (1989) Demarginalizing the intersection of race and sex: A black feminist critique of antidiscrimination doctrine, feminist theory and antiracist politics. *The University of Chicago Legal Forum*, 140, 139–67.

Crenshaw, K.W. (1991) Mapping the margins: Intersectionality, identity politics, and violence against women of color. *Stanford Law Review*, *43*(6), 1241–99.

Draškić, M. (1994) *Transseksualitet i brak.* Belgrade: Nomos.

ERA. (2020) Statement by ERA and its member organisations regarding the rise of trans-exclusion and anti-gender narratives in the region of Western Balkans. Retrieved on 26 December 2020 from https://www.lgbti-era.org/news/statement-era-and-its-member-organisations-regarding-rise-trans-exclusion-and-anti-gender

Fanon, F. (1961/2004) *The wretched of the Earth.* New York: Grove Press.

Foucault, M. (2003) *Society must be defended: Lectures at the College de France, 1975–76.* New York: Picador.

Gržinić, M., Kancler, T., and Rexhepi, P. (2020) Decolonial encounters and the geopolitics of racial capitalism. *Feminist Critique.* Retrieved on 28 September 2021 from https://feminist.krytyka.com/en/articles/decolonial-encounters-and-geopolitics-racial-capitalism

Hodžić, A., Poštić, J., and Kajtezović, A. (2016) The (in)visible T: Trans activism in Croatia (2004–2014). In B. Bilić and S. Kajinić (eds) *Intersectionality and LGBT activist politics: Multiple others in Croatia and Serbia* (pp 33–54). London: Palgrave Macmillan.

Hura, R. (2016) Against bisexual erasure: The beginnings of bi activism in Serbia. In B. Bilić and S. Kajinić (eds) *Intersectionality and LGBT activist politics: Multiple others in Croatia and Serbia* (pp 55–76). London: Palgrave Macmillan.

Istinomer. (2011) 'Šačica' izmanipulisanih ili stotine hiljada ogorčenih. Retrieved on 28 September 2021 from https://www.istinomer.rs/amnezija/sacica-izmanipulisanih-ili-stotine-hiljada-ogorcenih-6-deo/

Kancler, T. (2013) Post-Soviet imaginary and global coloniality: A gendered perspective – An interview with Madina Tlostanova. Retrieved on 28 September 2021 from http://www.kronotop.org/ftexts/interview-with-madina-tlostanova/

Kancler, T. (2016) Body politics, trans* imaginary, and decoloniality. Paper presented at the conference 'Decolonizing Transgender in North', 4th Nordic Transgender Studies Symposium, The Centre for Gender Studies, Karlstad University, Sweden.

Krznar, T. (2021) (Ne)mogućnosti emancipacije: Promišljanja društvenih uvjeta konstrukcija spolnosti u djelu hrvatskog filozofa Milana Polića. *Nova prisutnost*, *19*(1), 77–95.

Kulpa, R. (2014) Western leveraged pedagogy of Central and Eastern Europe: Discourses of homophobia, tolerance, and nationhood. *Gender, Place, & Culture: A Journal of Feminist Geography*, *21*(4), 431–48.

Kulpa, R. and Mizielińska, J. (eds) (2011) *De-centring Western sexualities: Central and East European perspectives*. London: Ashgate.

Lugones, M. (2008) The coloniality of gender. *Worlds & Knowledges Otherwise*, *2* (Spring), 1–17.

Milanović, A. (2015) *Reprezentacije transrodnih identiteta*. Belgrade: FMK.

Milanović, A. (2019) *Medijska konstrukcija drugog tela*. Belgrade: Orion Art.

Milekić, S. (2021) Intentional amnesia: Croatia's attempt to erase Yugoslavia. Retrieved on 28 September 2021 from https://balkaninsight.com/2021/03/04/intentional-amnesia-croatias-attempt-to-erase-yugoslavia/

Mizielińska, J. and Kulpa, R. (2011) 'Contemporary peripheries': Queer studies, circulation of knowledge and East/West divide. In R. Kulpa and J. Mizielińska (eds) *De-centring Western sexualities: Central and East European perspectives* (pp 11–26). London: Ashgate.

Mlađenović, L. (2012) Notes of a feminist lesbian in anti-war initiatives. In B. Bilić and V. Janković (eds) *Resisting the evil: (Post-)Yugoslav anti-war contention* (pp 127–36). Baden-Baden: Nomos.

Morokvašić, M. (1986) Being a woman in Yugoslavia: Past, present and institutional equality. In M. Gadant (ed) *Women of the Mediterranean* (pp 120–38). London: Zed Books.

Muñoz, J.E. (2009) *Cruising utopia: The then and there of queer futurity*. New York: New York University Press.

Nord, I. (2013) An overall success with some geopolitical limitations: Review of the Transgender Studies Reader 2. *Lambda Nordica*, *3–4*, 177–84.

Nord, I. (2019) Routes to gender-affirming surgeries: Navigation and negotiation in times of biomedicalization. In G. Griffin and M. Jordal (eds) *Body, migration, re/constructive surgeries* (pp 209–24). London and New York: Routledge.

Pearce, R., Erikainen, S., and Vincent, B. (2020) TERF wars: An introduction. *The Sociological Review Monographs*, *68*(4), 677–98.

Pirnar, M. (2006) *Tok/protitok: konstrukcija in reprezentacija homoseksualne identitete v 20. stoletju*. Ljubljana: Založba ŠKUC.

Plummer, K. (2010) Generational sexualities, subterranean traditions and the hauntings of the sexual world: Some preliminary remarks. Retrieved on 28 September 2021 from https://kenplummer.com/publications/

Polić, M. (1988) Emancipacijske mogućnosti transseksualnosti. *Žena*, *46*(1–2), 96–115.

Puar, J. (2007) *Terrorist assemblages: Homonationalism in queer times*. Durham: Duke University Press.

Quijano, A. (2000) Coloniality of power and Eurocentrism in Latin America. *Nepantla: Views from South*, *1*(3), 533–80.

Quijano, A. (2007) Coloniality and modernity/rationality. *Cultural Studies*, *21*(2), 168–78.

Rakić, Z., Marić, J., Slijepčević, D., Vujović, S., and Perović, S. (1993) *Polni identitet i promena pola.* Belgrade: BIGZ.

Rexhepi, P. (2018) The politics of postcolonial erasure in Sarajevo. *Interventions*, *20*(6), 930–45.

Rogoznica, N. (2011) Cijela je Hrvatska od početka jedna klerikalna namještaljka. *Zadarski list.* Retrieved on 28 September 2021 from https://www.zadarskilist.hr/clanci/09062011/cijela-je-hrvatska-od-pocetka-jedna-klerikalna-namjestaljka

Sears, A. (2005) Queer anti-capitalism: What's left of lesbian and gay liberation? *Science & Society*, *69*(1), 92–112.

Sernatinger, A. and Echeverria, T. (2013) Queering socialism: An interview with Alan Sears. *New Politics.* Retrieved on 28 September 2021 from http://newpol.org/content/queering-socialism-interview-alan-sears

Stryker, S. (2006) (De)subjugated knowledges: An introduction to transgender studies. In S. Stryker and S. Whittel (eds) *The transgender studies reader* (pp 1–17). New York: Routledge.

Stryker, S. and Aizura, A.Z. (2013) Introduction: Transgender studies 2.0. In S. Stryker and S. Whittel (eds) *The transgender studies reader* (pp 1–12). New York: Routledge.

Stubbs, P. (2020) Socialist Yugoslavia, the Global South and the Non-Aligned Movement: The limits of Yugocentrism. Retrieved on 28 September 2021 from https://www.youtube.com/watch?v=s94vaVINHoA&list=UUwM2JKE3w1-sv-3pqaHheKw

Tlostanova, M. (2014) Towards a decolonisation of thinking and knowledge: A few reflections from the world of imperial difference. Retrieved on 28 September 2021 from https://www.academia.edu/10142502/Towards_a_Decolonization_of_Thinking_and_Knowledge_a_Few_Reflections_from_the_World_of_Imperial_Difference

Transserbia.org (2022) Snimak: Transkultura i umetnost u Srbiji. Retrieved on 28 December 2021 from https://transserbia.org/trans/transrodnost/1915-trans-kultura-i-umetnost-u-srbiji

Valentine, D. (2007) *Imagining transgender: An ethnography of a category.* Durham: Duke University Press.

Videkanić, B. (2020) *Nonaligned modernism: Socialist postcolonial aesthetics in Yugoslavia, 1945–1985.* Montreal: McGill-Queen's University Press.

Vidić, J. (2021) Identitet i iskustva stigmatizacije transrodnih osoba u Srbiji. [Unpublished doctoral dissertation]. Faculty of Philosophy, University of Belgrade.

PART I

Lives

1

Transgender lives in North Macedonia: citizenship, violence, and networks of support

Slavcho Dimitrov

It would be impossible for someone visiting Skopje, the capital of North Macedonia, to go for a walk in the city centre and not notice – probably with mixed feelings – numerous monuments that arose within the *Skopje 2014* urban renewal project spearheaded by the populist government of the VMRO-DPMNE.[1] In this jumble, which mimics the colonialist grandiosity of Western European capitals, one can also find *Porta Macedonia*, a triumphal arch completed in 2012. On its top, there are sculptures of a boy and a girl pointing both forwards and backwards, to the future and the past of North Macedonia and expressing the heterosexual form of the binary gender framework immersed in reproduction.

One could hardly understand such architectonic choices without considering a complex range of dimensions that make up the country's present political moment: multicultural ethnic composition marked by affective politics of uncertainty around national identity, a relatively recent independence (1991), an ethnically motivated armed conflict in 2001, and the ongoing disputes with the neighbouring countries such as Bulgaria and Greece involving also the politically influential Orthodox Church. In such a milieu, gender and sexuality serve as sites for displacing social anxieties and inequalities brought about by capitalist adjustments and economic devastation, which also shifted the gendered division of family labour and destabilised the traditional role of men as 'breadwinners'.

With this image in mind, it is not surprising that transgender people in North Macedonia face a high degree of invisibility. This is not only due to the gendered power relations and unequal distribution of resources but also to knowledge/power production and continuous erasure of the 'transgender phenomenon' (Stryker and Aizura, 2013) as a subject matter of research. Transgender people are 'the absent other', a constitutive impossibility within the societal and cultural production of the human, normatively defined through the universalised and naturalised gender binary categories. In this regard, transgender people's appearance in the public sphere and the media is rare, superficial, or sensationalist. Trans persons fall through the cracks of the traditional division of gender roles and inequality between men and women as questioning and violating these social positions is punished by stigma, ridicule, and violence.

Moreover, such traditional cultural registers and practices are reproduced within the legal framework. Up until 2018 there was no law regulating protection against violence and discrimination on the grounds of gender identity. In the past three years, limited but significant efforts have been made to legally protect gender identity from discrimination and make it a category that could mobilise national policies and actions. However, there is still no legal gender recognition framework that would enable transgender people to align the information in their personal documentation and civil registries with the gender they identify with.

The situation in the academic community is no different. Where present in academic works, textbooks, and literature, trans people are either pathologised or criminalised (Coalition Margins, 2019; Coalition Margins, 2020). There is a lack of qualitative research in which transgender people would themselves appear as experts and offer an analytically sound insight into the everyday practices, identities, diverse, and complex models and forms of embodiment, as well as their lived experiences and needs.

For many years, reports and analyses done by (non-specifically LGBT-oriented) human rights NGOs (non-governmental organisations) have pointed to a high level of violence and discrimination against LGBT people as well as to the lack of political will to protect them/us (Dimitrov and Kolozova, 2012; Cvetkovich and Dimitrov, 2015; Dimitrov, 2015). However, even a cursory look at that material shows that the T is either lacking from the acronym or is located on the margins. That is why the initial attempts to increase trans visibility were made by LGBT activist organisations that offered analyses of the existing legal framework with regard to transgender people and the obstacles they encounter within the health system (Boshkova and Raiden, 2016, 2017).[2] The data derived from these analyses is disconcerting as it shows that transgender people are forced to submit false information due to fear of being condemned: they face obsolete and intrusive psychiatric approaches as many psychiatrists 'advise' getting used to living with their gender assigned at birth instead of affirming their gender identity; transgender people struggle with medical services, especially accessing hormone therapy and are exposed to humiliating treatment due to the incompatibility between their documents and their appearance. Of course, there are also positive examples, but they remain in the shadows of multiple negative experiences with both the general public and the healthcare system facilities (Boshkova and Raiden, 2016).

Given this situation, in 2017–18 I was prompted by the Coalition Margins to embark on a research project that would offer an insight into the experience of transgender people in North Macedonia. On the one hand, I explored the main topics and milestones of transgender identity formation while bearing in mind the complex social dynamics and inter-subjective relations. On the other hand, I examined the intimate, yet socially determined, embodied, and affective experiences of citizenship of transgender people. These are seen not solely in terms of legal status and regulation of rights and duties but as the everyday affective and embodied experience in the social and public space, constituted and regulated by state policies and mundane power operations (Berlant, 1999; Muñoz, 2020). I also engaged with the question of how transgender people form networks of care and support in adverse circumstances. The current text focuses on the last two aspects of the original research project and also gives an account of the ways in which intersectionally sensitive and trans-led activism has recently started to develop announcing better futures for the trans population in the country.

Citizenship, affective experiences, and socialisation

Citizenship is a performative and affective practice (Joseph, 1999) imbued with symbolic, representational, cultural, and idealised notions that draw the boundaries of the 'good citizen' and create the conditions for national belonging. Citizenship is a 'category of feeling', a performative practice of 'national sentimentality' (Berlant 1997) that, while eschewing the politics on behalf of idealised private life, thus masking social inequalities, conflicts, fractures, hierarchies, and violence, is regulated and articulated around the normative axes of gender and sexuality underpinning the logic of the national future. The normative gendered national fantasies and performances of citizenship provide 'processes of valorisation that make different populations differently legitimate socially and under the law' and use 'cruel and mundane strategies both to promote shame for non-normative populations and to deny them state, federal, and juridical supports because they are deemed morally incompetent to their own citizenship' (Berlant 1997, p 8).

Within this context, I explored how the persistent, and not always visible or recognised, mechanisms of power operate in the social field, the administrative system, and institutions, as well as relations within everyday interactions, which cannot be comprised within a traditional understanding of power, seen exclusively as the government or as the punitive, negating, repressive legal system. The experiences of unequal treatment, exclusion, and humiliation of transgender people bear witness that the invisible webs of power affect the experiences of citizenship and everyday opportunities of transgender people (Spade, 2011). In this regard, I place such experiences under the interpretative framework of gender discipline (Foucault, 1990, 1991, 2007), as the assemblage of assumptions, norms, and techniques by means of which individuals interpret, frame, understand, and conduct their own and others' behaviours, bodies, and subjectivities, by setting gender as the regulatory optics, or to use Lauretis' terminology, different gender technologies (Lauretis, 1987).

In the second empirical section I focus on the biopolitical aspects of gender violence and the various strategies through which the access to public space and freedom of movement in line with one's gender identification, the access to health services and provision of a mentally sustainable and bearable life, and the distribution of security, are unequally distributed among the different segments of the population, focusing on how they affect the everyday lives and wellbeing opportunities of transgender people. I start from the thesis that different power technologies assume the *a priori* existence of natural categories, which are the source or condition for performances, permitted acts and actions, possibilities for body transformation, various behaviours, and administrative categorisations. I claim that such assumptions create the categories they assume to follow, that is, the gender binary, and on this basis, they consequently organise the various possibilities for the different, sexually marked bodies. The strategies for population management, or the security apparatus, according to Foucault, operate at the level of the effective reality of things (Foucault, 2007). This approach enables us to see how the administration and regulation of gender is harming trans people, organises their vulnerability, uses laws as tactics in the name of its goals, and redirects our attention toward various administrative legal procedures, regulations, and rules, which often stay out of sight in the 'big picture' of anti–discrimination legislation and legislation regulating hate crimes.

Things become additionally complicated when one considers the existing division between procedures that are reconstructive and procedures that belong to aesthetic surgery, according to which the status of the procedure and related expenses are determined by the Health Insurance Fund. As argued by Preciado (2013, p 116), such divisions bear witness that two:

> distinct regimes of power-knowledge traverse the body and that they construct the nose and the genitals according to different somato-political technologies. Whereas the nose is regulated by a pharmacopornographic power in which an organ is considered to be private property and merchandise, the genitals are still imprisoned in a pre-modern, sovereign, and nearly theocratic power regime that considers them to be the property of the state and dependent on unchanging transcendental law.

On the other hand, such fragmentation of the body and its reunification in totality as biopolitical fiction bears witness to the meaning of the heterosexist imagination, embodied in the pinnacle called reproduction, as a defining framework for understanding, division, and regulation of bodies, as male and female, as unchangeable, or subject to permissible change only when its purpose is confirming the ideal of sex or to reconstruct the bodies in accordance with this ideal. Ultimately, the productive function of such divisions, by excluding certain bodies, such as transgender and sex-ambivalent bodies, from the system for distribution of body biotechnologies, at the expense of said bodies, enables the maintenance of the fiction of biological, pre-technological, pre-cultural, and pre-political pureness of sex- and gender-normative bodies (Preciado, 2013).

Methodological considerations

I collected data through semi-structured, in-depth interviews with 23 participants from around the country: 14 were assigned male at birth; seven identify as women; three as other, explaining that sometimes they feel both as a man and a woman, or neither; two as transgender women; one as a crossdresser; and one as a man but assuming the role of a drag queen for experimentation and pleasure. Out of nine interviewed people who were assigned female at birth, five identify as men, one as other (as 'both a man and a woman'), two identified as transgender men, and one identified as gender non-binary. For the purpose of this text I gathered more data through distributing a questionnaire to representatives of three feminist activist organisations, one sex workers' collective, and the first and only non-formal trans grassroots group TransForma.

Gender police, discipline, and violence

All of the participants have experiences of being forced to perform gender norms and have undergone verbal, psychological or physical violence. The spaces of disciplinary technologies of gender span various segments of the social field, starting from

(a) the seemingly private space of the family, where my participants are often subject to violence, mostly from their fathers; then
(b) schools, as a disciplinary arranged structure in line with disciplinary normatives, in which socialisation spaces and methods of the teacher–student relations are organised in accordance with the gender binary and segregation;
(c) the streets and public spaces where everyone surveils everyone else, and looks, remarks, and humiliation are the means of punishment and correction;
(d) the hospitals and public facilities where duty bearers and public servants use the parents of children as mediators for confirmation and correction of the normal gender performance of transgender children;

(e) the wider family, concerned about the 'normal' reproduction of offspring and heritage; and all the way to

(f) all cultural agents, including the media.

In the words of two participants:

> 'People have been commenting and mocking me my entire life. Random people ... For years I was terrified of sitting at the back of the bus, because if kids my age gathered, they would mock me. Maybe it's because they noticed my insecurity, I don't know and I don't bother, but regardless of whether I was passing by a school, or in a bus, or ... whenever I went to get food, I wasn't even spoken to as male yet, but when walking out of the store, I heard them laughing: "Oh, so that was a girl." Also in job interviews, when they measured me up head to toe, like I was an alien. My latest experience was when I was looking for an apartment to rent ... I was walking toward the bus, I was listening to music and some high school boys were sitting nearby, they kept saying crap ... they started laughing.' (F., trans man)

> 'I was subject to physical violence since a very young age. First to domestic violence, by my father, who was very violent. This was just the beginning of everything that followed, the violence I faced in the streets. As I grew, there was more and more of it. When I was 11, particularly traumatic things happened, I was chased by a group of boys, around 20–25 boys who wanted to beat me up. I was afraid to go to school because I would get beaten. I went with fear, I went everywhere with fear, running, rushing ... And whenever I went, there was always a problem with me. There was always someone who had a problem with me. There was always someone who didn't like me, someone bothered by me, wanting to beat me up.' (Sh., trans woman)

These 'correctional' measures, pointing in the 'right direction' for achieving 'normal' gender embodiment, have long-term consequences both for mental health and the chances for development and social fulfilment. Such violent technologies of gender normalisation do not mark the body merely with a threat of punishment, but they also slowly exclude it, without utilising directly visible measures thereof, and by doing this, they exclude it from the equal distribution of opportunities. Many participants confirmed that as a result of exposure to humiliation, they withdrew themselves from further socialisation, experiencing anxiety, depression, and suicidal thoughts. Participants also pointed out that some of them left education, started skipping classes, or moved to another school. "I experienced most discrimination at school. Both elementary and high school. Mostly elementary. I didn't even finish high school. I mean I did, but not with regular classes, because I couldn't stand it" (A., trans woman).

In a long-term perspective, these experiences of humiliation, shame, and identity threats mobilise 'self-fulfilling prophecies' in which assumptions and stereotypes, or traumatic experiences are reflected in future achievements (Major and O'Brien, 2005). Along with scarce amounts of financial and cultural capital in the family, such experiences may also be associated with interrupted education and lead to lower employment rates. Most of the participants are unemployed, while a small portion have temporary engagements, mostly in NGOs. In the cases of participants with university-level education, there is a correlation between educational success and support by their families, as well as the existence of networks of care and support, as scarce as they might have been, or perhaps acquired after many years of struggle for recognition.

'Earlier the feeling of being in danger was much more intense, so I suppressed it with opiates. My struggle with addiction is, of course, a consequence of me being transsexual. I was using opiates for ten years. Fifteen I think. Almost fifteen years, my entire life, so to speak. This must not remain hidden. I am still using opiates because of being transsexual.' (A., trans woman)

Two participants, one transgender man and one transgender woman, who are also sex workers, spoke about an experience of rape, a traumatic moment they did not wish to discuss further, which was also the reason why they were reluctant to answer questions related to intimacy and sexuality. The vulnerability to violence is much higher for transgender women sex workers because they intertwine their transgender identity with the potentially dangerous provision of sexual services.

There are particularly disturbing experiences of transgender people who express their gender identity but they do not 'pass' as 'unambiguously' men or women. One participant, a transgender man from a small town, spoke about a series of experiences of brutal violence in public space:

'I just went home for the weekend and I had an unpleasant experience. I was attacked by 10 people around 30 years old, and we know each other … I really don't know why they did that. I didn't do anything. I didn't even respond, nothing, I didn't even try to defend myself because against 10 people … They started talking to me, they punched me and hit my leg with a crowbar, then threw lit firecrackers at me. They really freaked me out. I had to run away … I've had other scary situations, which ended up with 6 months probation for them, I was badly beaten up and they weren't held accountable. They also used cold weapons. I was terribly beaten. I have the medical paperwork from it … They were not some light injuries, they were serious. I had facial fractures. I went to the police, and it got worse. The police said "It happens, they're kids." They got six months of probation. That was it.' (T., trans man)

Many participants felt threatened in everyday situations and vulnerable when organising their daily routines. The unpredictability of everyday situations is a reason for not only continuously managing their gender identity and related information displayed in public but also constant monitoring of signs of potential attack. And ultimately, because of the manner of tackling the identity and existential threat as stigmatised bodies, transgender participants often withdraw and disengage their efforts from domains in which they are negatively stereotyped or when they are afraid they might be a target for discrimination, humiliation, or violence.

Gender administration and unequal access to biotechnology

In this section I turn my attention to the gender administration aspects of my participants' lives, especially in terms of access to toilets and biotechnology. The 'toilet issue' refers to the humiliating, corrective, and violent treatment against trans people, when using sex-segregated public toilets. The experiences, gender identifications, and body projects of transgender people challenge these normative assumptions, but this criticism comes at a price. Many participants, who express their gender identity in public spaces as well, spoke of negative experiences when using toilets in line with their gender identification and pointed out that they were treated as a security threat. In such instances, transgender men are perceived as not-men-enough and as too manly and not-women-enough, depending on the toilet they choose to use. T., a trans man, spoke about the following situation:

'Recently at the mall I got kicked out of the men's room. So I had to go to the ladies' room. I went in to wash my hands … I wasn't even going to use the toilet stall, I just wanted to wash my hands. In the men's room I almost got beaten up: "The hell are you doing here? Get out." So I did. And so I went to the ladies' room, and a woman came out of a stall and started screaming at the top of her lungs. She was hysterical, everyone was turning and listening, they were coming in and looking at me. "Maniac, maniac, maniac!" She kept shouting "maniac" and hit me with her purse. I said, "Madam, calm down, I'll explain, I'm female." "Don't lie to me, you rapist!" Maniac, she kept screaming and hitting me with her purse. I couldn't get away, she was pushing me. She was older, I even felt uncomfortable defending myself. So this guy came up in the end: "The hell are you doing here?" He was around 50. "Lemme see your ID!" so I showed it to him and he saw I am female: "Dear God, things like this are actually being born," or something like that. And I just walked out, but that was scary. I mean, it was terrifying for me.'

One of the most frequent problems had to do with personal documentation and misrecognition, a result of the misalignment of the data on their sex in their personal documents, their gender expression, and public presentation. These problems arise in different situations, institutions, organisations, and agencies, where personal documentation is needed to identify the service beneficiary. Participants pointed to different contexts in relation to this issue, for example banks, public transport, medical facilities, communication with police officers ... With almost no exception, these situations are stressful and humiliating, because my participants are continuously forced to explain and defend their identity. Some of the participants who have not experienced such a situation still feared it might happen to them and were particularly concerned about encountering a police officer.

Considering the lack of legal framework for the protection of transgender people or gender recognition, transgender people find themselves in a limbo that prolongs their uncertainty. Practices show a misaligned and unequal treatment of similar or different cases (Boshkova and Raiden, 2017). While changing name in personal documentation is relatively easy, with even the Ministry of Interior explaining that this change is permissible in order to confirm the gender of the person submitting the request, the change of the sex marker within the unique personal identification number and the ID is particularly difficult because decisions of the Civil Registry Office are inconsistent. In one case, the Office permitted a person to have their sex marker changed, while in an identical case, another person was not allowed, with the Office explaining that they did not have surgery. In two other cases, with persons applying for changes submitting adequate medical documentation, the Office proclaimed itself incompetent and denied their requests. For these two negative decisions of the Civil Registry Office, the Administrative Court reached positive verdicts in favour of the applicants and instructed the Office to perform the change of sex markers. Despite the success of these two cases, these people had to struggle for several years in order to realise their basic rights and live with dignity and safety (Boshkova and Raiden, 2017).

Another domain operated by the biopolitical regulatory mechanisms for maintaining the separation of femininity and masculinity is the domain of healthcare services and health insurance for different types of health services. Apart from the lack of sufficiently trained staff and developed mechanisms for coordination among different sectors and specialists for performing gender confirmation surgeries, the biopolitical regulation of sex seems like one of the key obstacles in the provision of adequate and necessary healthcare of transgender individuals. Namely, if we exclude those cases where the problem is either lack of biotechnologies or human resources, the available administrative apparatus decides about availability of these biotechnologies along the normalising gendered axis. This is in accordance with the initial assumptions regarding the sexed body, which are historically specific, socially organised, and much more complex than the reductionist bi–partisan framework of their normative analysis (Preciado, 2013).

There are plenty of examples in this direction: I can mention oestrogen and testosterone, as well as variations of hormone products, available to biologically 'normal' male and female bodies, in accordance with the ICD diagnoses, and covered by the Health Insurance Fund in line with the Diagnosis Related Group (DRG) system, with numerical codes. These hormone products are often prescribed to cisgender persons for treatment of various health conditions, but they are not on the list that would make them available to transgender persons. Furthermore, many of the gynaecological surgical procedures performed at the Gynaecology and Obstetrics Clinic, based on previously established medical indications, are also procedures that are performed during gender confirmation surgeries but yet again, these procedures are not available to transgender persons nor are they covered by the Health Insurance Fund. Even in situations where patients do not have health insurance, there are no administrative obstacles for cisgender women, provided that they can afford to cover the costs themselves. However, even this option is unavailable to transgender people because they cannot receive a diagnosis on the basis of which doctors would perform the. Moreover, silicone prostheses for trans women, for example, are technically possible, but get rejected as invalid because of a lack of relevant diagnoses (Peev in Boshkova and Raiden, 2016). The clear sex–based biopolitical investment in the administrative regulation of the availability of biotechnologies for different bodies is reflected in the fact that many of the surgical interventions are available on the list of diagnoses and covered by the Health Insurance Fund in cases of infants with 'hermaphroditism', in accordance with the classification, that is, in cases when sexually ambivalent bodies are subject to enforced physical intervention with the purpose of aligning their different bodies with the idealised and normalising frameworks of maleness and femaleness.

All the afore mentioned shows that for most interventions there is an administrative obstacle faced by transgender people because the Health Insurance Fund does not identify them as basic health services for this purpose. This way, even without the direct, visible, and recognisable application of technologies of violence and exclusion of transgender people, they become victims of the unequal distribution of opportunities and chances for a dignified life. There is a division in the supposedly unified population, between those worthy of care, safety, and benefit, and those left on the margins and their own resources.

Networks of care and support

Considering all the aspects of everyday violence, correction, humiliation, and body regulation, one wonders about where transgender people find strength, energy and care. According to the statements and stories told by trans people in this research, it is hardly likely that the response would point to the state institutions, including schools, expert staff in schools, or other representatives of the state apparatus. With almost no exception, my participants confirm that they do not trust the police, and therefore do not report their experiences of violence or discrimination. The participants state that their lack of trust in the police is due to personal experience or the experience of their close friends or acquaintances. Many of them confirmed that in situations when they tried to report violence or threats to the police, they either faced additional ridicule and humiliation or the police did not undertake any measures, or if they did, they still tolerated the perpetrators and minimum sentences were given even in cases of brutal violence. These experiences are even more present among transgender sex workers, all of whom had suffered humiliation by the police when they were actually looking for protection.

Apart from a small number of those who received support in the gendering or gender confirmation process by their parents and close ones, almost all participants stated that their main source of support were other trans people, or sometimes gay or lesbian friends. Socialising with other trans people is a source of support, a safe space where they can openly talk about their problems, and a place where they can express their gender identity. For participants who only express their identity to a select audience, LGBT social circles are among the rare places where they can express their identity at all. Friendships and communication with other trans persons generate informal support networks where they exchange information and acquire gender capital, as well as receive information on all aspects of the transition process. This is particularly important if we consider the lack of information on transgender issues in the education process or in the media field (with the exception of some rare examples). Considering the forced self-isolation faced by many of the transgender people, at least in one phase of their lives, these friendships and relations are an escape from the 'psychological ghetto'. Many participants stated that they see their activist role precisely in connecting and helping other trans persons who do not yet have the courage to accept their transgender identity, who are afraid of expressing freely, or who doubt their mental health.

'Finally, I can understand and talk to these people, without having to explain myself for ages, about what this means, and all that. And immediately, we have mutual support, absolutely. Advice and what not, and also when I started meeting others, my friend and I had already started hormone therapy. We started on the same day, and we had already overcome many things. We were quite liberated, so we ... or I can speak for myself ... I was some sort of support for others. So yeah, great. Awesome! Very positive, very liberating.' (S., non-binary trans man)

Considering the average or below-average social status of most of the participants, as well as the fact that many of them live in different towns outside of the capital, a large portion of the communication and support networks is maintained via the internet and various social networks, due to the lack of possibility for them to meet.

All these experiences are also a reason for identification with the trans community, that is, self-perception as a part of this community. There was notable disidentification of many participants with the LGBT community, mostly due to the different forms of experienced exclusion, lack of understanding, and ridicule of their identity by cisgender gay men. This problem was pointed out by a large majority of the participants, while some trans men spoke of unpleasant experiences with lesbians.

'I think LGB is kicking us out of the community. They're throwing us out, so you can't feel it's a joined fight, when there are people fighting against others. You can't really feel like you're part of it. Realistically speaking in terms of LGBT, all human rights activists also fight for trans rights. I'm not questioning this at all. But LGB people aren't fighting for us, they even discriminate against us a lot.' (T., trans man)

Among participants who expressed a sense of belonging to the trans- or LGBT community as well as intense experiences of communication, networking, solidarity, and friendships with other trans people, there is a visible correlation with the higher degree of self-confidence, determination, and knowledge about the processes of gender transformation and identification, as well as about gender confirmation procedures. There was also visible correlation in regard to having concrete responses to the key issues and priorities of trans people.

Some participants said that even after several years, they still struggle with their friends about the recognition of their gender identity. This problem is a daily struggle in their broader families too. Of course, this does not exclude friendships with straight or cisgender people that represent a source of support for some of my participants. These friends tend to be women as cisgender men are mostly associated with misgendering practices, including shaming and humiliation. Only one trans man stated he maintains friendships with straight cisgender men, but in these friendships he is not open about his transgender identity as he can 'pass' as a man. Another participant, a post-operative transsexual woman, who denies her transgender history, spoke of more frequent socialisation with cisgender women, before whom she hides her transgender trajectory and identity.

Conclusion

Compared to other countries in the post-Yugoslav region, in particular Serbia, Croatia, and Slovenia, LGBT activism in Macedonia is younger, beginning in 2006 with the formation of the Association for Free Sexual Orientation – MASSO. After 2008 several other LGBT and queer CSOs and groups have been initiated, including Coalition MARGINS Skopje, the LGBTI Support Center, LGBT United Tetovo, Subversive Front, LEZFEM, and the National Network for Fighting Homophobia and Transphobia. (Miškovska-Kajevska, 2016). Within this short trajectory, as in other Central and Eastern European countries, '"bisexuality" and "transgender" were included alongside lesbian and gay politics beforehand, discursively, without any signals from bisexuals and transsexuals claiming their rights to be included' (Mizielińska, 2011, pp 92–3). Since the beginning of LGBT organising, Coalition MARGINS Skopje and the LGBTI Support Center have devoted attention to trans issues and visibility, although direct participation and public visibility and appearance of trans people was lacking. These organisations, and later the others that formed, were advocating for inclusion of gender identity in non-discriminatory legislation, organising debates, films screenings, public discussions, media talks, and art and cultural programmes including transgender artists and topics, and offered legal and psycho-social help for transgender persons. Some of the participants in my research confirmed that the support they received from activist organisations was important. These collectives were their first opportunity to meet other trans people, resolve their 'gender uncertainty', see themselves within the transgender identity position and relieve themselves of the feeling of 'being alone in the world'.

Starting from 2011, Coalition Margins created a space and hosted the formation of the first trans group that in 2018 would become an activist collective, TransForma. With the support of the existing initiatives, the trans group produced videos, handbooks, and help literature for transgender people along with organising support groups for trans people and their parents. As a trans group for support led by the trans activist Igor Raiden, this group operated for a while within the LGBTI Support Center, initiating contacts and trainings with/for psychologists, psychiatrists, and representatives of different medical professions and teams and activist groups from Belgrade. These collaborations with medical professionals have been continuously sustained and have led to a group of supporters within the State Clinic, helping transgender people to navigate the labyrinths of the health system in order to receive the needed health services without discrimination.

From 2018 the non-formal group has started with public activities, making its work and efforts more visible by also naming themselves as TransForma. Although the group is still not officially registered, it has initiated a series of activities in the past two years, by setting its focus mostly on strengthening the capacities and knowledge of transgender people for activism, advocacy, strategic litigation, and artovos. The group has also organised a public video campaign on trans visibility in 2019, having for the first time three transgender individuals and activists speaking publicly. In 2019 TransForma organised the first Trans Visibility March in Skopje, a few months before the first Pride Parade in the same year.[3]

In the last few years, trans activism has been merging its struggles through intersectional alliances, not only with the lesbian and gay movement but also with the struggles for equality of sex workers and women's and gender equality. STAR STAR is a sex workers' collective that provides various services and advocates for the rights of sex workers, also reaching transgender sex workers but even more importantly initiating different activities and projects related to the intersections of transgender people's visibility, rights and health. Lila Milik, a transgender woman, one of the founders of TransForma, and one of the few publicly visible trans persons is also a sex worker and part of the STAR STAR sex workers' collective. Although most older women's equality organisations offer limited support for trans issues, several younger feminist organisations and groups have unequivocally supported transgender people's struggles and incorporated transgender women as a visible and constitutive component of their work and activities. Тиииит! Инк. (Tiiiit!Inc.), a feminist organisation that initiated the first feminist cultural festival, for example, includes trans issues regularly in their festival programmes, while transgender rights and critique of the gendered system is a constitutive part of their feminist position, which 'represents a joint platform for all gender-marginalised identities and opposes patriarchal society and its negative effects on women, trans women and the LGBT community in general'.[4] Together with the team behind PeachPreach, a women's storytelling event that has gained great popularity, they have invited trans people to participate and share their stories, while PeachPreach also organised the first trans slam PeachPreach event in February 2020. REAKTOR – Research in Action is another gender equality-focused organisation supporting the same principles, investing efforts in their work, research, and advocacy work to bring to light non-binarity and the struggles of the most marginalised women (mostly trans women).[5] MEDUSA, self-defined as a platform for girls, women, and gender and sexual minorities is another feminist group that understands the struggles for women's equality as constitutively intertwined with the struggle of trans women.[6]

Given that trans visibility and trans activism are recent, future research could devote more attention to the questions related to trans identity from the perspective of the strategic construction of political and cultural resistance, both collectively and individually. The political struggle creates the conditions for a certain socially oppressed group to learn the histories and strategies of its own oppression, to develop consciousness-for-itself as a group, and to institute its own subjectivity in relation to history and knowledge. As much as political identity, gender identity also represents a creative response of trans people to the structural conditions that colour their existence and serves as a site of transformation. My research participants have confirmed that the trans support group and social and political organising of trans people are valued sources of support care, knowledge, and survival. Considering the rise of trans activism in the past few years, it remains to be seen how this movement will organise itself, what interpretative tools for self-identification it will produce, and what paths of resistance it will pursue with the view of improving the status of trans people in the country.

Acknowledgements

I would like to thank all the participants who shared their intimate stories for the purposes of this research. I am also grateful to Igor Raiden for his help with arranging the interviews – his struggle for and devotion to the transgender cause is a great source of inspiration.

Notes

1 Internal Macedonian Revolutionary Organization – Democratic Party for Macedonian National Unity is a major political party in North Macedonia.
2 For several years, the Skopje Pride Weekend was the only cultural and artistic platform where a Macedonian audience could encounter the cultural production of trans people and meet some of the most prominent trans artists in the world. For more information on the festival's concept and programme visit the Facebook page of Skopje Pride Weekend at: https://www.facebook.com/skopjeprideweekend/ or the website of Coalition Margins, the festival's organiser, at: http://coalition.org.mk/?lang=en
3 I would like to thank Lila Milik for recounting this brief history of TransForma to me. Our interview was conducted in Skopje on 20 June 2020.
4 Jana Kocevska, TIIIIT!Inc. Interview conducted in Skopje on 22 June 2020.
5 Marija Bashevska, REAKTOR-Research in Action. Interview conducted in Skopje on 21 June 2020.
6 Kalia Dimitrova and Ena Bendevska, MEDUSA. Interview conducted in Skopje on 22 June 2020.

References

Berlant, L. (1997) *The queen of America goes to Washington City: Essays on sex and citizenship.* Durham and London: Duke University Press.

Berlant, L. (1999) The subject of true feeling: Pain, privacy, and politics. In A. Sarat and T. Kearns (eds) *Cultural pluralism, identity politics, and the law* (pp 49–84). Ann Arbor: The University of Michigan Press.

Boshkova, N. and Raiden, I. (2016) *Analiza na zdravstvenite potrebi i dostapnosta na zdravstveni uslugi za trans lugeto vo Makedonija.* Skopje: Koalicija Margini.

Boshkova, N. and Raiden, I. (2017) *Analiza na pozitivni praktiki na pravno priznavanje na rodot.* Skopje: Koalicija Margini.

Coalition Margins/Коалиција МАРГИНИ. (2019) *Годишен извештај за состојбата со човековите права на маргинализираните заедници.* Скопје: Коалицуја МАРГИНИ.

Coalition Margins/Коалиција МАРГИНИ. (2020) *Годишен извештај за состојбата со човековите права на маргинализираните заедници.* Скопје: Коалицуја МАРГИНИ.

Cvetkovich, I. and Dimitrov, S. (2015) Heteronormative agnotology: The performative of silence and ignorance in Macedonian media. In T. Rosić, J. Koteska, and J. Ljumović (eds) *Representations of gender minorities in media: Serbia, Macedonia and Montenegro* (pp 93–110). Belgrade: FMK.

Dimitrov, S. (2015) The triumphant distribution of the heteronormative sensible: The case of sexual minorities in transitional Macedonia, 1991–2012. In C. Hassentab and S.P. Ramet (eds) *Gender (in)equality and gender politics in South-Eastern Europe* (pp 231–54). London: Palgrave Macmillan.

Dimitrov, S. and Kolozova, K. (2012) Sexualities in transition: Discourses, power and sexual minorities in transitional Macedonia. In K. Daskalova, C. Hornstein Tomić, K. Kaser, and F. Radunović (eds) *Gendering post-socialist transition: Studies of changing gender perspectives* (pp 151–82). Vienna: Erste Foundation.

Foucault, M. (1990) *History of sexuality: Volume one: An introduction.* Harmondsworth: Penguin.

Foucault, M. (1991) *Discipline and punish: The birth of the prison.* London: Penguin Books.

Foucault, M. (2007) *Security, territory, population: Lectures at the Collège de France 1977–1978.* Basingstoke: Palgrave.

Joseph, M. (1999) *Nomadic identities: The performance of citizenship.* Minneapolis, London: University of Minnesota Press.

Lauretis de, T. (1987) *Technologies of gender: Essays on theory, film, and fiction.* Bloomington: Indiana University Press.

Major, B. and O'Brien, L.T. (2005) The social psychology of stigma. *Annual Review of Psychology, 56,* 393–421.

Miškovska-Kajevska, A. (2016) Growing oppression, growing resistance: LGBT activism and Europeanisation in Macedonia. In B. Bilić (ed) *LGBT activism and Europeanisation in the (post-)Yugoslav space: On the rainbow way to Europe* (pp 81–116). London: Palgrave Macmillan.

Mizielińska, J. (2011) Travelling ideas, travelling times: On the temporalities of LGBT and queer politics in Poland and the 'West.' In J. Mizielińska, and R. Kulpa (eds) *De-centering Western sexualities: Central and Eastern European perspectives* (pp 85–106). Farnham: Ashgate.

Muñoz, J.E. (2020) *The sense of brown*. Durham and London: Duke University Press.

Preciado, B.P. (2013) *Testo junkie: Sex, drugs, and biopolitics in the pharmacopornographic era*. New York: Feminist Press.

Spade, D. (2011) *Normal life: Administrative violence, critical trans politics and the limits of law*. Durham: Duke University Press.

Stryker, S. and Aizura, A.Z. (2013) Introduction: Transgender studies 2.0. In S. Stryker and S. Whittel (eds) *The transgender studies reader* (pp 1–12). New York: Routledge.

2

The resilience of trans existence through solidarity in Montenegro: (non)pathologising narratives of transgender lives

Jovan Ulićević and Čarna Brković

'First of all, I am proud to stand here with you today. I remember as if it were yesterday, when I first came to the community as a child, and clearly stated that I would never walk in a Pride Parade, because I didn't get the purpose of that walk. I proudly say that I stand here today as, still a child, in my fourth Pride. A child whose childhood was damaged just because I was different from others. Today I understand the gravity of this walk and its steps. This walk, this Pride gives me back the childhood that was denied to me ... I stand here today to demonstrate that they did not break me; that with every breath, every morning coffee, and every step I will shine the light of my struggle. Our struggle.'[1]

These words were uttered by Nikola Ilić, a trans activist, during his speech at the seventh Montenegro Pride, held in Podgorica, the capital of Montenegro, on 21 September 2019. The whole speech illustrates the long way that Nikola has travelled since he joined the local trans support group in October 2017. From a high-school kid who lived in the dorms and "felt huge repulsion towards ... LGBT people generally", as he said during our interview, Nikola has become an openly trans young man and a trans activist who occasionally runs the support group, speaks in the public venues, and cultivates relations of care and respect among trans people in Montenegro. For him, as for many others in this context, trans activism has provided a means to work simultaneously on personal healing and on changing the fabric of the Montenegrin society. Trans activism in this context means more than reworking the coordinates of sex and gender in the public arenas; it also provides a means to claim back one's childhood and life damaged by transphobia.

Nikola's path reflects broader fast-paced transformations of trans activism in the country. The first organised meetings of trans people in Montenegro started in 2013, within the framework of a self-support group founded within the LGBTIQ+ association *Queer Montenegro*. This self-support group has been a place of healing, resistance, learning, and teaching, (re)shaping narratives about trans and gender diverse people and nurturing resilience. It has also turned out to be the backbone of trans activist endeavours in the country. The self-support group led to the creation of an informal activist trans group called Transovci (Transians) in 2015, which then grew into a formally registered NGO called Spektra in 2017.

This chapter explores social conditions that have enabled trans people to start making political claims for greater visibility, recognition, and respect in Montenegro. In order to explain why trans activism has been focused from the very beginning on personal healing and on social transformation, we trace a relatively short history of public discussions about trans people and issues that have been led in Montenegro in the last 20 years. In those discussions, led largely in the comments section of the Montenegrin internet and news portal *Vijesti*, we mapped four discursive standpoints, which we call transphobic nationalism, pathologising compassion, liberal standpoint, and intersectional standpoint. We understand the term 'standpoint' as a particular way of making connections between notions that reflect and enable a certain understanding of the world – or as a discourse in emergence, in Foucault's (2002) sense.

From the perspective of the transphobic nationalist standpoint, trans people were positioned as 'foreign' to the Montenegrin political community, that is, as an 'import' brought about by the West and the EU integrations. Pathologising compassion included an expression of sympathy for the trans people, in a pathologising, patronising, and passivising manner. From a liberal standpoint, trans people were discussed as individuals who needed and deserved better human rights protection, particularly better cultural visibility and recognition. An intersectional standpoint was articulated mostly by the trans people themselves, often by those who were members of the self-support group and, later, Spektra. Here, trans people were understood as needing material support as well as better cultural recognition and as people whose existence interwove gender and sexuality in complex ways with other aspects of their social positions and personhood, including class, race, ethno-nationality, and so on. From the intersectional standpoint, emphasis was placed also on the socio-economic grievances that are shared between trans and cis people in Montenegro.

A newspaper interview with Marko Bojanić: pathologising compassion

In August 2009, an interview with Marko Bojanić, a transgender man, was published in newspaper *Vijesti*.[2] This was the first time any LGBTIQ+

person told their personal story in a public venue in Montenegro.[3] The interview presents a prime example of the standpoint we call pathologising compassion, as we will explain below. Marko is not the first trans person from Montenegro who has gone through a gender-affirming process: he states that he was familiar with three people who performed it before him. Before 2012, when the law on health insurance was amended to provide public healthcare coverage of 80 per cent of costs of medical transition, five persons from Montenegro underwent the transition process.[4] Only one of those five people still lives in Montenegro, not revealing their gender identity to anyone.[5]

At the time of the story being published, Marko Bojanić was a 37-year old transgender man, born in Podgorica and based in Rome, Italy. In the interview, Marko lets the readers know that he left Podgorica when he was 19 because his family did not accept him. They forced him to dress in 'female dresses', he said, and his father beat him. Marko states that he had support from his mother but that she was not able to act upon it and to stand by him. Marko went to Belgrade and Sarajevo to study economics because he 'could not stand anymore to be seen as a freak' (*nijesam više mogao da podnesem da me gledaju kao čudaka*). He was seeking other transgender persons from Podgorica. At that time, he could find information about them only in the newspapers and from medical doctors.

In the interview, Marko describes how he started his transition in 1999, by going to a psychiatrist twice a week for 90 minutes. The psychiatrist conducted different types of analysis and Marko had to pay between €30 and €50 for every session. After some time, Marko went to doctors in Italy who engaged in a different process and started hormonal treatment. He paid for this from his own pocket too: €150 per injection. Marko paid for all the costs of the transition by himself. The journalist who interviewed Marko insisted on finding out the price of surgeries. Marko refused to provide this information, as is stated in the article. Marko did not problematise the length, the high price, and the rigid criteria for initiating the transition process. He said that he was happy to just be able to undergo the process. He had one surgery performed in Rome and another one, genital reconstruction, in Belgrade. Marko mentioned his friendship with the doctor who performed the second surgery, Sava Perović, a well-known specialist for gender-affirming surgeries and a pioneer in his work in the former Yugoslav region (Vidić and Bilić, this volume). Relationships between transgender persons and doctors are frequently described in trans storytelling in former Yugoslav countries as 'friendships'. Such an interpretation of a professional relationship illustrates the sense of gratefulness that trans people feel for the mere fact of being able to transition. It also leaves the monopolistic and capitalist character of trans-specific healthcare unproblematised.

Another newspaper article followed Marko's interview.[6] In that second article, Dr Sava Perović says that he performs one in every two to three gender-affirming surgeries pro bono – because they are so expensive and he is aware of economic hardship many trans people endure. Dr Perović added that the price of the gender-affirming surgeries is significantly lower in Serbia than abroad. He addressed the difficulties he faced at that moment to provide the gender-affirming medical interventions within the public healthcare system, due to the unwillingness of the hospital management. This has changed over time. The larger problem nowadays seems to be that a medical team in Belgrade, led by Dr Đorđević, has monopolised trans-specific healthcare, performing surgeries both in the public healthcare system and in the private clinics (Vidić and Bilić, this volume). This affects many trans people throughout the former Yugoslav region because of the lack of medical practitioners educated about trans-specific healthcare.

The first newspaper interview also provides a glimpse into the pain and violence Marko experienced in Podgorica. Marko describes how he was excluded from the funeral of his mother, adding that he was treated with disgust and rage by his relatives, who also made it clear that he was not welcome in the family anymore because of who he is. Furthermore, Marko described a particularly violent situation when his father tried to kill him by burying him alive. He survived with the help of a neighbour. While the article describes in vivid detail the challenges and difficulties that Marko had faced, it ends on an empowering note, suggesting that Marko is finally living the life he wanted, not caring about other people's opinions, and that he is happy and successful in his personal and professional life.

While the article clearly has a friendly and sympathetic tone, its goal seems to be to present Marko as akin to a 'normal person', rather than as already a regular man in his own right. This is the characteristic of pathologising compassion. From this standpoint, a clear boundary between cis and trans persons is maintained by positing trans people as an object of charitable compassion. The background assumption is that trans people are ill, that they need medical help to get better, and that, therefore, they deserve compassion. For instance, the story is described in the newspapers in a sensationalist manner as 'exclusive' and as a 'confession', implying that trans experiences are both extraordinary and shameful. The terms 'born in a wrong body' (*rođen u pogrešnom tijelu*) and 'biological mistake' (*biološka greška)* are used in the article, while the term 'transsexuals' is portrayed as 'outdated'. The article includes a subtitle, 'Those born in the wrong body used to be killed' (*Rođene u pogrešnom tijelu nekad su ubijali*). The subtitle is extracted from a depiction of a conversation between Marko and the grandmother who supported him. He recollected the words of his grandmother, who said that, in the past, in the Montenegrin villages, 'people like him' (*ljude poput mene*) used to be imprisoned in the wooden houses and held without water and food, until they died. This is a relatively strange claim, since pastoralist communities in the mountainous parts of the Balkans included a place to articulate gender that both confirmed and overcame the heteronormative binary. Namely, gender landscape of Balkan mountainous communities in the 19th and 20th century included a practice of 'sworn virgins', or people who were recognised as women at birth, but who were socialised as men for various reasons (Grémaux, 1996, see also Limani, this volume). The story represents trans people as not belonging to the traditional life in Montenegro, which contradicts the general potential for queerness that Balkan rural life contained (see also Hadžiristić, this volume). This sense of foreignness of trans people and issues is strengthened in the article by using the words 'transdžender' and 'transdženderizam', which is the Montenegrin transliteration of English words 'transgender' and 'transgenderism'.

The subsequent article about Marko, called 'The illness must be cured' (*Bolest se mora liječiti*), pathologises Marko's identity to a far greater extent. The article features an interview with Dr Sava Perović and compliments Marko for being a 'passing' trans man. Both the journalist and Dr Perović mention that Marko does not show he is transgender in his appearance and gestures, and they discuss this as an admirable trait. The article portrays Marko as a proud Montenegrin, whose ancestors were well known for their courage and military accomplishments. The fact that Marko's wedding followed traditional Montenegrin customs is discussed positively, as an indication that his national sense of belonging is in 'the right place'. The wedding included musicians, folklore dancers, and many invitees, which indicates it was a fairly expensive event.

Despite the pathologising and normative manner of writing about Marko's gender identity and expression, this article had an impact on other transgender persons in Montenegro. For instance, Jovan Džoli Ulićević, one of the authors of this text, mentioned publicly many times that the interview with Marko was his first encounter with the storytelling and information about transgender people in Montenegro, which empowered him to start working as an activist – leading to the founding of a self-support group and his public coming out in 2016.[7]

The founding of Spektra and the performance *Masks*

[8]One aim of the activist/self-support group Transovci[9] was to create a space where transgender and gender diverse people in Montenegro could start creating their own narrative about themselves, away from pathologising and patronising perspectives on trans people and towards a perspective that stresses diversity, self-determination, and empowerment. After organising several visibility actions, Transovci hosted the first regional event that brought

together transgender, gender diverse, and intersex people from across the former Yugoslav countries – Transposium.[10] During that event, organised in March 2017, with the logistical support of Queer Montenegro, Transovci announced that they were founding the first trans-led organisation that would deal with the protection and promotion of the human rights of transgender, gender diverse, and intersex people called – Association Spektra.[11]

After Spektra was officially registered, ten members of Spektra shared their stories publicly, including trans men (Teodor Stojanović, Nikola Ilić, Dante Ognjanović, Aleksa Radonjić, and Jovan Ulićević), trans women (Lara Mirović, Vanja, and some other trans women), and non-binary people (Katja Jovanović). Spektra members who were willing to become visible and talk openly in the public have been very diverse: there were people of various gender identities, age groups, people from rural areas, sex workers, and people who migrated to Montenegro from other countries in the region (for example, Serbia).[12] The members of Spektra have also regularly reacted to the cases of human rights violations of transgender people. For instance, Spektra reacted when a trans woman was denied the right to change her name;[13] when the issue of intersex persons was opened to the public for the first time;[14] when the World Health Organization depathologised trans identities;[15] when the right to privacy of trans women in the Public Health Center Podgorica was violated; when amendments to the Law on Health Insurance provided a completely free gender-affirming procedure; when a trans man was attacked in Kolašin in 2019, and so on.

One of Spektra's most important events was a performance called *Masks*. This was the first public and artivistic gathering of trans and gender diverse people in Montenegro, organised in Podgorica in November 2018 to mark the Transgender Day of Remembrance (TDOR). It was then repeated in the town of Kolašin, as a reaction to the violence inflicted upon a trans man who lived there. This performance inspired trans groups across the region to organise it in Belgrade and Zagreb (see Milanović, this volume). TDOR was marked in 2019 by the performance *331* in Podgorica. Although it gathered around 50 visitors, including allies and the general public, it did not provoke a live discussion in the public venues.

The performance provoked lively discussions on portals and in the social media. In one long discussion in the comments section of the daily *Vijesti*, we can find all four above-mentioned standpoints. The most dominant aspect of the public discussions after the performance included transphobic nationalism and pathologising compassion. Transphobic nationalism standpoint was reflected in comments and arguments that focused on the presumed 'Western influence', praising Russia, Putin, and the ban of 'gay propaganda'. This echoes transphobic nationalist discourses elsewhere too, which also rely on the 'storyline' of needing to protect 'traditional values' from outside interference (Edenborg, 2021). The same standpoint was taken by the commenters who lamented upon the money that is 'spent by NGOs' in order to 'exploit the differences and minorities', as well as by those who complained because of 'too much exposure' of trans people:

tandrket, portal *Vijesti*
14-11-2018 06:21h
In MNE you can't cross the street without someone pointing at your flaws, neither straight nor gay people are protected from this, but you don't see the other ones requesting some bigger rights. (…) There are some people who honestly support this, but mostly this is about profits on projects of different NGOs. The more the people respond to this, the more they will emphasize the "differences".

Pathologising compassion was present among the commenters who claimed to 'accept' trans persons but placed trans persons in the fixed position of the Other. They often did so by presenting their own attitudes as the 'common sense' of the society, for whom trans people present a 'foreign tissue'. Although these commenters emphasised that trans people are 'not to blame' for being the way they are, they framed trans people as those who constantly try to be removed from the 'healthy tissue' of society.

Robespierre____, portal *Vijesti*
14-11-2018 02:27h
… a weak one should not be attacked, that is the basis of our somewhat forgotten humanity. However, every one of us has the right to choose what they want in their surroundings. Society (from the perspective of the majority) does not want these kinds of people and writing essays on the topic of humanness is in vain, that is what I am talking about. This is about, as I already said, recognizing something which is a foreign tissue, I am not saying they are to blame for what they are.

Robespierre____, portal *Vijesti*
14-11-2018 01:48h
I understand their situation, they are rejected by the family and society, often being targeted by insults … You understood me wrong, I was not speaking in the name of the whole society, I was just stating the facts about that relationship between the society and transgender people. Let me repeat, whatever they do, they will never cross the barrier between them and society, because the community feels their behaviour as an absolute distortion of the natural law; from that perspective, their integration into the society remains an eternal Sisyphus's work.

Liberal standpoint can be illustrated by the comments of one particular author who claimed to be involved with LGBTIQ+ activism. One of the main characteristics of this standpoint is the call to tolerate differences, grounded in a clear human rights approach, and aimed at countering arguments that minority is taking the rights of the majority.

> Commenter portal *Vijesti*
> 14-11-2018 01:37h
> That what you talk about is discrimination. We don't have to love some group, but we must not belittle it, exclude it from society. We must understand that not all people are the same and that there are so many variations that none of us is the same. Therefore, let us show tolerance. Regarding the society, believe me, in your environment, surely, there is an LGBT person. It is just that you are not aware of that. People are afraid to show to you who they actually are because of your attitudes.

Intersectional standpoint was put forward by trans people and Spektra's activists. While we have not conducted quantitative research, we suggest that the intersectional standpoint was the least present in the comments section on the *Vijesti* portal. We found only a handful of comments that reflected this perspective; for instance:

> Commenter portal *Vijesti*
> 14-11-2018 01:39h
> We all have multiple identities, not only one.

Some of the responses to this comment illuminate a confusion that some members of the broader public articulate when faced with an intersectional perspective:

> zbun_mali, portal *Vijesti*
> 14-11-2018 01:22h
> … how do you score if someone is Roma, and at the same time LGBTIQ? Does one negate the other? Do not fool around.

The 'score' in this comment is related to the idea that minority identities and the practice of various forms of minority belonging bring 'benefits' through the mechanisms of protection of minority rights.

The question of this commenter demonstrates confusion, since one of the key points of intersectional analytics is that being Roma *and* LGBTIQ+ at the same time differs from being either Roma or LGBTIQ+ separately, in terms of how a person experiences discrimination in society (cf. Crenshaw,

1991). It needs to be said here that Roma and Balkan Egyptians have been racialised as 'Black' in Montenegro. While racial formations throughout Europe need to be triangulated, for they include Euro-Whiteness, Eastern European dirty-Whiteness, and Blackness (Parvulescu, 2015; Baker, 2018; Böröcz, 2021), the forms of oppression and discrimination of the LGBTIQ+ Roma and Balkan Egyptians are specific and rarely addressed through the dominant LGBTIQ+ anti-discrimination mechanisms in the country. This remains an important task for the strengthening of an intersectional approach to trans activism in the country.

Who is entitled to full public healthcare?

Public discussions of healthcare insurance law

In 2018, Montenegrin Ministry of Healthcare proposed amendments of the Law on Health Insurance, which among other things, aimed to cover expenses for the gender-reaffirming treatments from 80 per cent to 100 per cent. This provoked a reaction from transphobic nationalists. In March 2019, an NGO-turned-political-party called 'Alternative Montenegro' sent a request to the Montenegrin Ministry of Healthcare asking for several changes of the Law on Healthcare Insurance. One request was 'to remove sex change from free[16] healthcare insurance' and another one to increase three 'free IV fertilization attempts' to five.[17] The reasoning for the request of this NGO was the following:

> free healthcare protection financed by the Montenegrin tax payers should cover only procedures and treatments which protect life, the creation of life, and things that affect health of Montenegrin citizens. Sex change is an expensive procedure that is not caused by someone's endangered health. Also, sex change does not give the patient the ability to reproduce.

Ministry of Healthcare ignored the request.[18] However, the request attracted a lot of attention in the social media. People commented from all four positions we mentioned above. This discussion also crystallised a broader trend of far-right actors to misuse trans people and trans questions to claim justice from transphobic nationalist perspectives. We will now take a closer look at some of the discussions provoked by the amendments of the Law on Health Insurance in order to illustrate this trend.

Transphobic nationalism: trans rights as pressured from the West

Alternative Montenegro:	This is a consequence of a much bigger problem, and that is that we do not have

	enough money for basic healthcare in the Fund. The cause of this problem is well-known.
Facebook user AJ:	This is what I am talking about. To pay 100% for sex change, but for a trip to Belgrade for a medical treatment, you should pay from your own pocket!!!
Alternative Montenegro:	The pressure from the West and organizations they finance.
Facebook user AJ:	Lesbo-feminist and gay lobby.

This snippet from an internet conversation on the Facebook page of Alternative Montenegro illustrates that, from the perspective of the peripheral nationalist groups, respecting healthcare rights of trans people is not just elitist and decadent, but also fundamentally foreign. Alternative Montenegro claims that trans (and generally LGBTIQ+) issues are not indigenous to the country, but imported from Europe and the West by the Montenegrin political and NGO elites.

While such claims are wrong, they actually follow the dominant discursive framing of sexuality and geopolitics, whereby there is a clear conceptual link between 'Europe', 'progress', and 'LGBT human rights' on the one hand and 'Balkans/Russia', 'backwardness', and 'traditional family' on the other. This positioning of sexuality and geopolitics is not specific to the peripheral nationalist groups – it reflects the discourse of pro-European Montenegrin politicians as well. The only thing Alternative Montenegro did was to turn the moral valence of this dominant discourse about Europeanisation on its head.

While the EU representatives never directly discuss what sort of family is desirable in its member states, the fact that they take certain forms of LGBTIQ+ activism (that is, Pride parade) as a measure of 'European progress' of a country makes the EU complicit in this discourse. As Bilić and Stubbs (2016, p 233) argue, the EU in South-Eastern Europe:

> uses the long and troubled accession process to disseminate discursive tools employed in LGBT activist struggles for human rights and equality. This creates a linkage between 'Europeanness' and 'gay emancipation', which elevates certain forms of gay activist engagement and, perhaps also non-heterosexuality more generally, to a measure of democracy, progress, and modernity. At the same time, it relegates practices of intolerance to gays to the status of non-European primitivist Other who is inevitably positioned in the turbulent past that should be left behind.

Here we draw on a long list of authors who suggest that Europeanisation had ambivalent effects on LGBTIQ+ politics in (South)East Europe: it increased visibility of sexual and gender minorities, but it was also alienating in a very particular way (Dioli 2009; Johnson 2012; Bilić 2016; Bilić and Kajinić 2016; Bilić and Radoman 2019). As Renkin (2009, p 25) argues, 'LGBT people appear here as a kind of "indicator species" for the postsocialist creation of inclusive society – for "normal" social progress.' Namely, the EU-conditioned progress of Balkan countries in the negotiations over European accession on adopting several laws that aim to improve the position of LGBTIQ+ people and on holding Pride Parades. This pushed most Balkan governments, including the Montenegrin one, to adopt the requested laws and to secure Pride Parades in order to meet expectations of their European supervisors – rather than in order to protect their citizens. This was a dangerous twist in reasoning – here, the state decides to protect LGBTIQ+ people for the sake of the EU negotiations and the country's claim to Europeanness, rather than because of the specific problems that LGBTIQ+ people face in everyday life. This twist has had ambivalent, both positive and negative effects: it raised visibility of LGBTIQ+ issues, but also effectively erased LGBTIQ+ people and their agency from the picture (Renkin, 2009).

Importantly for our chapter, Alternative Montenegro did not create this discursive link between 'Europe' and 'LGBT human rights'; it simply turned its moral valence upside down. From their perspective, what EU takes as progress in human rights (for example, full public healthcare for gender reaffirming treatments) is actually backwardness that needs to be stopped. The 'West' is presumably pressuring Montenegro to provide full public healthcare for gender reaffirming treatments, although there are groups more deserving of full public healthcare, such as children – and this motivated peripheral nationalists to organise and 'fight back'. Alternative Montenegro see themselves as fighting the elite imposition of a particular gender regime from above (Europe, the West, and the Montenegrin liberal elites).

Misusing trans issues to claim justice: competition over public healthcare support

We suggest that *Alternative Montenegro* and the social media commenters who supported them (mis)used trans issues and people in order to articulate a criticism of the Montenegrin public healthcare system and the redistribution of resources within it. The public discussions revolved around the question of who has the moral right to claim public support for healthcare treatments abroad: the Law that was adopted in 2019 made some healthcare treatments abroad eligible for public support (for example, gender reaffirming treatments for trans people), but it did not cover expenses of many other medical treatments that had to be conducted abroad. Transphobic nationalists saw this selectivity as wrong. The populist, right-wing standpoint of transphobic nationalism used the language of gender to express grievances over extreme levels of economic inequality and a very quick class differentiation that took place in Montenegro between 2006 and 2018.

Speaking from the position of transphobic nationalism, social media commenters quickly created a discursive opposition between 'free sex change' and 'sick children whose treatment is paid for via SMS [short message service]':

> Facebook user DS: Those who are not happy with their gender should finance themselves, since they repeatedly claim that they and those like them are healthy.
> Alternative Montenegro: Exactly. We have no doubts that, one day, if Montenegro progresses economically, such topics will become relevant. But not now, while we pay for the medical treatment of the children via SMS!
> Facebook user NH: Exactly. And just look at how many children wait for donations in order to get treatment.[19]

This brief conversation between FB users on the Alternative Montenegro page evokes the figure of sick children as more deserving of public healthcare than trans people. In the hegemonic system of gender representations in Montenegro, trans people who are undergoing gender reaffirming treatments are placed opposite the innocence ascribed to the figure of a 'sick child'. The figure of a 'sick child' is sexless, genderless, and innocent. In contrast, the figure of a 'trans person' is marked by their wilful decision to medically intervene in their body and sex to reaffirm it. Both figures need medical treatment abroad but presumably only one of them gets public healthcare support for this – which again makes it impossible for trans people to claim innocence.

The figure of a 'sick child' has become potent in the Montenegrin social imagination, through the so-called 'humanitarian actions'. Humanitarian actions are a form of raising monetary donations to people (often children) who need medical treatments abroad (Brković, 2016a; Brković, 2016b). The money for treatments abroad is usually raised informally, from people's friends, family, and local communities. Humanitarian donations made via SMS to specially registered humanitarian phone lines are a successful way of raising money during humanitarian actions. That some people need to finance their medical treatments abroad through humanitarian actions is a source of anger in almost all of the post-Yugoslav states. The healthcare system of the Socialist Federative Republic of Yugoslavia (hereon: SFRY) provided virtually universal access to a wide spectrum of services, including specialised medical treatments abroad. However, this is not the case anymore. Neoliberal transformation, which followed the fall of socialism, profoundly transformed the contracts between citizens and their states on a global level. As anthropologists of the state have demonstrated, the state did not vanish under neoliberalism; instead, it became selectively present (for example, Read and Thelen, 2007; Collier, 2011; Muehlebach, 2012). The Montenegrin state did not withdraw from welfare: it became involved in its organisation in a selective manner. For instance, the state significantly restricted access to healthcare abroad for the majority of medical treatments for the majority of citizens, but it included gender reaffirming treatments (which also have to be done abroad) in the full public healthcare. As a result of this selectivity, some needs of trans people were included (gender-reaffirming treatments), but many other needs of trans people remained excluded (almost all medical treatments that could not be done in the country). Since Montenegro is a small country, with 650,000 inhabitants, the scope of healthcare people can get in the country is rather limited. This means that many Montenegrin citizens have had to pursue healthcare abroad – and often to pay for it from their own pockets. Montenegrin citizens largely feel entitled to full and free healthcare protection and they consider its contemporary absence as unjust.

This sense of injustice was misdirected towards the trans people. For instance, one particularly vocal person argued for 'the rules of triage'. She asked 'whether the rights of any marginalized group are more important than a six-year-old child with a cancer who needs money for surgery abroad?' In her view:

> priorities exist everywhere. Priorities are pregnant women, people with internal haemorrhaging and bleeding. These sorts of decisions must be made. I also think that the Fund should take into account that – if it gives 11,000 EUR for sex change to a person whose life is not in an immediate danger – it should prioritize and donate this money to a child who needs a bone marrow transplant which could save its life. This is prioritizing.[20]

This quote illustrates well that this public discussion was ultimately about who is morally deserving of the full public support. This was a discussion about socio-economic redistribution within the polity and how to organise it in a moral manner, which we will go back to in more detail in the conclusion. The discussion expressed grievances of the rising socio-economic inequality and changes in state roles and responsibilities – and it did so in the most transphobic way imaginable.

Intersectional standpoint

Trans activists, such as Jovan Džoli Ulićević, responded to the above-described accusations and narrative attacks on trans people by articulating an intersectional standpoint. Reminding the Montenegrin public that poverty is one of the main problems for trans people too – since trans people face discrimination when searching for accommodation and work due to their gender expression – Jovan and other trans people made visible that socio-economic grievances are shared across genders and cis/trans distinctions. Trans people invited the Montenegrin public to stop a capitalist-minded competition in victimhood and to start articulating solidarity across identitarian divisions.

Spektra counteracted this transphobic nationalist imaginary in two ways. First, it used the discourse of human rights to justify the claims of trans people on public healthcare. Second, it inscribed trans people into the Montenegrin polity by reminding everyone that trans people share the same economic problems as all other Montenegrin citizens. For instance, Jovan responded to the attacks in the social media by saying that:

> as long as we talk about money, instead of wellbeing of the people, we will keep thinking that one group threatens another. And this prevents us from seeing that we are all in the same trouble ... I will claim until my last breath – we all can work together on creating a better society, or we can keep competing who has it better and who has it worse, we can keep fighting and working against one another, and then the society will get better – never.[21]

With these words, Jovan evoked solidarity and common struggle of differently positioned people and groups for a better society. This was also a call to the Montenegrin public to stop the capitalist-inspired competition in victimhood. Having 'Who is more morally deserving' as the key underlying question of this discussion on healthcare insurance pits people who need support against one another. Trans activists such as Jovan suggested a different approach based on mutual solidarity and support. This intersectional standpoint was largely ignored by the transphobic nationalists; however, it picked up the interest of other NGO activists in the country. Arguably, it was this discussion that made various human rights workers in the country aware of the limitations of the liberal standpoint and of the importance of the intersectional standpoint (Novović, 2021). If we ask what can be done in Montenegro to break the impasse that positions LGBTIQ+ issues as a matter of 'Europeanness' (and therefore as ultimately 'foreign' to the Montenegrin social context), our answer would be to keep emphasising that redistributive injustices affect LGBTIQ+ people too and to explore more what this solidary struggle across differences may look like in terms of activism and in terms of politics.

Conclusion

What made trans people such a good target for the transphobic nationalists? We suggest there are two reasons, which have to do with what Nancy Fraser (2003) calls the politics of recognition and the politics of redistribution.

In Fraser's reading, since the 1980s there has been a 'shift in the grammar of political claims-making' (Fraser, 1997, p 2) from a socialist political imaginary, which is primarily concerned with the problem of redistribution of wealth and resources, to a politics of identity in which the central problem of justice is cultural recognition. Politics of recognition, or identity politics has become 'the paradigmatic form of political conflict in the late twentieth century' (Fraser, 1997, p 11). The contemporary globally dominant mode of political struggle is 'not between "classes" but between "cultural groups"', which have been mobilised 'under the banners of nationality, ethnicity, "race", gender, and sexuality' (Fraser, 1997, p 11). In other words, problems of redistribution (political and economic restructuring, reorganisation of the division of labour, and so forth) are often hidden by the problems of recognition (cultural and symbolic representation of various senses of self).

This global shift in the grammar of political claims-making took place in former Yugoslav countries as well. During the 1990s, socialist Yugoslavia fell apart through a series of nationalist wars, which had a twofold effect: one, they transformed Yugoslav ambiguous political community into several discrete ethno-national collectives (Sorabji, 1995; Bugarel, 2004), and two, they contributed to the violent dispossession and privatisation of resources (Duijzings, 2003). Furthermore, simultaneous post-war and post-socialist transformation, followed by processes of democratisation and Europeanisation, gave clear primacy to the issues of cultural recognition. Socio-economic dissatisfactions could not be directly addressed through any of these processes and they often got expressed in the language of race, culture – and sometimes even gender.

This is what happened in Montenegro too. It was not an exhibition of photographs of trans people held at the centre of the capital in 2018[22] that provoked the open attack of the (clearly transphobic) Alternative Montenegro. Instead, the attack was provoked by the increase of public healthcare support of the gender-reaffirming treatments. *Alternative Montenegro* ignored the attempt to improve cultural representation of trans people through an exhibition; it reacted transphobically to the change in redistribution of public support. Their attack demonstrates that socio-economic dissatisfactions in contemporary Montenegro are not just ethnicised, or racialised, but also 'gender-ised'. The genderisation of socio-economic inequalities was expressed by defining LGBTIQ+ human rights as an 'elitist' and 'decadent' project different from the 'normal' gender regime of 'decent', 'hard-working people'. It also involved a complaint about including the trans people but not the 'sick children' into the public coverage of the healthcare abroad.

'Genderisation' of socio-economic grievances demonstrates that gender is an unsettling category today. The unsettling of gender reflects a broader unsettling of ideology that characterises life in contemporary Europe. The strengthening of anti-trans (TERF) feminist positions, transphobia on the left, and similar combinations of progressive and reactionary (or even far-right) standpoints illustrate a broader ideological confusion that has enveloped Europe over the last ten years. We seem to be living in what Gramsci (1930) described as the 'age of monsters', or a moment of crisis that 'consists precisely in the fact that the old world is dying and the new world struggles to be born; in this interregnum a great variety of morbid symptoms appear' (see also Fraser, 2019). The contentions over trans people in Montenegro indicate that we are living in such a moment of morbid symptoms and ideological monsters. However, we do not know when the 'new world' will be born, or what ideological shape it will have. It is important to remember this depends also on us. The periods of crisis are dangerous, but also full of possibilities. This is why articulating an intersectional standpoint now is crucial. We need to consider the conditions under which it is possible to articulate joint struggles across racial, class, ethno-national and other vectors of distinction in order to create political and economic structures that can support decent and dignified life for all.

Notes

[1] Nikola's speech at Montenegro Pride 2019: https://www.youtube.com/watch?v=1pH7 c9xV0uc

[2] 'Muškarac nakon četiri operacije', *Vijesti*, 10 August 2009, printed edition.

[3] This fact was not recognised in 2011, when Zdravko Cimbaljević came out publicly as a gay man. Cimbaljević claimed to be the 'first LGBT person who publicly came out', which indicates how invisible trans people were in public discourse at the time. It also suggests that LGBTIQ+ people were primarily portrayed through sexuality.

[4] Amendments to the Health Insurance Act from 2019 enabled a completely cost-free gender reassignment procedure, with financial participation that needs to be defined by the Ministry of Health.

[5] This information has been described in 'Short review on some aspects of the position of transgender persons in Montenegro' by Aleksandar Saša Zeković, 2011. As a resource, he notes personal contact with transgender persons and medical experts. Available online at: http://www.hraction.org/wp-content/uploads/asz-transgender-lica-report.pdf

[6] 'The illness must be cured: Profesor Dr Sava Perović, doctor who was the first who performed sex-change surgery in the ex-Yu region', *Vijesti*, 11 August 2009, printed edition.

[7] 'Ekipa koju s ponosom zovem svojom', Diskriminacija.ba portal, 14 November 2014. Available online at: https://diskriminacija.ba/ekipa-koju-sa-ponosom-zovem-svojom. This was one of the first storytellings by Jovan, anonymously, using the pseudonym Dorijan at that moment. See also: 'U ovoj zemlji je teško voljeti sebe', Dan, 4 April 2019, printed edition.

[8] 'Transovci' could be translated into English as 'transians' and it is a play on the word 'Martians'. The name *Transovci* was a reaction to the invisibility of trans people and to the idea that trans people did not traditionally belong to the Montenegrin society. The allusion to 'Martians' indicates that trans people appropriated this sense of exclusion from the Montenegrin polity and decided to show their visibility and existence. The name itself was suggested by Teodor Stojanović, one of the founders of the group.

9   Available online at: https://mondo.me/Info/Drustvo/a584749/Transpozijum-krajem-marta-u-Podgorici.html
10 The event was organised Trans Aid for the first time in 2014, and then handed it over to the regional organisation Trans Network Balkan in 2015.
11 The name *Spektra* was created by Ivana Vujović, director of NGO Juventas. Founders of Spektra were brainstorming with friends and allies about a name, which could reflect diversity, and after Ivana's suggestion, it was adopted unanimously. The word purposefully has the grammatical female gender (in Montenegro, the noun 'spectrum' has the grammatical male gender), with the intention to show resistance to the dominant male culture.
12 Still, to this day there have been no publicly trans, inter, and gender variant (TIGV) people of an older age, with disabilities, or TIGV people of colour (ex. Roma people).
13 Ulićević: MUP zabranom promjene imena krši građanska prava, *Vijesti online*, 07 May 2017. Available online at: https://www.vijesti.me/vijesti/drustvo/81918/ulicevic-mup-zabranom-promjene-imena-krsi-gradanska-prava
14 Jedna od 2000 beba je interpolna, *Vijesti online*, 3 April 2017. Available online at: https://www.vijesti.me/vijesti/drustvo/86740/jedna-od-2-000-beba-je-interpolna
15 Transrodne osobe više nijesu na listi bolesnih, *Vijesti online*, 21 June 2018. Available online at: https://www.vijesti.me/vijesti/9101/szo-transrodne-osobe-vise-nijesu-na-listi-bolesnih
16 They are not free, but covered by the public healthcare insurance.
17 Available online at: https://www.facebook.com/alternativacrnagora/posts/2243206272392352
18 Available online at: https://www.facebook.com/alternativacrnagora/posts/2317833404929638
19 Comments on the Facebook post: https://www.facebook.com/alternativacrnagora/posts/2243206272392352
20 Comments on the Facebook post: https://www.facebook.com/alternativacrnagora/posts/2243206272392352
21 Available online at: https://www.facebook.com/alternativacrnagora/posts/2243206272392352
22 U subotu izložba fotografija trans osoba 'Vidljivi_e', available online at: http://prcentar.me/clanak/u-subotu-izloba-fotografija-trans-osoba-vidljivi-e/211; Otvaranje izložbe 'Vidljivi_e', available online at: https://asocijacijaspektra.org/2018/04/16/otvaranje-izlozbe-vidljivie/

References

Baker, C. (2018) *Race and the Yugoslav region: Postsocialist, post-conflict, postcolonial? Race and the Yugoslav region.* Manchester: Manchester University Press.

Bilić, B. (ed) (2016) *LGBT activism and Europeanisation in the (post-)Yugoslav space: On the rainbow way to Europe.* London: Palgrave Macmillan.

Bilić, B. and Kajinić, S. (eds) (2016) *Intersectionality and LGBT activist politics: Multiple others in Croatia and Serbia.* London: Palgrave Macmillan.

Bilić, B. and Radoman, M. (eds) (2019) *Sisterhood and unity: Lesbian activism in the (post-)Yugoslav space.* London: Palgrave Macmillan.

Bilić, B. and Stubbs, P. (2016) Beyond EUtopian promises and disillusions: A conclusion. In B. Bilić (ed) *LGBT Activism and Europeanisation in the (post-)Yugoslav space: On the rainbow way to Europe* (pp 231–48). London: Palgrave Macmillan.

Böröcz, J. (2021) 'Eurowhite' conceit, 'dirty white' resentment: 'Race' in Europe. *Sociological Forum, 36*(4), 1116–34.

Brković, Č. (2016a) Scaling humanitarianism: Humanitarian actions in a Bosnian town. *Ethnos: Journal of Anthropology, 81*(1), 99–124.

Brković, Č. (2016b) Depoliticization 'from below': Everyday humanitarianism in Bosnia and Herzegovina. *Narodna Umjetnost, 53*(1), 97–116.

Bugarel, K. (2004) *Bosna: Anatomija rata.* Belgrade: Fabrika knjiga.

Collier, J.S. (2011) *Post-Soviet social: Neoliberalism, social modernity, biopolitics.* Princeton and Oxford: Princeton University Press.

Crenshaw, K. (1991) Mapping the margins: Intersectionality, identity politics, and violence against women of color. Stanford Law Review, *43*(6), 1241–99.

Dioli, I. (2009) Back to a nostalgic future: The Queeroslav utopia. *Sextures, 1*(1), 24–42.

Duijzings, G. (2003) Ethnic unmixing under the aegis of the West: A transnational approach to the breakup of Yugoslavia. *Bulletin of the Royal Institute for Inter-Faith Studies, 5*(2), 1–16.

Edenborg, E. (2021) Anti-gender politics as discourse coalitions: Russia's domestic and international promotion of 'traditional values'. *Problems of Post-Communism,* online first, 15 October, 1–10.

Foucault, M. (2002) *The archaeology of knowledge.* London: Routledge.

Fraser, N. (1997) *Justice interruptus.* New York: Routledge.

Fraser, N. (2019) *The old is dying and the new cannot be born.* London: Verso.

Fraser, N. and Honneth, A. (2003) *Redistribution or recognition? A political-philosophical exchange.* London: Verso.

Gramsci, A. (1930/1971) *Selections from the prison notebooks.* New York: International Publishers.

Grémaux, R. (1996) Woman becomes man in the Balkans. In G. Herdt (ed) *Third sex, third gender: Beyond sexual dimorphism in culture and history* (pp 241–84). New York: Zoone Books.

Johnson, N.D. (2012) We are waiting for you: The discursive (se)construction of Belgrade Pride 2009. *Sextures, 12*(2), 6–31.

Muehlebach, A. (2012) *The moral neoliberal. Welfare and citizenship in Italy.* Chicago: The University of Chicago Press.

Novović, A. (2021) Queer je biti svoj i imati kičmu: Intervju sa Jovanom Ulićevićem. Retrieved on 1 October 2021 from https://portalkombinat. me/queer-je-biti-svoj-i-imati-kicmu/

Parvulescu A. (2015) European racial triangulation. In S. Ponzanesi and G. Colpani (eds) *Postcolonial Transitions in Europe* (pp 25–46). New York: Palgrave.

Read, R. and Thelen, T. (2007) Introduction: Social security and care after socialism: Reconfigurations of public and private. *Focaal: European Journal of Anthropology*, *50*, 3–18.

Renkin, H. (2009) Homophobia and queer belonging in Hungary. *Focaal: European Journal of Anthropology*, *53*, 20–37.

Sorabji, C. (1995) A very modern war: Terror and territory in Bosnia-Hercegovina. In R.A. Hinde and H.E. Watson (eds) *War: A cruel necessity?* (pp 80–95). London: Tauris.

3

Transgender and non-binary persons, mental health, and gender binarism in Serbia

Jelena Vidić and Bojan Bilić

Over the last three decades Serbia has been characterised by profound and occasionally violent social change.[1] In such a politically dynamic milieu little attention has been paid to trans issues and there are for the time being no systematic studies exploring the entanglements between transgender and gender non-binary (TGNB) persons, trans activism, and mental health. Our chapter starts filling this lacuna by combining both quantitative and qualitative data and offering an account of mental health-related challenges faced by trans people. After three introductory sections in which we provide an overview of research on TGNB mental health, describe the interface between transgender lives and the Serbian legal and health systems, and briefly present the history of transgender activist organising in the country, our analysis unfolds in three inter-related streams: first, we offer descriptive statistics arising from a 2019 survey about TGNB persons' needs and experiences: there we argue that in spite of legal and medical advancements, the right to gender self-determination is contentious and dependent upon the highly centralised health system which is still inadequately equipped to serve the population in question. In the second part, we draw upon the first author's year-long experience as a psychotherapist working with transgender clients in an activist organisation providing psychological support outside of the public healthcare system and gender medical team (thus not having a gatekeeping function). We examine some of the most recurrent issues that appear in individual clinical work with trans people emphasising how social status and geographical location modulate non-normative gender expression and the capacity to deal with the accompanying mental distress. In the third, final part, we turn to the transgender self-help group operating within the framework of the Belgrade-based activist organisation Geten (formerly known as Gayten-LGBT[2]). Above and beyond its empowerment function, we claim that this group constitutes an epistemic community that generates embodied knowledge about transgender lives that still lacks wider understanding and social recognition. We point to potential policy implications of such insufficiently visible community-based strategies for improving transgender health and highlight the necessity of the official (mental) health institutions to incorporate them into their practice. While this group helps its members navigate the labyrinths of psychiatric/medical power, it does not always manage to wriggle out of normative gender binarism that pervades its wider socio-political space. In this regard, our trilateral approach enables us to start tracing the genealogy of gender binarism within the Serbian medical setting. We claim that despite significant improvements of the situation of TGNB people concerning psychiatric gatekeeping and legal gender recognition, TGNB community in Serbia is still marginalised with mental health being one of the most affected areas. With this in mind, we conclude by arguing in favour of a non-binary understanding of gender as a basis for gender-affirming (mental) healthcare.

TGNB people and mental health

Gender is a fundamental social category that organises personal and interpersonal experience throughout the life-course and helps us make sense of the social world by serving as a primary criterion for classifying people (Fassinger and Arseneau, 2007). TGNB persons have a gender identity that differs from the one assigned at birth. Such persons undermine traditional gender norms and may problematise deeply entrenched binary understandings of gender (gender benders, genderqueer, agender, bigender, third gender, and so on) according to which human beings are divided into men and women. TGNB people have recently gained global visibility accompanied by high levels of transphobic discrimination in a range of contexts including family, peer groups, educational institutions, workplace, partner relationships, and public space (Turner et al, 2009; Grant et al, 2011; Testa et al, 2012; Bockting et al, 2013; Robles et al, 2016). Various forms of anti-trans prejudice interfere with TGNB persons' access to basic human rights including medical and counselling services (Smiley et al, 2017).

Discriminatory attitudes that devalue TGNB persons may lead to different forms of stigma, such as harassment and violence as well as to self-stigma (as an internalised anti-trans prejudice). A systemic bias based on the idea that gender identities are assigned at birth and are not a matter of self-identification may negatively affect TGNB people's mental health. Indeed, the growing body of research related to the mental health of TGNB population has shown that they are at disproportional risk for negative mental health outcomes when compared with the general population (Grant et al, 2011; McNeil et al, 2012; Bockting et al, 2013; Budges et al, 2013; Smith et al, 2014; Smiley et al, 2017; White and

Fontenot, 2019). TGNB persons are more likely to become estranged from their families and may be more easily rejected by their peers and their wider social environment which, in turn, compromises their emotional wellbeing (McCann and Sharek, 2016; Aylagas-Crespillo, García-Barbero, and Rodríguez-Martín, 2018; White and Fontenot, 2019). High levels of stigma and discrimination, compounded with material hardship, may lead to anxiety, depression, suicidal ideation and attempted suicides, and various life-threatening behaviours (for example, substance use), particularly among transgender youth with insufficient parental support (Simons et al, 2013; McConnell, Birkett, and Mustanski, 2016; Robles et al, 2016; Veale et al, 2017; Taliaferro, McMorris, and Eisenberg, 2018; Valentine and Shipherd, 2018). Thus, a study conducted in Ireland (Transgender Equality Network Ireland, 2013), for example, showed that 78 per cent of transgender people had considered suicide. The situation is exacerbated by the fact that healthcare services are often not sensitive towards transgender issues and that psychotherapists lack skills for working more effectively with transgender clients (McCann and Sharek, 2016; Ho and Mussap, 2017; Valentine and Shipherd, 2018).

Moreover, TGNB people may be reluctant to seek mental health assistance due to fear of discrimination and rejection in medical settings that have a long history of trans pathologisation. All the way until 2019, the International Classification of Diseases (ICD) categorised various transgender and non-binary identities under the code F64 (gender identity disorders within the broader category of disorders of adult personality and behaviour). This was described as a disorder characterised by:

> a desire to live and be accepted as a member of the opposite[3] sex, usually accompanied by a sense of discomfort with, or inappropriateness of, one's anatomic sex, and a wish to have surgery and hormonal treatment to make one's body as congruent as possible with one's preferred sex. (WHO, 2016)

Such a psychopathologising view of TGNB persons assigns great importance to psychiatrists who are responsible for giving the diagnosis and monitoring their patients for at least a year before allowing them to proceed to endocrinological and surgical treatment, in order to prevent regrets, but also as a form of social control aiming to maintain the gender binary. This includes the so-called real-life experience or real-life test referring to a period during which transgender individuals had to live full time in their preferred gender role (understood in a normative and binary way) and by doing so demonstrate that they are sure about and can be socially functional in their self-identified gender (WPATH Standards of care, first to fifth edition; for example, Breger et al, 1979; Levine et al, 1998). During such a period they often cannot change their legal documents regardless of numerous difficulties they encounter in social life due to a lack of legal gender recognition.

The 11th revision of the International Classification of Diseases, which came into effect on 1 January 2022, has de-psychopathologised trans identities by removing them from the chapter on mental and behavioural disorders. Following decades of intense activist mobilisations and scientific research indicating that a higher level of mental health difficulties in TGNB people should be understood as a consequence of adverse life experiences due to prevailing stigmatisation (Robles et al, 2016), this revision has redefined gender identity-related health by eliminating diagnostic grounds for social and institutional stigma of mental disorder and marking a paradigm shift from a disease-based model to an identity-based model (Reisner et al, 2016a). According to the new classification, gender incongruence has moved into the chapter dealing with conditions related to sexual health. This has been done in order to ensure that transgender people will continue to have access to gender-affirming healthcare that can be covered by health insurance. Such emancipatory measures may further encourage the use of a 'participatory population perspective'[4] (Reisner et al, 2016b) that would lead to interventions specifically tailored to the needs of TGNB persons and increase the representation of TGNB individuals among health and mental health providers.

TGNB people in Serbia: laws, health, and discrimination

Until January 2019, there was no formal procedure in Serbia that would enable legal recognition of gender identity and allow changes of name, gender, and personal data (including the unique identification number/unique master citizen number that contains information about gender). The long-term practice, which did not have sufficient legal grounding, made document updates entirely dependent on surgical interventions that also included obligatory sterilisation. The Family Law that is currently in force enables name change for persons older than 15, but civil registrars usually refuse to do a name update in those cases in which a chosen name does not correspond to the gender registered in legal documents. It is for this reason that TGNB persons opt for gender neutral names (such as Vanja or Saša) as a temporary solution until they meet the requirements for full legal gender recognition. Until January 2019 it was possible to update a person's name and identification number in legal records only with a medical certificate stating that the person has gone through a 'complete gender-affirming surgery'. However, given that there were no legally binding protocols, the procedures and the conditions that had to be met were not standardised and differed from one case to another and across the country. The extent of such administrative difficulties and disturbing treatments (for example, asking for additional certificates from forensic pathologists to prove that the person's genitalia were 'adequate') has been captured by a study that showed that TGNB people in Serbia perceived them as their major problem (Zulević, 2012).

A step forward was taken in March 2012 when the Constitutional Court decided that registrars were the only competent authorities for changing gender-related information in legal records. It was also stipulated that a statement issued by a hospital regarding gender-affirming surgery performed on the patient needs to be recognised by registrars as sufficient evidence for an update of records. However, this decision has not managed to standardise legal practice and people were still facing various obstacles during legal gender recognition (Vidić, 2020a). Thus, in 2018 the Law on the Birth Registry (Službeni glasnik, 2018) was revised and in January 2019 a new rulebook was adopted that regulates the matter of name and gender change.[5] The rulebook stipulates that records should be amended on the basis of a certificate issued by doctors working in relevant hospitals (which effectively means only by those who are members of the Belgrade-based team working with the TGNB population to which we turn below). For such a certificate to be produced, the person eithers needs to be on hormonal therapy for at least a year or to have gone through gender-affirming surgery. Both options also presuppose psychiatric–psychological evaluation and monitoring as a starting point of a medically assisted transition. Even though it is better than legally unregulated practice that required forced sterilisation, the current legal solution has serious disadvantages: it medicalises legal matters, pushes the person into the healthcare system via psychiatric encounters (which also used to add to the gender-related stigma the stigma of being a psychiatric patient) and presupposes recourse to hormonal treatment that changes the body.

Regardless of the fact that gender-affirming surgeries have been taking place in Serbia for more than three decades (Vujovic et al, 2009), the operation of the Belgrade Team for Gender Identity was officially regulated only in 2012. Before that, persons interested in undertaking gender-affirming surgery were dependent on a narrow circle of medical experts in the domain of 'gender dysphoria' (Zulević, 2012; Marković Žigić, Zulević, and Maksimović, 2015). This not only often meant that the surgeons arbitrarily determined surgery prices that were too high for the majority of TGNB persons (when that service still had not been covered by the national health insurance system) but that medical interventions were performed in inadequate circumstances, sometimes outside of the regular working hours, without the necessary permissions and the knowledge of other employees and without proper documentation or post-operative care (Zulević, 2012;

Đurić, 2012).[6] In her study about the problems that TGNB individuals in Serbia face in various spheres of life, Zulević (2012, p 41) reports the experience of one patient:

> My surgery was scheduled for Friday at 9pm … I was already lying on the operating table when the doctor came in to tell me that we had to postpone the operation and that I should come back in three days … I had an impression that no one was supposed to know that my surgery would take place.

Particularly during the highly taxing 1990s, characterised by soaring inflation, international isolation, and rampant impoverishment, doctors employed by the national health institutions routinely diverted their patients to the private sector in which they also worked. This was also done in those cases in which the required services could have been offered by the state system, so that TGNB clients were unduly put under much stronger financial pressure (Đurić, 2012).

Another set of problems had to do with the fact that gender-affirming surgeries are relatively rare, so they are treated as exclusive opportunities for training medical students and junior surgeons. As a result, operating rooms could become crowded interfering with the patient's privacy and comfort. As one interviewee told Zulević (2012, p 41):

> The atmosphere in the operating room was like that at a football match. No one ever asked me for permission and I had an impression I was left with no choice. There were so many students bending over me to watch that one of them leaned on my head and I had to tell him to move so that I could breathe normally. In such a commotion one of them also bumped into me … I felt as if I was in a circus … but I did not protest because I feared they might refuse to perform the surgery.

With time the situation has improved and surveys register higher levels of TGNB persons' satisfaction with healthcare provisions (Zulević, 2012). In 2012 the Ministry of Health established the National Expert Committee for Transgender Disorders, which was renamed the National Committee for Transgender Conditions in 2017 as a response to the request that Geten sent to the Ombudsperson. At one of their initial meetings, the Committee adopted its rules of procedure and decided upon its area of competence stipulating that the following conditions had to be met for a person to be allowed to surgically align their physical appearance with their gender identity: first, the person needs to be more than 18 years old; second, they need to provide at least two referral letters by two independent psychiatrists following psychiatric monitoring not shorter than a year; and third, they need to be on a suppressive-substitutive hormonal therapy for at least a year. The Health Insurance Ordinance entrusts the Committee with the task of determining whether the conditions have been fulfilled. Upon receiving a favourable decision of the Committee, the patient is sent to a tertiary referral hospital with 65 per cent of the costs covered by the insurance and 35 per cent by the patient themselves. In contrast to surgical interventions, the costs of hormonal therapy, its availability, or quality are still not legally regulated regardless of the fact that transgender persons are expected to receive it for the rest of their lives. While previous legal solutions took into account only those individuals interested in completely transitioning from one discrete gender category (man or woman) into another, the Belgrade medical team has recently been moving towards more individualised treatments. Only up to a few years ago it was impossible to obtain a favourable referral letter from a psychiatrist for hormone treatment unless the person stated that they wanted complete genital surgery and referred to themselves in binary categories. Hormonal treatment is now also increasingly available to those who claim non-binary gender identities.

Making legal recognition of gender dependent on complete medically assisted transition did not take into account the social aspects of the lives of TGNB persons going through such a process. Many TGNB people who opt for partial or complete gender-affirming treatments take hormones that lead to bodily changes and may live for years with gender expression that is incompatible with the one stated in their personal documents. Such prolonged incompatibility in the context in which there is a widespread perception that there should be a close relation between body, identity, and documents makes TGNB persons vulnerable to various forms of violence and discrimination undermining their physical and mental wellbeing. In this regard, according to a survey done by Transgender Europe in cooperation with Gayten-LGBT (later named Geten) in 2014 and 2015 (Vidić, 2020a), one fourth of all reported incidents were categorised as cases of discrimination (66 per cent of which were in one way or the other associated with the legal recognition of gender), 37 per cent pertained to physical violence, 21 per cent to verbal threats, and 8 per cent to sexual harassment. Similarly to other countries, trans women in Serbia were exposed to violence more than trans men as they were victims in 79 per cent of all transphobic incidents. Perpetrators also belong to different groups and include: administrative workers (16 per cent), health workers (8 per cent), policemen (25 per cent), while they are unknown in 29 per cent of cases. As in other examined countries, the percentage of incident reporting is very low due to lack of trust in institutions and expected transphobic reactions by those who should offer support and protection.

Trans activism in Serbia

Autonomous feminist activism has been developing in a more intense manner in the Yugoslav space all the way since the late 1970s, while the first LGBTIQ+ initiatives appeared throughout the 1980s, mostly along the route Ljubljana–Zagreb–Belgrade (Bilić, 2012, 2020). Activist efforts became difficult and sporadic in the beginning of the 1990s as Yugoslavia witnessed a political and economic crisis and eventually disintegrated through a series of decade-long armed conflicts. The first Serbian initiative for gay and lesbian rights – Arkadija – was launched in Belgrade in 1991 (the organisation was officially registered only in 1994 following a revision of the Penal Code, which decriminalised homosexuality). Even though Arkadija did not explicitly address the issues of TGNB persons, along with other anti-war and peace-oriented endeavours, it did represent a refuge for sexual and gender difference, which was severely marginalised in times of strong militarist and patriarchal sentiment.

It was only after October 2000 and the removal of the authoritarian regime of Slobodan Milošević that a new impulse appeared in the domain of LGBTIQ+ legal and social emancipation. In this context, Gayten-LGBT was established in Belgrade in 2001 as the first all-inclusive activist organisation paying particular attention to the rights and culture of trans, intersex, and queer persons. The organisation struggles to acknowledge their sexual, gender, ethnic, 'racial', age, health, and class differences, and was founded by its current coordinator Milan Agatha Đurić (see Đurić, this volume), a pioneer of transgender mobilisation in the Yugoslav space and one of the earliest members of Arkadija.

Over the last years, Geten has been active in drafting a bill that would regulate the domain of gender identity and the rights of intersex people starting with the right to self-determination as the fundamental guiding principle.[7] Taking into account the latest developments in the sphere of TGNB human rights and health, this bill envisions a legal gender recognition based fully on self-determination and a straightforward procedure for updating name and gender on legal records, introducing the option 'other' for non-binary people. This draft also proposes regulation in the sphere of trans people's legal continuity as well as their rights and obligations before, during, and after hormonal-surgical treatments. It forbids all forms of discrimination on the basis of gender or sex and envisions psycho-social support to trans and intersex persons and their families. It also accounts for the possibility for trans and intersex persons to access medically assisted procreation technologies.

Along with their legislative work and other intersectionally sensitive activities, Geten offers a framework for the operation of a self-help TGNB group (see Đurić, this volume). This group was started in August 2006 as the first self-help initiative for TGNB people in the Yugoslav region. It is estimated that until 2019 more than 120 persons, coming from a range of countries, have been in one way or the other associated with it. This is an open group that on average gathers twice per month and welcomes members with varying degrees of commitment. The operation of the group is based on the principles of support, self-esteem, safety, and self-realisation. Topics that are usually discussed in group meetings include but are not limited to the sphere of rights and administration, transphobic discrimination, partner relations, sexuality, and family life. We take a more detailed look at some aspects of the work of this group in the following sections of the chapter.

Methods

In this chapter we rely upon three major kinds of empirical data: a survey with TGNB individuals, observations from year-long clinical practice with TGNB clients unrelated to the evaluation preceding medical transition, and semi-structured interviews with members of the self-help group. We address each of these in further detail. First, in 2019, Geten conducted a survey, co-coordinated by the first author, about the needs of TGNB persons in Serbia (Vidić, 2020a). The aim of the study was to gain an insight into the current status of TGNB individuals in the domains of education, employment, healthcare, and legal gender recognition. The online survey was shared via Geten's social networks and trans-affirming mailing lists between 15 August and 30 October 2019. The questionnaire included a combination of open- and closed-ended questions: seven questions referred to general personal data (gender, age, residence, belonging to minority groups, ability, citizenship), three questions to financial situation, six questions to education (highest educational level, current education status, gender expression during education, potential discrimination and violence in the educational system, dropping out of school), eight questions to employment (current employment status, gender expression as well as potential discrimination and violence at work), four questions to the need for legal, psychological, and peer support, and two questions to the perception of safety at home and in public space. A separate section was dedicated to trans-specific healthcare tapping respondents' experience and level of satisfaction with health services, discrimination, and violence in healthcare environments and their perceived priorities in the domain of trans healthcare. At the end of the questionnaire, all of the respondents had an opportunity to add their experiences, perceptions, and comments that were not captured by the survey. The questionnaire was filled by 90 respondents from around Serbia, but 18 of them were eventually excluded from the sample for not fulfilling the criteria for the participation in the survey (not giving consent, identifying as cisgender, or responding in a derogatory and mocking way).

In our analysis we offer summaries (descriptive statistics) about the sample and the most relevant examined dimensions.

Second, when it comes to clinical work, we rely on the experience of the first author who is a psychologist and certified psychotherapist working in this capacity within Geten. TGNB clients are mainly young adults (up to 30 years old) in the process of education or with an incomplete faculty degree and without financial independence from their families. They constitute a heterogeneous group with regard to their gender identity (both trans men and women and non-binary people), needs, and/or plans for medical gender confirmation procedures and stages of the process itself. Sessions are usually held once per week and last 50 minutes, while occasional consultations last between 50 minutes and one hour. Therapeutic work is psychodynamically oriented and based on gender-affirmative approach. In this chapter we will focus on the work with ten TGNB clients during the period of three years.

Third, in order to get an insight into the ways in which TGNB people narrate and make sense of their experiences, we draw upon ten semi-structured interviews with members of the Geten self-help group for TGNB people. The interviews were conducted by the second author in December 2019 with group members all of whom at the time resided in Belgrade (even though they may not be from there originally). The participants were recruited through the snowball sampling. The interviews lasted between 45 minutes and two hours and were recorded with an mp3 voice recorder. Every interview started with an opportunity for the interviewee to narrate a biographical episode associated with their self-help group participation. This was then explored in further detail on the basis of an interview guide. All of the interviewees received verbal information concerning the design and procedure of the study and gave their informed consent. The interviews were subsequently transcribed and analysed by using inductive thematic analysis with a view of identifying predominant themes in the dataset.

Finally, we complement our empirical corpus with other sources, including unpublished surveys as well as published research and newspaper interviews with trans activists.

Results

Survey

The examined sample (N=72) consisted of 31 per cent trans women, 35.2 per cent trans men, 29.6 per cent non-binary persons, and 4.2 per cent who perceive their gender in a different way. A vast majority of respondents is younger than 35 (82 per cent) and living in a town with more than 100,000 people (60.6 per cent); almost one fifth of respondents (18.3 per cent) belong to an ethnic, 'racial', or religious minority (including atheists, Romani people …), and 4.2 per cent stated to have some sort of a disability.[8] The majority of respondents face different financial difficulties: more than one third of those older than 18 do not have any regular monthly income with only ten of them having a salary higher than the national average; one half of the sample is unemployed, 31 per cent has a (temporary) job, and 11.3 per cent own their own business. Two thirds report that their households experience difficulties when trying to make ends meet. In terms of education, the majority of respondents finished high school (50.7 per cent) or university (31 per cent) while one half were in the educational system at the time of the survey.

Respondents encountered different forms of discrimination and violence in various domains of everyday life. Almost one half (45.1 per cent) report that they never felt safe to express their gender identity at school, while only one fourth were never discriminated or exposed to violence by peers, teachers, or other school staff. Among the most frequent forms of violence were requests for normative gender expression (for example, 'the principal kept forcing me to have a haircut and verbally attacked me on numerous occasions regarding the way I dressed or looked'), ridiculing, physical or sexual abuse, and death threats mostly coming from fellow students. With this in mind it is not surprising that 33.8 per cent considered leaving school while 12.7 per cent actually did so. Fear of violence is the major reason for dropping out of school, whereas the decision to persevere is backed by internal motivation ('nothing in the world will put me off doing what I like') or existential concerns ('what could I do without a degree?').

Gender stigma has a negative impact on their professional lives as well. Perceived/anticipated stigma is evident at the work place: 62 per cent of respondents think that they do not have equal chances of finding a job in comparison with the members of the majority population with the same professional qualifications. Less than a half of the respondents are open about their gender at work so that 'everybody knows it' (20.4 per cent) or that 'most people know it' (22.7), while 36.3 per cent state that 'nobody knows about it' or 'only a few persons of trust'. Among those with work experience (currently employed or unemployed), 38.4 per cent had been exposed to gender-related violence or discrimination in the workplace and 21.7 per cent decided to quit their jobs because of it. One respondent stated that she left her job because she did not want to be treated as a man and another one was told he should come back 'once he has become a man'.

Four out of ten respondents (39.4 per cent) claim to have had difficulties in everyday life due to documents that do not align with their current gender identity and one fourth (25.4 per cent) suffered discrimination or violence because of this. Such discriminatory acts mostly pertain to minor resistances and misunderstandings (like police or administrative personnel not believing that survey respondents were actual owners of their legal documents), but a more serious issue is that inadequate documents prime

TGNB individuals to expect negative reactions and therefore avoid social situations in which legal documents would need to be shown. In this regard many respondents talked about their reluctance to visit a medical doctor because they assumed that there would not be sufficient knowledge or that they would encounter transphobia.

The majority of respondents felt a need for legal counselling (57.7 per cent) or psychotherapeutic assistance (63.4 per cent) in the year that preceded the survey. Nine out of ten respondents (90.1 per cent) stated that it was important for them to learn about the experience of other TGNB people or to confide in another TGNB person (85.9 per cent). Less than one half of the sample (45.1 per cent) have already used some form of trans specific (psychiatric, endocrinological, or surgical) healthcare (31 per cent have not so far, but plan to do so, 23.9 per cent have not and do not intend to) and one half of those (48 per cent) were either very dissatisfied (22.6 per cent) or dissatisfied (25.4 per cent). When it comes to psychiatric/psychological support as a part of trans-specific healthcare, 36.6 per cent of respondents were dissatisfied with them whereas 31 per cent were either satisfied or very satisfied and 32.4 per cent stated that the question did not apply to them. Such a high level of dissatisfaction with the psychological support is particularly worrisome in the light of a European survey in which Geten was the national coordinator for Serbia, which showed that TGNB people from Serbia had the highest percentage of suicidal ideation among the five examined countries (including Georgia, Poland, Serbia, Spain, and Sweden; Smiley et al, 2017): 85.9 per cent of respondents (55 persons filled the questionnaire and 38 ended up in the analysed sample) reported that they thought seriously about ending their life, 73.7 per cent multiple times, and 13.2 per cent once (Smiley et al, 2017). In the year that preceded the 2016 survey, 39.4 per cent of respondents stated that they thought seriously about ending their life. The same survey also demonstrated that 57.6 per cent of trans people with suicidal thoughts did not seek any help. Among those who did, 21.2 per cent did so among their peers, friends, or family, and only 12.1 per cent looked for support from a mental health professional.

Both surveys (2017 and 2019) demonstrate that TGNB people in Serbia share the predicaments of the general population in terms of poverty and unstable and badly paid employment. However, these social status parameters are aggravated by high levels of transphobic marginalisation and discrimination in practically all spheres of life, including both private and public spaces. Living in a centralised state in which all relevant institutions are located in the capital, many TGNB persons are deprived of their right to professional healthcare. The sphere of mental health is particularly affected as the wide majority of TGNB people are not sufficiently familiar with such services or do not have an easy access to them. This is not only due to a shortage of qualified mental health professionals trained in gender-affirmative approach and a virtual absence of TGNB mental health workers apart from those included in the medical gender identity team but also to more widely held prejudicial attitudes towards those seeking mental health assistance. In the following section, we review some of the most frequent issues that appear in individual clinical work with TGNB clients.

Clinical work with TGNB clients

Geten has a broad and well-developed system of psychosocial support for LGBTIQ+ people, provided both by peers and mental health professionals. An LGBTIQ+ helpline and trans support group were founded in 2006 and have been available to LGBTIQ+ people for the past 16 years, and in the past decade team members have been providing psychosocial support via email and Facebook. In 2014 Geten introduced individual consultations, counselling, and psychotherapy with certified psychotherapists, and in the past couple of years this form of support was also provided as a separate activity on TIQ chat. Besides that, team members support the community by organising various benefit parties (mainly to provide financial support to TGNB individuals for medical interventions), support in the form of communication and advocacy with various institutions, advice on the matter of legal gender recognition, and so on.

In this section we will focus more on the support provided by mental health professionals. In the past six years more LGBTIQ+ people started contacting the organisation asking for counselling and in 2014 the first author, supported by the rest of the team, started providing psychological support in a more systematic manner as a part of her engagement within the organisation. Due to the increase in demand for this kind of support, another psychotherapist joined the team in 2019. In 2019, 310 individual sessions were provided by the two psychotherapists. Support is mainly offered in the form of psychotherapy, ranging from several months to several years. Due to limited resources, the continuous support soon had to be restricted to only students and unemployed LGBTIQ+ people, and LGBTIQ+ people in a better financial situation can schedule one consultation or ask for referral to some of the LGBTIQ+ affirmative psychotherapists working in private practice with reduced prices.

Concerns raised in therapy are to a certain extent similar to those raised by their cisgender peers; however, different manifestations of stigma, and particularly self-stigma, are colouring interactions with the environment and client's self-image. Given that the majority of clients seeking psychotherapeutic assistance are adolescents or young adults, it is not surprising that the most prevalent topics they raise are those related to the intersection of their families of origin with their gender identity. People who have not shared their transgender identity with their parents are exploring the topic of coming out and potential consequences; people who did come out are questioning whether their parents truly accept them for who they are. Having in mind either the absence of transgender topics in general public or their presentation in a sensationalist and pathologising way and the predominance of traditional patriarchal upbringing, many clients are preoccupied with actual and anticipated parental reactions and are extremely vigilant for signs of rejection. In this regard, in the therapeutic setting, one repeatedly encounters prevailing guilt (stemming mainly from the internalised anti-trans prejudice) that clients feel in the first place towards their parent/s. They are contemplating the consequences their (trans)gender identity and, for some, a decision to start and continue medical gender affirmation process, not just for themselves, but also for the everyday life and feelings of their parents and close family members. In these considerations they empathise with their families anticipated discomfort in interactions with broader social environment.

At the same time, young TGNB adults are quite often angry at their parents for the lack of understanding and support for the struggles they are going through but usually find it difficult to fully accept and express that anger. Stories may differ from family to family: some parents are reacting with open rejection and pathologisation of their identity; others are offering financial and logistic support but avoid providing emotional support and acceptance, thus leaving their child to struggle alone; some parents are trying to distance themselves from the process and avoid any conversation about the topic of gender or gender confirmation surgery and others are supportive in various ways but never ask questions first. Having this in mind, it is not surprising that young TGNB adults often question the sincerity of their parents' support, not just as a consequence of perceived stigma but as a result of their own experiences and interaction. Silence about the (trans)gender identity and the parental lack of initiative to start a conversation on that topic is especially challenging and interpreted as the lack of true acceptance and support. This struggle between guilt and anger results in silence and feelings of helplessness. These feelings are often generalised to both parents, even though – as with cisgender people – one's relationship with each of the parents is different and so are their expectations, fears, and hopes from them, as well as each parent's reactions to their child's gender identity.

Psychotherapeutic work with transgender clients in the circumstances of intense and long-term transgender psychopathologisation reveals the silver lining of a diagnosis: receiving a (psychiatric) diagnosis for many clients means that their gender identity and expression have been finally recognised and acknowledged. Given the strength of the medical/psychiatric discourse, it is often a diagnosis that gives legitimacy and provides a framework within which transgender experience can acquire meaning and imbue the client with a sense of control over their lives. Psychiatric diagnosis relocates distressing transgender experience from the spheres of sin, criminality, or caprice where it has been traditionally located into the domain of medicine. This shift may attenuate some TGNB persons' feelings of guilt because their condition becomes a matter of scientific knowledge within which, as they expect, it will be professionally 'treated' rather than mocked, punished, or excluded. As long as the person is willing to succumb to the role of a patient, the medical discourse 'promises' not to consider them responsible for their 'condition' as well as to make it possible for them to reintegrate into the binarily gendered world following surgical interventions. Some people reported that healthcare providers further nourished that attitude, saying that they will 'stop having' the psychiatric diagnosis after their last gender confirmation surgery.

The period surrounding gender-affirming surgery is saturated with different meanings, both for trans people and their parents. Some clients report that their parents refuse to use the correct name and pronoun up until the surgery, as if this final body modification is the only and true determinant of their identity. There are different ways to understand this: as the need to keep what they believed was the identity of their child for as long as possible; as the hope that their child will change their mind in the last moment before the irreversible surgical intervention; but also as a manifestation of their understanding of the gender as determined by genitalia and the need for their child's identity to be verified by external authority (medical and/or legal). This corresponds with the importance of genital surgery for (some) trans people as well: waiting for the surgery is often exhausting, filled with uncertainty and fear that something might happen and delay the process even more. During this period it is often difficult to focus on anything else and make any long-term plans – the moment of surgery is decisive in their life, the turning point after which (as the person perceives it) everything will be different and easier. This dream of the 'new life' often leads to disappointment – even though the long-waited process of medical affirmation of gender is finally over, the following days and months bring back the same unresolved issues that the person has to face and deal with. What is important to understand is that this moment depends on somebody else: it is determined by different medical authorities (referral letter from two psychiatrists and one endocrinologist is required), schedules of the surgeons who will perform the surgery, and the number of surgeries determined by the Ministry of Health. These administrative procedures put a person in a passive role and it might be difficult to maintain the sense of agency in this process.

The question of the dis/continuity of life is also important for some people: what has happened before they started living their current gender is forever lost in the past that should be forgotten. This moment – the beginning of an authentic life – may be different for different people but often is connected with the perception of the important other(s), with their current self finally being seen and mirrored by others (Fraser, 2009). This sense of dis/continuity that may be nurtured, but also disrupted by important others, poses a great challenge to a person, struggling to find their own narrative and be able to tell their life story with a deeper level of integration.

We should perhaps emphasise again that this psychotherapeutic support is provided within an activist organisation, free of charge and without any connection with the official (mental) healthcare system. This setting enables people to openly discuss different issues regarding their mental health and transgender identity without the fear that these thoughts and considerations will be interpreted as indicators that they are not 'trans enough', not 'psychologically stable enough' (to start with medical treatment), which might result in the delay of referral for the hormone treatment or different surgical interventions. Unfortunately, TGNP persons often share with their chosen psychotherapist outside of the medical team that they refuse to discuss their mental health issues (for example, overwhelming anxiety, depression, or suicidal ideation) or certain doubts about their identity or upcoming procedures with their psychiatrist from the gender identity team due to this fear, and thus are not able to receive adequate psychiatric support (including pharmacotherapy) that might reduce suffering, improve their mental health, and provide guidance in the process of medical transition.

Self-help group

Geten offers psychological support to TGNB persons in the form of individual counselling/psychotherapy as well as through the operation of a self-help group. As we have explored some of the major issues encountered in individual clinical work with TGNB population in Serbia, in this section we take a look at the Geten self-help group, the oldest of its kind in the post-Yugoslav region. The group, which gathers around twice per month, constitutes a fluid initiative and its membership fluctuates: for example, there are those who only attend a few meetings around their surgical transition as well as those involved for a few years regardless of any medical procedures. On the basis of our dataset generated through both our own semi-structured as well as published interviews with group members, we have identified three inter-related elements of group operation, which we would like to examine in further detail. These are: (1) information, support, and community, (2) navigating the medical/psychiatric system, and (3) dealing with gender binarism.

Information, support, and community

Joining the self-help group[9] can take place through various channels, but it most frequently occurs upon recommendation by current members as this ensures that the group stays a safe place for all of its participants. When someone wishes to join, the coordinators conduct an initial interview with the interested person with a view to evaluating their motivation. A new member then is often the first one to introduce themselves to other members of the group and share their experiences and expectations. In accordance with its guiding principle 'Support, self-esteem, security, and self-realisation', the group explores topics ranging from the body, identity, family relations, education and employment, transphobia and discrimination, transition experiences, sexuality, partner relationships, and relevant legislation. In this regard, the group operates as a safe-haven for TGNB people from both Serbia and other countries and it tries to forge cooperation with similar initiatives across the region and internationally. One of the most important, or at least most explicit, functions of the group is that it provides support and offers information about TGNB-related issues. As one interviewee states:

> It is the sense of community that the group gives that was important when I decided to join … A sense of belonging … The possibility to exchange experiences … It is easier to complain about bad experiences, like those with doctors, when there is someone who has gone through the same things as you have … So the group is an opportunity for us to learn about how others are coping with their problems … Sometimes you hear something positive, other times more negative, but regardless of that, there is someone you can identify with and someone who can understand you … What was crucial for me about the group participation was the fact that the group is a place where I could meet more trans people than anywhere else … Different trans people … There is that dimension of safe space … Especially when you do not know anyone … All of a sudden there is a room full of trans persons. (Personal communication, December 2019)

However, some interviewees talked about how there are limits to what can be actually shared among group participants. These mostly pertain to mental health-related difficulties that are not frequently brought up within the group and also because some group members may not be sure about how to name their emotional states. It seems that some participants avoid dealing with their psychological burden because they have a hard time establishing trust with their psychiatrists or they prefer to discuss it in individual psychotherapy/ peer counselling like the one we explored in the previous section.

My impression is that people think quite little about psychology and things related to it … I only realized what was happening to me when my psychiatrist told me 'look, that is a panic attack', so if people have emotional problems, maybe they talk about that with psychiatrists … But, on second thought, I doubt that anyone goes to confide in their psychiatrists … They go more to say 'please give me hormones, give me something for depression'. (Personal communication, December 2019)

The fact that psychological distress is rarely touched upon in discussions within the group or, for that matter, with a psychiatrist, reflects broader social patterns of stigma that is still attached to mental issues in contemporary Serbia, which has over the last three decades been strongly impoverished and repatriarchalised (Bilić, 2012). In the words of one group member:

I think we are far from having a support group which would actually deal with people's psychological issues associated with being trans … But this applies to Serbia, more generally, regardless of whether you are trans or not … For example, I have experience with depression and when I go to my GP to ask for medication, she tells me 'oh, but you are too young to be depressed … why are you asking for this?' like … what the heck … as if I was just bored, so let's take some antidepressants … as a country we are still far away from knowing about the importance of mental health care. (Personal communication, December 2019)

Given that the group is a self-support group, which means that it is not led by professional psychotherapists and does not insist on regular attendance, according to some interviewees, many of its members may not be immediately aware of the beneficial effects the group meetings have on their mental health. In this regard, one interviewee stated that the protective dimension of the group is something he noticed only in hindsight as he 'looked back at his participation' (personal communication, December 2019).

Navigating the medical/psychiatric system

While raising personal issues related to mental health within the group may be contentious, there is much more consensus about the capacity of the group to help its members prepare for confronting the medical system, above all psychiatrists and endocrinologists. In this regard, many group members talk about their negative experiences in the medical domain. Regardless of whether they approached it in their capacity as patients or activists (or both), they felt that their knowledge was underappreciated and that medical power overrode their accounts of their own lives. In the words of one group member:

> The Ministry of Health is the most conservative, not only here but in the region more generally ... the door is completely closed ... there are committees that write bills about us but do not consult us at all ... not a single trans person participates in that ... so people think they do not have any rights and they are not used to reacting or complaining. (Personal communication, December 2019)

The issue of power and its abuse is also reflected in the interactions with specific trans-specific healthcare providers.

> There is only one endocrinologist ... if you complain about her, then how will you deal with your hormonal treatment? So doctors are really masters of fear ... there is constantly a risk that you may stay even without that one doctor and then you say 'ok, let me bear with this, endure, stay silent, then at least I will manage to do what I want to do' ... as long as they have so much power, they do not have any incentive to change anything ... so there needs to be a shift in power relations ... they are constantly fragmenting the community because they have so much power ... they speak constantly in the media about trans issues ... the focus is so much more on doctors than on activists ... if you come to them and say 'wait, in my life it's not like that', doctors says 'how can you teach me about that when I know better, I am a doctor' ... for example, if you go to see an endocrinologist and you do not address her as 'professor', she does not look at you ... you must not say 'doctor', but 'professor' ... these are horrible complexes they have. (Personal communication, December 2019)

With this in mind, preparing for an encounter with a psychiatrist and eventually meeting one (especially until 2019 and the latest policies of the World Health Organization) can be an intense and anxiety-fraught experience. This is due to the fact that a psychiatric assessment and the diagnosis are critical for receiving hormonal treatment and eventually proceeding towards surgery. Psychiatrists are mainly responsible for deciding the 'appropriate' moment for initiating hormonal therapy: thus, they can unnecessarily delay that process and amplify anxiety without providing sufficient information. In this regard, Đura Đuričić, one of the current co-coordinators of the self-help group, states:

> I went to see a psychiatrist in one of the health institutions with a view to beginning my transition process. It was already there that I felt

disappointed because I had expected some sort of psychotherapy which I did not get. The whole process of starting hormonal therapy took me entire six years which was rather atypical and led me to anxiety as well as more pronounced gender dysphoria and depression. Such feelings did not help at the time when it was necessary for me to continue with the transition process. ... During the transition, meetings with the psychiatrist take place once per month or less. I think that is too little for this kind of problem when we need to be supported and get advice. I believe that there should be a specific department dedicated exclusively to trans health so that there are sufficient slots and sessions with the psychiatrist and so that we do not have to compete for those slots with other patients. (As cited in Jeremić, 2017, online)

The self-help group serves as a platform for sharing knowledge about the medical procedures, 'required' behaviour on behalf of the people forced in the role of patients, and expected behaviour for healthcare providers. While considering a gender-affirming surgery, group members turn to their peers to learn about their experiences with overcoming the psychiatric 'hurdle'. This often means that, as is the case with TGNB people across the globe, group members engage in the gender confirmation process as a kind of performance where they are playing the role they believe is expected from them to successfully 'pass the test' and gain access to surgical procedures. As one interviewee states when describing the initial meeting with a psychiatrist:

you need to say the right words, you need to act the norm ... one guy in the group talked about how he was told by the psychiatrist 'you need to cut your hair, to go fishing' ... it is incredible how stereotypical their protocols are ... in the group we discuss this and aim to tell people how things stand ... then it is their decision whether they want to lie or not ... we are not encouraging anyone to lie but people do need to know how things work ... they should know that they are taking that risk ... some people have very fragile mental health exactly because they are not taking hormones and the whole process is being delayed ... so they are waiting and cannot find a job. (Personal communication, December 2019)

Having in mind the long history of psychiatric gatekeeping and the 'one-treatment-fits-all' approach, characterised by the lack of sensitivity to individual needs of different people, group members are often willing to engage in this performance. As a consequence of such 'artificial' interaction, mental health-related knowledge is generated within the official medical system not on the basis of the real experiences and needs of transgender people, but on their attempt to conform to the perceived and internalised expectations of the medical authority, which leads to further alienation from care providers. This is especially problematic given that members of the group also state that they feel 'used' by medical professionals curious about TGNB persons. Đura Đuričić, states:

> [When I went to see a psychiatrist] my impression was that I was there because of the doctor, helping him to get more information about transgender condition rather than to be helped myself. From the very beginning I knew who I was and what I wanted and I did not need a doctor's endorsement, I did not have any doubts about the surgery. (As cited in Jeremić, 2017, online)

This idea that TGNB persons are 'used' as sources of information that is then processed without their direct involvement or benefit also appears in relation to another TGNB group that is led by a psychiatrist working at the national clinic. One self-help group participant went to a few meetings of the other group only to notice that the group leader (psychiatrist) was overly distant allowing conflicts among group members to surface in an aggressive manner. This interviewee states:

> I had a feeling that we were like guinea pigs there ... like here you are, you should talk and I will observe and learn on the basis of your behavior how a trans person should look like, how they should behave ... her understanding of the trans issue can be reduced to binarity ... that is the only thing she has learned from the book that they are using ... there is another psychiatrist who is learning a bit more, but she is also quite conservative ... I heard these psychiatrists complaining that people just disappear after their surgeries and never show up again leaving them without any feedback ... and they would need that feedback for the Ministry ... yeah, but I wonder why they disappear. (Personal communication, December 2019)

When asked about the differences between the two groups, the self-help group and the one at the clinic, the interviewee who briefly participated in both says that the one led by a psychiatrist is attended more by those people who do not approach the medical model critically or are much less likely to put it in question. Thus, this interviewee also points to an increasing critical consciousness among the trans people towards the healthcare that is being developed in the activist context that is, in the context of the group. He states:

> those going to the other group have a more 'medical' outlook ... some of those who are coming here also have that 'outlook', but they are open for communication and it is possible to explain to them that

that way of looking at things is not the only one ... I don't have in mind only gender binarism but the idea that transgender is a mental disorder ... I met a lot of trans people used to the idea that they had a mental disorder ... I remember one guy lying next to me at the hospital when we had our surgeries and he held such a worldview ... I was shocked ... one trans girl came saying 'I am lesbian, I do not have any problems with my genital organs and I do not want a surgery' ... after she said that three persons reacted immediately saying 'Then, you are not trans, you have issues', so such patronizing stupidities were said ... and the group leader did not react to that at all ... even though the girl was there for the first time ... that was one time I witnessed such a thing whether members of the group tried to impose on other how they should feel and after that I stopped going there ... it looked like the group coordinator's role was only to observe and to learn. (Personal communication, December 2019)

Dealing with gender binarism

As is obvious from above, throughout the interviews, gender binarism appears as the dominant issue that group members have to negotiate both in their personal lives as well as in group meetings. In her study with 28 members of the self-help group done in 2012, Zulević noted that the majority of those who joined went through the complete process of surgical gender affirming even though the group also welcomed those who were not interested in medical interventions or at least not in a complete physical transition. 'Incomplete' bodily modifications, however, were not legally allowed in Serbia at the time of Zulević's research and partially done surgeries[10] were more a consequence of the lack of financial means for covering all of the necessary interventions. In this regard, legal regulation reflected deeply entrenched perceptions about the social world being divided into two genders, which have to a great extent persisted up to this day colouring the operation of the group. In the words of Aleksa Milanović, a long-term group member:

A huge number of trans people, especially in Serbia, want to enter into transition as soon as possible, to get a diagnosis quickly, start with hormones, do surgeries and blend into the society ... They do this in order to protect themselves and decrease discrimination. In the West, also a huge number of people want to go into the process of gender affirmation, but there is also a huge number of those who do not want to modify their bodies, but do want to change their gender identity. I personally have not done any medical interventions, my transgender identity comprises me using masculine pronouns and a name which is considered masculine in my environment. (As cited in Galić, 2018, online)

The adherence to the idea of gender binarism would perhaps not be so strong within the group were it not reinforced by the dominant psychiatric discourse encountered, in one form or the other, by many TGNB persons across the region. As one person states:

psychiatrists are, in principle, promoting the following view: you have gender dysphoria, you have the so-called F64 diagnosis and your cure for that is surgery ... once your surgery is done, that diagnosis will disappear, meaning that you are no longer trans ... you are then a man or a woman ... but it's not like that only in Serbia. (Personal communication, December 2019)

Gender binarism is reflected in the psychiatrists' prototype of an ideal candidate for hormone-surgical treatment: as a person who finds their identity in gender binary and traditional gender roles, including heterosexual orientation.

We recently had a regional meeting and many people said that those who would admit to their psychiatrists that they were non-binary would unnecessarily prolong their hormonal treatments and the whole procedure ... it is similar with non-heterosexual information ... maybe it is now a bit better than it used to be, but it is still like that ... interestingly enough, psychiatrists still tend to ask you also about your sexual orientation ... like who you go out with ... even though that is completely irrelevant.

The fact that many people do not only sever their links with their psychiatrists, as one group member pointed out above, but also stop coming to group meetings[11] once their gender-affirming surgery has been completed, testifies to the power of binary gender conceptions among the group members. They seem less interested in being associated with the Belgrade trans collective when they start feeling more secure about being a man or a woman (for example, there is currently only one person who continued to attend the meetings after surgery). The pressure to conform to the gender norm – which constitutes the basis for (internalised) transphobia – manifests itself during or around group meetings marginalising, in turn, non-binary persons. As one member states:

transphobia is appearing within the group as hypermasculinity or hyperfemininity ... like one trans woman telling another that she 'does not look like a woman enough' ... like she is not wearing makeup or taking care of her looks ... the argument is that by not presenting herself as a 'woman enough', she makes it easier for others to understand that she is actually trans ... however, I should add that people rarely raise such issues in group discussions, it is more something that is said 'on the fringes' and individually, but not when we are sitting in a circle ... It is for sure that there is not enough space within the group for non-binary people, probably also because there are so few of them ... so in the 90 per cent of cases, the discussion within the group slides into the medical issues ... non-binary people who are not interested in any surgeries can get a bit bored. (Personal communication, December 2019)

When asked whether there are any generational differences regarding the need to conform to gender norms, especially in view of recent intensification of trans activist engagement on the global scale, one group member states:

In the group there are people from 18 to 50 years of age ... there is a generational difference in the sense that younger people do not really perceive doctors so much in terms of their authority, but older people still do ... they see them a lot as an authority ... so young people are generally more informed and open ... and especially more open to dating other trans people as well as to experimenting with various ways of expressing their gender identity ... this was not so much the case with my generation. (Personal communication, December 2019)

Irrespective of the fact that it may still be unsure about how to confront the challenge of reproducing gender norms that are at the root of gender-related oppression, the Geten self-help group represents a crucial convergence point for TGNB people in Serbia and the region. In the local milieu still characterised by high levels of transphobia, there is hardly another place with such a concentration of trans-related knowledge. In this regard, the group goes beyond an immediate empowerment to constitute an epistemic community engaged in developing a critical and analytical perspective vis-à-vis the norms of medicine as well as in continually negotiating and acknowledging embodied trans experience. While the group for the time being lacks wider social visibility, the experience of its members has informed the legal solutions that Geten has proposed to destabilise the gender norm and advance the social status of TGNB people in the country. With the legal weakening of the psychiatric dimension in TGNB lives, it is to be expected that the official institutions providing trans (mental) healthcare will increasingly turn to such community initiatives for information and advice.

Conclusion

The field of transgender health has been recently going through an unprecedented change brought about by decades of sustained trans activist engagement. As an identity-based model of trans health is slowly replacing a disorder-based model, TGNB persons' experiences with health provisions are improving. This is clearly visible in the highly dynamic political context of today's Serbia in which issues encountered by TGNB individuals differ greatly as a function of the period in which they started socially and/or medically affirming their gender over the last three decades. However, in spite of the evolution in the domain of surgical interventions and the higher visibility of trans-related topics in the media, trans mental health has remained an area that warrants further attention. Our trilateral approach, comprising a survey with TGNB persons, observations from clinical work, and interviews with members of the self-help group, points to the prevalence of negative experiences with and emphasises the necessity for improving mental health services. We have shown that the medical/pathologising outlook on trans lives based on the idea of gender binarism is still surprisingly resilient posing an obstacle to TGNB people's willingness to seek mental health assistance.

The hegemony of the medical model in Serbia, in contrast to some other post-Yugoslav states,[12] cannot be separated from the fact that gender-affirming surgeries have been regularly taking place in Belgrade since the 1980s. Given that groundbreaking surgical interventions had started years ahead of any activist claims for transgender liberation, the rapidly accumulating medical knowledge has quickly gained the upper hand over the voice of trans persons themselves.[13] The first more differentiated as well as publicly and collectively articulated trans grievances appeared only in the wake of democratic changes that started with the fall of the Slobodan Milošević regime in October 2000. By that time the medical discourse on 'transgender condition' had been already firmly rooted not only in psychopathology but also in the idea that sex and gender are overlapping binary categories. Sava Perović, Professor of Urology at the University of Belgrade Faculty of Medicine, was at the helm of the team that started performing gender-affirming surgeries. In an interview, conducted in 2003, once he had already earned an international reputation for his work, Dr Perović talked about a patient who in the early 1980s approached him with a request for a surgical intervention that would change his genital organs. Dr Perović stated:

'I refused that first patient three times, but then primarius doctor Zoran Rakić, who was dealing with the issues of transsexualism sent me a letter in which he explained that what was at stake was indeed a real medical disease (prava medicinska bolest) and that it had to do with a gender identity disorder. It was a male person with a female brain and the changes were in the (brain) cortex. I was looking for a solution in the existing literature, but given that I could not find anything, I decided to perform a surgery on the basis of my knowledge. It was successful and after it I started a series of such surgeries here (kod nas) and published a paper about a new surgical technique in the world leading journal of plastic and reconstructive surgery. Ever since then our clinic has been visited by foreigners who want to be operated and I am invited to clinics around the world. At the same time, wars broke out here leading to isolation and everything that happened to us, but nevertheless, I managed to obtain visas and continue performing surgeries.'

Dr Perović understood that being unable to fully affirm one's gender due to social constraints was a source of mental distress[14] and that a multidisciplinary approach was the only viable strategy towards effective trans healthcare (Kovačević, 2003).[15] However, even though he had a lot of media presence and became a member of the Serbian Academy of Sciences and Arts on the basis of his surgical innovations, he kept – in accordance with the then global trends – positioning trans people in pathologising contexts without acknowledging discrimination or problematising the way in which the social environment proscribed gender variance. He never demanded legal action that would improve the social status of trans people or at least the way in which his colleagues perceived them (Đurić, 2012). Dr Perović was known for his insistence that people willing to undergo gender-affirming surgery should not be allowed to do so if they admit that they would be homosexuals after they transition. In a lecture for the general public which he gave at the National Library of Serbia in 2005 he expressed such a stance saying that some members of staff at his clinic refused to enter a room with trans patients because they considered them homosexuals (Deve, 2005; Đurić, this volume; Đurić, 2012). Given that Dr Perović was the leading figure in the trans domain in Serbia and internationally as well as the principal mentor for urogenital surgeons at the Belgrade Faculty of Medicine, his rather conservative ideas about gender diversity had a profound impact on the national medical science for almost three decades. There is still only one medical gender team in the country reflecting high levels of Serbian state centralisation and perpetuating the fissure in access to healthcare between urban and provincial/rural populations.[16] On the other hand, it is also important to keep in mind that position of members of the medical gender team among the broader medical community. The very fact that the work of the team was officially recognised by the relevant medical professional organisation only in 2012, when the Committee was founded, is an example of the associated stigma they faced among their peers.

The most active period of Dr Perović's professional life to a great extent coincided with the intense process of repatriarchalisation that preceded and accompanied the wars of the Yugoslav succession and the fall of Yugoslav socialism. The late 1980s and the early 1990s witnessed a rapid dismantling of the emancipatory achievements of the socialist regime that particularly affected the area of reproduction and gender relations. After sustained policy measures that aimed at improving the social status of women and decriminalise homosexuality in the second half of the 20th century, all of the (former) republics went through a 'calcification' of gender roles undergird by sensationalistically propagated demographic concerns. Given that the unprecedented modernisation impulse of the socialist regime never really managed to destabilise deep patriarchal roots, nationalist politics that culminated in an armed conflict also manifested themselves in the form of 'gender wars' (Slapšak, 2013, p 255) comprising high levels of misogyny, homophobia, and transphobia. In such challenging circumstances, some of the already fragile streams of Yugoslav feminist engagement could not altogether resist the patriarchal assault and ended up assuming radical feminist positions unsupportive of the transgender cause (Bilić, this volume; Bilić, 2020). This was also aggravated by strong neoliberal tendencies of activist professionalisation that radically narrowed and fragmented the field of political struggle by zooming in on particular identities and increasingly foreclosing the possibilities of intersectionally sensitive initiatives. Such a situation dispersed TGNB people and contributed to their marginalisation by depriving them of a feminist refuge.

Once nationalism subsided as the central axis of official political life towards the end of the 1990s and in the early 2000s, some of its strongest elements survived by withdrawing into the fields of psychiatry and psychology. The sphere of mental health, always already immersed in political contestations, became a new discursive battleground on which conservative/traditional perspectives about what constitutes 'normal' gender and sexuality expression clashed with much more subdued but resilient liberal currents. Mental health professionals were no longer crucial only for 'managing' personal destinies but were effectively turned into a 'bulwark' against the 'decadent influences of the West', which were supposedly determined to deal a final blow to the already weakened 'traditional' Serbian family. In this regard, professional medical/psychiatric organisations may show serious delays in absorbing emancipatory LGBTIQ+ legal norms due to the power that middle-class heteronormative (male) psychiatrists tend to hold in patriarchal environments.[17] Given that they are generally perceived as 'objective' experts without immediately visible political commitments, conservative mental health professionals may be influential in framing public debates around LGBTIQ+ issues in a way that modulates progressive legislation and truncates its potential to diffuse across the social field. Mental issues, thus, have a hard time detaching themselves from the layers of social stigma that have thickened across decades characterised by violence, isolation, and authoritarianism.

In such circumstances, little reliable information about trans issues or gender and sexual non-normative identities, more generally, circulate within clinical or academic settings. LGBTIQ+ topics have been for a lot of time insufficiently or inadequately represented in Serbian higher education institutions,[18] mainly in the courses other than those dealing with mental health (such as biological psychology, gender studies, history of psychology) and in pathologising and insulting manner (for example, the major psychiatry textbook [Jašović Gašić and Lečić Toševski, 2007] used by both psychology and medicine students in which it is, for example, stated that trans people try to 'simulate the phenotype of the opposite sex'). With this in mind, it is not surprising that a recent survey about transgender health, which brought together Georgia, Poland, Serbia, Spain, and Sweden (Smiley, 2017), demonstrated that Serbia was the only country where no healthcare providers identified as trans. This remarkable lack points to the history of the health system's closure towards TGNB individuals and continues to obstruct their engagement with (mental) health services.

However, while the reluctance to seek professional psychological help is rather general, it is in the case of TGNB people exacerbated by the dual role of mental health professionals who do work in the sphere of trans-specific healthcare. For the time being, those people who are responsible to decide about access to hormonal treatment and surgical interventions are also supposed to provide psychological help to them, especially given the shortage of mental health professionals and the fact that many TGNB persons cannot afford private/individual psychotherapy. Such an arrangement can seriously affect the therapeutic alliance between the mental health professional and the client and may distance TGNB individuals from engaging with therapeutic services due to the fear of compromising their treatment (Smiley et al, 2017). It is therefore imperative to increase the number of mental healthcare providers and to arrange further training in the domain of trans-specific mental health services. In doing so, both state institutions and private practitioners can benefit from the knowledge that has over the last 20 years accumulated within LGBTIQ+ activist organisations and, in particular, the Geten self-help group.

Updating mental health services is particularly important in the period in which transgender has officially ceased to be a clinical category. In their *Guidelines for Psychological Practice with Transgender and Gender Nonconforming People*, the American Psychological Association (2015) states that a non-binary understanding of gender is fundamental to the provision of affirmative care for TGNB people. The Association calls for psychologists and other mental health professionals to take a leadership role in ending transphobic discrimination. Although significant advances in this direction have taken place over the last years, Serbia, along with many of its neighbours, has structural rule of law difficulties that distort law implementation. New non-discriminatory legal solutions are, nevertheless, crucial and it is to be expected that the bill about gender identity and the rights of intersex persons, proposed by Geten, should be adopted in the near future. It will constitute a platform upon which community-generated knowledge can be shared among all interested parties. Activist organisations' alternative forms of mental healthcare and support, which are in synchrony with the global movement for gender and non-heterosexual liberation, can certainly help to transform mainstream mental health policies rendering them more sensitive to the needs of TGNB individuals.

Acknowledgements
The survey about the needs of TGNB persons in Serbia was co-conducted by the activists Dimitrije Đurić and Saša Demian Lazić, under the supervision of the first author and with input from the rest of the Geten team.

Notes
[1] This is an extended version of the paper: Vidić, J. and Bilić, B. (2021) TGNB persons, mental health, and gender binarism in Serbia. *Journal of Gay and Lesbian Mental Health*, 25, 2, 155–74. DOI: 10.1080/19359705.2020.1850596

[2] The name of the organisation was inspired by the androgynous world of Gethen from Ursula Le Guin's novel *Left Hand of Darkness*. In 2016, the organisation received the writer's formal permission to use Gethen (in Serbian, Geten) as its name, and in 2019 the name of the organisation was officially changed from Gayten-LGBT to Geten.

[3] ICD-10 still used the term 'opposite sex' assuming the gender binary; both DSM-V (2013) and ICD-11 use 'other gender'.

[4] According to Reisner et al (2016a), 'a participatory population perspective necessitates working with – and not through – local, national, and global transgender-led organisations in the conduct of research and evaluation, delivery of gender-affirmative clinical care, education and training, and policy and advocacy'.

[5] The law and the bylaw were adopted as a part of the accession process to the European Union. However, relevant non-governmental organisations were not invited to participate in the working groups, and the original version of the rulebook stipulated hormone treatment and (not either/or) surgical interventions as a requirement for legal gender recognition. The change from 'and' to 'either/or' was made in the last minute before its official adoption after Geten's urgently invited European NGOs and institutions to exert pressure on the working group with the view of giving up surgical interventions (basically sterilisation) as a requirement.

[6] Zulević (2012) notes that those TGNB persons who did their gender-affirming surgery before 2000 report that they were sometimes asked by the medical staff to give presents in the form of jewellery or other valuables so that the intervention could be performed smoothly.

[7] This bill is available in Transserbia (2019).

[8] The sample does not reflect the general population in this regard.

[9] The participants understand that one of the problems of trans organising is that it is very Belgrade-centred. As one group member states: 'mostly people from Belgrade come to the group ... or those who have moved to Belgrade ... so we cannot really reach those

who live in Niš or in other parts of Serbia ... we cannot do that ... how could we? We would need much more resources, funds, time ... So, in that regard, our situation here [in Serbia] is more complex than, for example, in Montenegro which is smaller and it may be easier to reach the capital ... Everything is more complicated the further you are from Belgrade' (personal communication, December 2019).

[10]   The option of partial transition was introduced by the fifth version of the WPATH standards of care from 1998. See Levine et al (1998).

[11]   One group member (personal communication, December 2019) states: 'until now it has mostly been the case that people, once they are done with the surgery, they also want to be done with that stage of their lives, they are not interested in mentioning it ever again, they think it would be the best if no one ever knew about them'.

[12]   This is due to the fact that in other capitals of the Yugoslav republics, gender-reaffirming surgeries were not possible throughout the 1980s and are still unavailable in some of them up to this day.

[13]   This may share certain affinities with the fact that the decriminalisation of homosexuality in Serbia, which took place in 1994, also did not stem from activist efforts but occurred rather as a result of a routine revision of the Penal Code. Such a legal act that preceded more visible forms of activism had a profound effect on the development of gay engagement in the following years: it prevented activists from going through a crucial public 'legitimisation' stage and left thick layers of social homophobia untouched while declaratively allowing homosexuality.

[14]   In the same article, it is stated (Kovačević, 2003, online): 'Sex change should certainly be accompanied by a complete personality change. That is why sex change should be done while the patient is still a baby and the environment does not know their sex. But when it comes to adults, psychological traumas are not negligible. We have seen that physical appearance, that is the external part, can be successfully modified. However, are there ways of changing the soul which is an integral part of one's personality? Even after thirty years in surgical wards, Dr Perović still has not found such a way: "That is almost impossible. On this level of medical development there are some biochemical studies that are trying to find the cause and target that [psychic, BB] aspect of the human being, but so far they have been unsuccessful."'

[15]   In the same interview, he stated (Kovačević, 2003, online): 'At the last world congress in which I took part, which was devoted to transsexualism, that is, to the disorder of gender identity, there was a whole team of experts including psychiatrists and psychologists, surgeons, social workers. Without a multidisciplinary approach, there can be no cure for such patients and that functions in the West, but here unfortunately not.'

[16]   Such an arrangement leaves a lot of space for the few specialised doctors to have a monopoly over the field of transgender health in Serbia. In this regard, Jelena Simić (On-Off, 2019, online), a member of the Geten legal team, states: 'Over the last 30 years, the major problem of trans people in Serbia was the legal lacuna ... You did not have a single legal document about trans persons. That changed in 2011 and that was a boom for us jurists given that in that year the law on health insurance was changed. ... After that, jurists became more flexible and started asking doctors how to regulate that field. ... I have to say that it is exactly our doctors, and their number is not that high, even though we were the first in this part of the world to deal with this question and reached a very high level ... unfortunately I have to say that the ethics of those [medical] experts failed in this case. In no way did they contribute to the improvement of the status of transgender people. It is exactly our psychiatrists and endocrinologists who are obstructing the procedure of legal recognition ... There is a monopoly of certain doctors who deal with these issues ... In order to control or to work in this field, you need to have specialized knowledge

… There are here few such doctors and they are playing the role of gatekeepers, they see themselves as guardians of the society, of social values … Even though they are members of eminent international organisations that deal with transgender conditions … So, if I can say so, it is really hypocritical that they are respected members of those organisations where practices and approaches are being improved over the last three decades … Thus it is certainly not a matter of a lack of knowledge … I can only express a doubt that there is that lucrative dimension which is quite pronounced among our doctors … Because if you have one endocrinologist in the whole country, even if the number of transgender people is not that great, try making an appointment in a state institution … All of the patients are being diverted to private practice.'

[17] For example, it took the Belgrade-based lesbian activist organisation Labris years of effort (until 2008) to persuade the Serbian Medical Society to acknowledge the World Health Organization's declassification of homosexuality (1990) as sexual deviation.

[18] In this regard, there are two studies conducted by the Gayten-LGBT team and coordinated by the first author: in 2015, 65 medical workers (GPs, specialists, and nurses) were asked about their attitudes towards LGBTIQ+ persons via an online survey (Vidić, 2020b). This study showed that the level of familiarity with trans issues was rather low – the participants answered correctly to around a half of 12 trans-related questions while no participant provided a correct answer to all of the questions. More than a half stated that a transgender person who has not gone through a surgical transition should be addressed in accordance with their legal documents. Even though the sample was self-selected, more than a half stated that they had never encountered topics around homosexuality or gender identity during their either general or specialist medical training. In the second, unpublished study conducted in 2017, 195 participants including students of psychology (70.3 per cent), social work (22.6 per cent), medicine (3.1 per cent), and law (4.1 per cent) were asked a set of questions regarding inclusion of LGBTIQ+-related matters in their curricula. A vast majority (73.8 per cent) stated that they encountered LGBTIQ+ topics at the faculty. When it comes to gender identity, more specifically, the examined students stated that the issue was covered in an affirmative way (32.3 per cent), neutral way (33.3 per cent), or in a pathologising way (6.7 per cent), while 22.1 per cent reported that the topic was not covered at all. When asked whether their courses covered the topic of working with transgender people, 56.9 per cent gave a negative answer, 12.3 per cent stated that it was covered in an affirmative way, in a neutral way (10.8 per cent), and in a negative way (8.2 per cent). One psychology student observed that non-heterosexual and trans people are mentioned only 'along the way', but that they are not formally included in the syllabi of any courses. The same participant emphasised that questions regarding LGBTIQ+ tend to be raised by students rather than by lecturers.

References

American Psychological Association. (2015) Guidelines for psychological practice with transgender and gender nonconforming people. *American Psychologist*, 70(9), 832–64.

Aylagas-Crespillo, M., García-Barbero, Ó., and Rodríguez-Martín, B. (2018) Barriers in the social and healthcare assistance for transgender persons: A systematic review of qualitative studies. *Enfermería Clínica*, 28(4), 247–59.

Bilić, B. (2012) *We were gasping for air: (Post-)Yugoslav anti-war activism and its legacy*. Baden-Baden: Nomos.

Bilić, B. (2020) *Trauma, violence and lesbian agency in Croatia and Serbia: Building better times*. London: Palgrave Macmillan.

Bockting, W.O., Miner, M.H., Swinburne Romine, R.E., Hamilton, A., and Coleman, E. (2013) Stigma, mental health, and resilience in an online sample of the US transgender population. *American Journal of Public Health*, *103*, 943–51.

Breger, J., Green, R., Laub, D., Reynolds, C, Walker, P., and Wollman, L. (1979) *Standards of care: The hormonal and surgical sex reassignment of gender dysphoric persons* (1st edn). San Francisco: Harry Benjamin International Gender Dysphoria Association.

Budge, S.L., Adelson, J.L., and Howard, K.A.S. (2013) Anxiety and depression in transgender individuals: The roles of transition status, loss, social support, and coping. *Journal of Consulting and Clinical Psychology*, *81*, 545–57.

Deve. (2005) *Razumevanje, predavanje u Narodnoj biblioteci Srbije*. Belgrade: Deve.

Đurić, M. (2012) Transpolnost u Srbiji. *Optimist*. Retrieved on 23 January 2020 from www.optimist.rs/transpolnost-u-srbiji/

Fassinger, R.E. and Arseneau, J.R. (2007) 'I'd rather get wet than be under that umbrella': Differentiating the experiences and identities of lesbian, gay, bisexual, and transgender people. In K.J. Bieschke, R.M. Perez, and K.A. DeBord (eds) *Handbook of counseling and psychotherapy with lesbian, gay, bisexual, and transgender clients* (pp 19–49). Washington, D.C. American Psychological Association.

Fraser, L. (2009) Depth psychotherapy with transgender people. *Sexual and Relationship Therapy*, *24*(2), 126–42.

Galić, N. (2018) Intervju sa Aleksom Milanovićem, aktivistom Trans mreže Balkan. Retrieved on 27 January 2020 from www.transbalkan.org/inter vju-sa-aleksom-milanovicem-aktivistom-trans-mreze-balkan/

Grant, J. M, Mottet, L.A., Tanis, J., Harrison, J., Herman, J., and Kesiling, M. (2011) Injustice at every turn: A report of the national transgender discrimination survey. Washington: National Center for Transgender Equality & National Gay and Lesbian Task Force. Retrieved on 27 January 2020 from www.thetaskforce.org/wp-content/uploads/2019/07/ntds_f ull.pdf

Ho, F. and Mussap, A.J. (2017) Transgender mental health in Australia: Satisfaction with practitioners and the standards of care. *Australian Psychologist*, *52*, 209–18.

Jeremić, M. (2017) Superheroj Đura: Budite svoji i ne odustajte. Retrieved on 27 January 2020 from www.transserbia.org/trans/transrodnost/1203-superheroj-djura-budite-svoji-i-ne-odustajte

Kovačević, L.J. (2003) Skalpelom kroz svet. Interview with Dr Sava Perović. *Planeta: Magazin za nauku, istraživanja i otkrića*. Retrieved on 23 January 2020 from www.planeta.rs/05/5naukakaozivot.htm

Levine, S., Brown, G., Coleman, E., Cohen-Kettenis, P., Maasdam, J., Pfafflin, F., and Schaefer, E. (1998) *The standards of care for gender identity disorders* (5th edn). Dusseldorf: Harry Benjamin International Gender Dysphoria Association.

Marković Žigić, D., Zulević, J., and Maksimović, K. (2015) Rad sa transseksualnim klijentima – specifičnosti tranzicije i izazovi nakon nje. In V. Miletić and A. Milenković (eds) *Priručnik za LGBT psihoterapiju* (pp 172–88). Belgrade: Udruženje za unapređenje mentalnog zdravlja.

McCann, E. and Sharek, D. (2016) Mental health needs of people who identify as transgender: A review of the literature. *Archives of Psychiatric Nursing*, *30*, 280–85.

McConnell, E.A., Birkett, M., and Mustanski, B. (2016) Families matter: Social support and mental health trajectories among lesbian, gay, bisexual, and transgender youth. *Journal of Adolescent Health*, *59*, 674–80.

McNeil, J., Bailey, L.. Ellis, S., Morton, J., and Regan, M. (2012) *Trans mental health and emotional wellbeing study 2012*. Retrieved on 5 February 2020 from https://www.scottishtrans.org/wp-content/uploads/2013/03/trans_mh_study.pdf Scottish Transgender Alliance; TREC, Traverse; Sheffield Hallam University, TransBareAll.

Miroslava Jašović-Gašić, M. and Lečić-Toševski, D. (eds) (2007) *Psihijatrija za studente Medicinskog fakulteta u Beogradu*. Belgrade: Medicinski fakultet.

On-Off (2019) Biti transrodan u Srbiji. Retrieved on 3 February 2020 from www.youtube.com/watch?v=aDZj-Z6ZNVU

Reisner, S.L. Poteat, T., Keatley, J., Cabral, M., Mothopeng, T., Dunham, E., Holland, C.E., Max, R., and Baral, S.D. (2016a) Global health burden and needs of transgender populations: A review. *Lancet*, *388*, 412–36.

Reisner, S.L., Keatley, J., and Baral, S. (2016b) Transgender community voices: A participatory population perspective. *The Lancet*, *388*, 10042.

Robles, R., Fresan, A., Vega-Ramirez, H., Cruz-Islas, J, Rodrigues-Perez, V., Dominguez-Martinez, T., and Reed, G. (2016) Removing transgender identity from the classification of mental disorders: A Mexican field study for ICD-11. *Lancet Psychiatry*, *3*, 850–59.

Simons, L., Schrager, S.M., Clark, L.F., Belzer, M., and Olson, J. (2013) Parental support and mental health among transgender adolescents. *Journal of Adolescent Health*, *53*, 791–3.

Slapšak, S. (2013) Žene, Jugoslavija, antikomunistička narkoza i novi kolonijalizam: Mape, putevi, izlazi. *Poznańskie Studia Slawistyczne*, *5*, 249–63.

Službeni glasnik RS. (2018) Pravilnik o načinu izdavanja i obrascu potvrde nadležne zdravstvene ustanove o promeni pola (br. 103). Retrieved on 20 February 2020 from www.pravno-informacioni-sistem.rs/SlGlasnikPortal/

Smiley, A., Burgwal, A., Orre, C., Summanen, E., Garcia Niento, I., Vidić, J., Motmans, J., Kata, J., Gvianishvilli, N., Hard, V., and Kohner, R. (2017) *Overdiagnosed but underserved: Trans healthcare in Georgia, Poland, Serbia, Spain, and Sweden – Trans health survey*. Malmö: TGEU.

Smith, E., Jones, T., Ward, T., Dixon, J., Mitchel, A., and Hilier, L. (2014) *From blues to rainbows: The mental health and well-being of gender diverse and transgender young people in Australia*. Australian Research Centre in Sex, Health and Society. Melbourne: La Trobe University and University of New England.

Taliaferro, L.A., McMorris, B.J., and Eisenberg, M.E. (2018) Connections that moderate risk of non-suicidal self-injury among transgender and gender non-conforming youth. *Psychiatry Research*, *268*, 65–7.

Testa, R., Sciacca, L., Wang, F., Hendricks, M., Goldblum, P., Bradford, J., and Bognar, B. (2012) Effects of violence on transgender people. *Professional Psychology: Research and Practice*, *43*(5), 452–9.

Transgender Equality Network Ireland. (2013) *Speaking from the margins: Trans mental health and wellbeing in Ireland*. Dublin: Teni.

Transserbia. (2019) Model zakona: Zakon o rodnom identitetu i pravima interseks osoba. Retrieved on 20 February 2020 from https://www.tran sserbia.org/files/9sep19_MODEL_ZAKONA_RODNI_IDENTITET_I_ INTERSEKS-1-3.pdf

Turner, L., Whittle, S., and Combs, R. (2009) *Transphobic hate crimes in the European Union*. London: Press For Change.

Valentine, S.E. and Shipherd, J.C. (2018) A systematic review of social stress and mental health among transgender and gender non-conforming people in the United States. *Clinical Psychology Review*, *66*, 24–38.

Veale, J.F., Watson, R.J., Peter, T., and Saewyc, E.M. (2017) Mental health disparities among Canadian transgender youth. *Journal of Adolescent Health*, *60*, 44–9.

Vidić, J. (2020a) Položaj i potrebe transrodnih i rodno nebinarnih osoba u Srbiji. *Psihološka istraživanja*, *24*(1). https://doi.org/10.5937/psistr a24-27858

Vidić, J. (2020b) Transrodnost u Srbiji u 21. veku – pilot studija o informisanosti i iskustvima zdravstvenih radnika u procesu prilagođavanja pola. *Engrami*, *42*(2), 6–22.

Vidić, J. and Bilić, B. (2021) TGNB persons, mental health, and gender binarism in Serbia. *Journal of Gay and Lesbian Mental Health*, *25*(2), 155–74.

Vujović, S., Popovic, S., Sbutega-Milosevic, G., Đorđević, M., and Gooren, L. (2009) Transsexualism in Serbia: A twenty-year follow-up study. *Journal of Sexual Medicine*, *6*, 1018–23.

White, B.P. and Fontenot, H.B. (2019) Transgender and non-conforming persons' mental healthcare experiences: An integrative review. *Archives of Psychiatric Nursing*, *33*, 203–10.

World Health Organization. (2016) *International statistical classification of diseases and related health problems* (10th edn). Retrieved on 28 September 2019 from https://icd.who.int/browse10/2016/en

Zulević, J. (2012) Istraživanje problema transeksualnih osoba u sferama školstva, rada I zapošljavanja, zdravstvene zaštite i državne administracije. In S. Gajin (ed) *Model zakona o priznavanju pravnih posledica promene pola i utvrđivanja transseksualizma. Prava trans osoba: Od nepostojanja do stvaranja zakonskog okvira* (pp 27–49). Belgrade: Centar za unapređenje pravnih studija.

PART II

Activisms

4

From survival to activism: tracing trans history in Kosovo from the 1970s onwards

Lura Limani

On 31 December 2019 an enthusiastic Blert Morina posted on his Instagram profile a photo of the Basic Court decision that obligated his local registry in Gjakova to change his name and gender marker[1] to fit his gender identity. Morina, a transgender activist who lives in Kosovo, had been in a legal battle with authorities for almost two years. Announcing the case decision in his favour, he wrote in English:

> For a long time I have been very uncomfortable in my own skin, in the company of girls, I was too boyish, while in the company of boys, I was not manly enough … I had to constantly explain myself to people, which made me very sad. Not to talk about how much I had to go through thoughts like who knew me as Blerta and who knew me as Blert … As much as we were aware of the whole process requiring a lot of work and energy during the process I often questioned myself if I should continue, because sometimes it became extremely difficult to balance work, transition and court battle … But we made it! (Morina, 2019)

Morina's case was hailed as historic by local and regional media: it was *the first* public case of a trans person demanding and being granted the right to the legal recognition of their gender. Indeed, it was initially reported as the 'first ever known request' in Kosovo for a formal change of name and gender marker (Halili, 2018a). In August of the same year, the Appeals Court upheld a Basic Court decision ordering the local civil registration office in Prizren to change the name and gender marker of an anonymous applicant (known later only as M.P.), after the Ministry of Internal Affairs had appealed the Basic Court decision (Travers, 2019). This case too was reported as a 'historic first' by the national television channel that broke the story (Klan Kosova, 2019).

But were either of these cases historic *firsts* for Kosovo? What can we even consider as a *first*, or what would count as *historic* in a context in which the history of LGBTIQ+ individuals and communities remains largely buried, unknown? Furthermore, how do we account for a historicity that is built upon 'historic moments' that are at times violent outings of queer people?

In a recent essay, writer and historian Morgan M Page problematises the perpetual rediscovery of trans people from the ex-GI incorrectly hailed by the *New York Daily News* as 'the world's first sex change' to the more recent reactions to Torrey Peters novel *Detransition, Baby* hailed as the first trans novel published by a major publishing house (2021). Page argues that such claims rely on active erasure of trans history that precedes us:

> It's historical narcissism as intoxicant, dropping into our collective bellies like parachuting molly in the clubs we can presently only dream about, one that brings a rush of hair-tingling excitement and media fanfare, but whose unfortunate side effect is a sort of cultural amnesia. In order for trans people to be constantly discovered, we must be always and immediately cast off, forgotten. (Page, 2021)

In the Kosovar context, 'historical narcissism' runs rampant: in a country that declared its independence from Serbia in 2008, everyone can be the first Kosovar at something or the other. Independence itself was marked with the unveiling of NEWBORN, a typographic monument in downtown Prishtina, reinforcing the mythmaking of the Kosovo state as something entirely new, divorced from its complex history.[2] When it comes to LGBTIQ+, particularly trans, individuals in Kosovo and their history, which this chapter attempts to tackle, the novelty seems to never wear off. Intermittently, a documentary, an article, or an interview with LGBTIQ+ individuals will appear, at times against the subject's will. At first, it will attract media attention, encourage a public debate, and incite some vitriol denying queer existence and disowning it as other, foreign. Inevitably, the story will disappear from the limelight, retreat without managing to enter our collective memory, only to be replaced by another sensational title and the ensuing fanfare about the next lesbian, gay, bisexual, trans, or intersex person who dares to come out in public. While one cannot expect journalists to do the work of historians, it is also often said that journalism is 'the first rough draft of history'.[3] In this regard, that draft remains fairly rough and consistently formulaic.

LGBTIQ+ stories are often told in structurally consistent narratives that employ elements of the fairy tale such as the happy ending, and even reference a fairy tale proper – the Albanian myth of 'crossing the rainbow' (*kapërcimi i ylberit*), according to which when a girl crosses the rainbow she becomes a boy. This motif is so popular that it appears and reappears in

LGBTIQ+ media coverage in Kosovo at least as early as 1978, when we encounter it in the so far earliest recorded reporting on a Kosovo transgender person, although the trope has also been utilised to symbolise coming out in general.[4] Nevertheless, while this leitmotif might resonate through stories and coverage across decades, the stories themselves are almost never presented as connected to each other.

The cultural amnesia that Page writes about is a form of epistemic injustice, namely the hermeneutical injustice 'of having some significant area of one's social experience obscured from collective understanding owing to a structural identity prejudice in the collective hermeneutical resource' (Fricker, 2011, p 211). Such an epistemic injustice occludes queer people from both knowing their history and having the hermeneutic resources to interpret their social experience. This chapter is an attempt to redress this epistemic injustice, providing an intervention into the historiography of LGBTIQ+ people in Kosovo and the wider region in general. It traces the earliest media report of the transition of a Kosovo transgender person, Misin Krasnić, back to 1978. This chapter also analyses the re-emergence of trans narratives in national Kosovar media with the public coming out of activists Lend Mustafa and Blert Morina in 2016 and 2017 and how it affected the methods and focus of LGBTIQ+ advocacy in the country. Through a discursive analysis of the media reports and semi-structured interviews with three of the transgender people whose stories mark the mostly unwritten history of trans people in Kosovo, this chapter presents itself as an intervention into the LGBTIQ+ historiography with personal stories being utilised to write a history from below.

Contextualising the LGBTIQ+ movement in Kosovo

The history of LGBTIQ+ individuals and communities in Kosovo continues to constitute a blind spot in academic research, despite a proliferation of media articles and television documentaries produced in the past few years. Existing critical contributions have focused on how LGBTIQ+ rights in Kosovo and human rights discourses have been utilised to construct a Muslim European identity in Kosovo and Bosnian narratives; or how the LGBTIQ+ struggle in the Balkans has been co-opted by the US American foreign policy to justify interventions abroad (Rexhepi 2016; 2017). Less has been written about how stories of LGBTIQ+ individuals appear in mainstream media in Kosovo and how these appearances are presented as novel and singular, cut off from any attempt at a genealogy of queerness in Kosovo as the history of challenging fixed notions of sexuality and gender.

One of the main reasons for this lack of research is the difficulty of conducting empirical research among a precarious and an insular community that has to negotiate survival in a conservative society with persisting hostile attitudes towards queer people. According to a poll by the National Democratic Institute (2015), 81 per cent of LGBTIQ+ people interviewed in Kosovo experienced psychological abuse or verbal harassment, and 29 per cent suffered from physical violence. When interviewed for television programs, news, and documentaries, most LGBTIQ+ individuals choose to tell their stories with disguised voices and faces to protect their identity.

In that sense, the emergence of a new generation of LGBTIQ+ activists, and in particular trans activists, who have turned their own transitions into battlegrounds for legal recognition and awareness raising campaigns marks a great turning point. The two activists, Mustafa and Morina, who came out around the same time, are both trans men who have given countless interviews, appeared in documentaries, and even chronicled their transition on YouTube. Their public activism represents a radical departure from the existing depictions of queer people as disembodied voices speaking to us from the dark, fearing for their lives. Their active involvement in the movement also shifted its focus as the two were able to turn organisational attention and resources towards addressing specific trans issues such as lack of medical expertise and regulations for gender dysphoria treatment in the country, as well as lack of legal provisions for trans individuals to have their gender identity formally recognised.

The patriarchal and patrilineal Albanian society is no stranger to the queering of gender: travellers, anthropologists, and journalists have documented in detail the phenomenon of 'sworn virgins' (in Albanian: *virgjëreshat e përbetueme;* or *burrneshat*) – women who assume the social role of men, which also requires them to swear to lifelong celibacy before the elders of the village or tribe (Dickemann, 1997; Young, 2000; Durham, [1908] 2013;). But while some anthropologists have either described 'sworn virgins' as cross-dressing women or as transgender individuals who have become 'social men' (Dickemann in Young, 2000, p 117), others have argued that 'sworn virgins' 'were recognised in their communities in the role of a distinct gender status, similar to what modern anthropologists describe as "third gender"' (Tarifa, 2007, p 88). Nevertheless, as Young, who managed to interview a few of 'the sworn virgins' herself, observes: neither Albanians in general nor the 'virgins' themselves would describe *burrneshat* as transsexuals, transgendered, or cross-dressers (Young, 2000). Both anthropologists and journalists who have recorded the phenomenon have also noted that it was dying out – in 2008, the youngest 'sworn virgin' who was interviewed was 54 years old (Tarifa, 2007, p 90; Bilefsky, 2008).

Furthermore, the gender bending in the case of 'sworn virgins' is limited as it only goes one way. It is advantageous for a woman in a patriarchal society to abandon her oppressive social role and status, while there are no folkloric anecdotes of men doing the opposite. The myth of 'crossing the rainbow' – folkloric in origin and predating the rainbow-flag taken up by the American LGBTIQ+ activists in the late 1970s – functions very much within the same logic: the proverbial girl wishes to become a boy to escape suffering. In a traditional *valle* from Tropoja, filmed in 1988, and performed to the song 'O ylberi me shtatë lara' (Oh, rainbow with seven colours) dancers can be seen whirling around with handkerchiefs in their hands, as the singer sings 'Oh, rainbow with seven colours, you have crossed white mountains/oh rainbow above the mountain/you turned our girl into a boy' (Dylberizm, 2019). As the female dancers close into a tight circle, the dance culminates with one of the dancers emerging dressed in traditional men's garb as a boy (Dylberizm, 2019).

Despite this latent fascination and a culture of gender queering, mapping out the modern history of LGBTIQ+ in Kosovo is difficult because there is no single all-encompassing account of either queer expressions and practices, or the LGBTIQ+ movement as a product of individual activism, informal groups, and established organisations. Most recently, in 2017, the Center for Equality and Liberty, CEL, produced a book *Lëvizja LGBT* (Qendra për Barazi dhe Liri, 2017), but the publication is far from exhaustive. Academic scholarship as well as publications produced by organisations largely ignore LGBTIQ+ individuals or activism before the Kosovo war. The earliest reporting of a transgender person I found, however, was from the daily national newspaper *Rilindja*, which had covered in a serialised longform article the transition of a transgender person from Peja in 1978. This case will be analysed in greater detail below, as it is instrumental for contextualising Kosovo's transgender history.

There is little documentation of LGBTIQ+ organising before the Kosovo war as well, although activists recount social gatherings and informal community organising that, like most activities by Albanian civil society during the 1990s, happened in private homes. Looking at such informal get-togethers as community-organising is pertinent as often the history of LGBTIQ+ movement in Kosovo is subsumed under the history of formal organisations. Women's rights activist Igballe Rogova recounts how in the mid-1990s, she and her partner hosted a small lesbian group in their home in Prishtina for parties, film screenings, and discussions (personal communication, 5 January 2021). The group had connections to the Serbian organisation for lesbian human rights, Labris, which supplied them with movies about gay rights, among other materials (Igballe Rogova, personal communication, 5 January 2021).

Incidentally, 'the first' same sex 'marriage' in Yugoslavia, occurred between Rogova and her then partner Rachel Wareham, a British national. Although same-sex marriage and civil unions were not legalised in Yugoslavia, the couple held a symbolic wedding banquet in Belgrade in August 1996 to formalise their bond in front of their friends. While the event was private, information about it leaked to the press and the weekly magazine *Koha* in Prishtina covered it, outing Rogova as gay (Igballe Rogova, personal communication, 25 January 2021). Rogova, who worked in grassroot women's organising in rural Kosovo at the time, considered leaving the country fearing persecution (personal communication, 25 January 2021). Rogova's story is indicative of just how difficult and problematic mapping out LGBTIQ+ history in Kosovo is. The genealogy of LGBTIQ+ communities and the activism for their rights, can be in part traced due to the violent outings of queer people, which then serve as historic moments on which the linear narrative 'it gets better' is anchored. The queer people whose histories escape this genealogy meanwhile remain in the shadows and provide us with the illusion of the perpetual necessity to discover anew non-heteronormative, non-cis bodies.

The history of LGBTIQ+ organisations in Kosovo is slightly better documented, but limitedly so. The first formal LGBTIQ+ organisation in Kosovo, the Center for Social and Group Development (CSGD) was established in 2003 and is active to this day. Since then, a handful of organisations, some established by a mix of local and international activists, have appeared. The Center for Social Emancipation (QESh), established in 2008, and Libertas, established in 2011, are, however, no longer active. The only other prominent organisation currently active is the Center for Equality and Liberty (CEL), established in 2013. These pioneering organisations were focused on providing direct support and a safe space for, initially, mostly the gay community. Unlike today, when most activities are centred in Prishtina, the first drop-in centre was opened in Prizren in 2004 (CEL, 2019, p 26). At the time, however, activists had a limited outreach and most of the community activities did not involve the lesbian community (CEL, 2019, p 27). Gradually, this shifted especially as lesbian activists assumed leadership positions in two of the organisations QESh and CEL.

Today, both CSGD and CEL operate drop-in centres in Prishtina, and plan to manage a space together once the municipality provides them with a location. In October 2020, the Municipality pledged 300,000 euros to build the first shelter for LGBTIQ+ individuals fleeing violence and harassment. The shelter will be run by the two organisations, which for years have been collaborating in advancing LGBTIQ+ rights and work on most projects either jointly or in close coordination (Arbër Nuhiu, personal communication, 14 January 2021). Both CSGD and CEL are also part of the ERA – LGBTIQ+ Equal Rights Association for Western Balkans and Turkey network – and collaborate closely in organising the Pride Parade in Prishtina. Indubitably, during the past two decades, interventions and actions for LGBTIQ+ rights, from online platforms to drag performances, have also been organised by informal groups and unassociated activists. More recently, in 2020, an informal and anonymous collective known as Dylberizm launched an online platform (dylberizm.com) to report on LGBTIQ+ issues in the Albanian language as part of their educational and advocacy efforts.

In addition to the incremental work with institutions, organisations have also managed to increase community visibility, despite backlash and at times violent opposition. In 2012, during the launch of an issue by the *Kosovo 2.0* magazine that focused on sex and sexuality, a group of around 30 people stormed the premises of the event beating up staff and destroying the stage (Demolli, 2012). The event was further obstructed by a protest of about 100 people who had gathered outside the building, some of whom yelled 'Out, pederasts' and 'Allahu Akbar' (Demolli, 2012). As a result, attendees had to be evacuated by the police, while the football fan group Plisat claimed responsibility on their Facebook page for the action against degenerate and anti-family 'cultures' (Demolli, 2012). Two days later, on 16 December, the office of the LGBTIQ+ organisation Libertas was attacked by seven people who threw tear gas through an open window (Civil Rights Defenders, 2012). One of the activists who had left the office was beaten severely by three or four assailants (Civil Rights Defenders, 2012).

Since 2007, organisations have marked the International Day Against Homophobia, Transphobia and Biphobia (IDAHOBIT) with public space interventions (placing posters and stickers), organising discussions, and sending public letters to institutions and media (Halili, 2020b). While at first requests to support IDAHOBIT officially were met with little enthusiasm by Kosovo institutions, in 2014 the three LGBTIQ+ organisations CSGD, CEL, and QESh, managed to organise the first public march in the pedestrian area in the centre of Prishtina (Halili, 2020b). The event drew the support of international representatives but did not gather a large crowd since it was not announced beforehand. In coordination with the Kosovo Prime Minister's Office, the government's main building was illuminated with the rainbow flag the same night – an activity that by now has become an annual tradition. Activists noted, however, that many people from the LGBTIQ+ community did not yet dare to march in public – instead they wore masks and costumes (Halili, 2020b).

The marches provided an opportunity for activists to signal to LGBTIQ+ individuals living in the closet that they were not alone and paved the way for organising the larger and publicly announced Pride Parades (Halili, 2020b). The first Pride Parade was organised in Prishtina in 2017 under the banner 'In the name of love' with hundreds of individuals in attendance. The organisation of the first Pride, documented through the short documentary series (four episodes) *The Sky Is Turning*, marks a turning point in the LGBTIQ+ movement. Intentionally, however, the organisers did not choose to have a political message or request but rather opted for a universal call to love (Bulent, 2018, Ep. 3). Although the parade itself was held in jubilation, after the event two incidents related to the Pride were reported, namely an individual being verbally harassed and another being physically attacked (Ahmeti, 2017). Since then, the Pride Parade has been organised four more times, most recently in July 2021, and before that, in October 2020 with attendees 'marching' in a car convoy in central Prishtina due to the COVID-19 pandemic.

Despite public outcry in opposition from some Muslim clerics and the small religious party Fjala (Morina, 2017; Duffy, 2018), Pride Parades in Kosovo have been organised without major incidents or counter-protests. They have also been conducted with the explicit approval and support of local institutions and international representatives, with Kosovo prime ministers and presidents, as well as US, French, German, British, and Italian ambassadors regularly in attendance. This uneventfulness is in contrast to other countries in the region. For example, Sarajevo hosted its first Pride in 2019 with 1,000 police officers protecting attendees from counter protests (Wood, 2019), while just a few days after Belgrade was announced as the host of EuroPride 2022, Belgrade's Pride Center was attacked by hooligans (Breue, 2020).

Even though festive decorations and music have accompanied the Prides, the events have nevertheless served as protests for LGBTIQ+ rights, with activists demanding institutional acknowledgment and inclusion. At first, the Pride marches were used as platforms to make general demands, rooted in the activist advocacy for the state to recognise LGBTIQ+ individuals as *citizens* with equal rights. In the second pride, activists demanded that state institutions 'not deny [their] identity, to offer equal opportunities and fulfill their responsibilities towards human rights' (Lendi Mustafa cited in Gashi and Travers, 2018). It was only in the fourth Pride march, that activists specified their demands. In the 2020 Pride Parade, activists drove around the city, honking their cars under the slogan 'I do' and demanding same-sex marriage to be included in the new Kosovo Civil Code. While the Pride Parades have indubitably increased visibility for the community and are well popular among LGBTIQ+ individuals (according to the NDI poll, 71 per cent of surveyed LGBTIQ+ people in Kosovo think that Pride has improved the position of the community), they also serve as a smokescreen of sorts. According to Arbër Nuhiu, director of CSGD, the parades provide an illusion that there have been major leaps and advancements in LGBTIQ+ rights in Kosovo, when in reality LGBTIQ+ individuals still face prejudice and discrimination (personal communication, January 14, 2021).

Becoming Alexandra Krasnić

The earliest journalistic reporting about a transgender person from Kosovo that I could find is an article published in nine instalments in the daily national newspaper *Rilindja* from November 1978. Written by Sadri Morina, a Radio Television of Prishtina journalist and a special correspondent for the paper for this 'exclusive' story, the series chronicles the transition of Misin Krasnić,[5] a Kosovo Roma man from Peja,[6] to Alexandra, and through his story introduces the novelty of gender confirmation surgery. Krasnić, who had graduated from a professional high school with a focus on economics in Peja, had moved to Slovenia in 1976 for work and began his transition to a woman in 1978. Today, Krasnić, a Slovenian national, has detransitioned and lives as a homosexual man in Austria.[7] In the section below, I analyse the article which 'announced', as he calls it, his transition to the Yugoslav public, and through excerpts of a semi-structured interview introduce an alternative reading of events (Misin Krasnić, personal communication, 1 February 2021).[8]

Krasnić's story is anything but common knowledge. In fact, my initial research and interviews with LGBTIQ+ activists in Kosovo led me to the conclusion that the earliest reporting of a Kosovo trans person was the television reportage of Edona James, a Kosovar-German transgender reality TV star. James, who was born in Kosovo but has lived most of her life in Germany, was introduced to the Kosovar audience in 2014 through the celebrity gossip show *Privé* as 'the Albanian who crossed the rainbow' (Privé, 2014). I first heard of Krasnić's story over a dinner with my mother and aunt, Myzafere Limani and Hazbije Krasniqi, who like him, are from Peja, a small town in western Kosovo. They both told me that when they had finished high school, a boy from their neighbourhood had undergone gender confirmation surgery. The story did not seem unusual or farfetched to me as during my research I had heard multiple stories of people transitioning or living as transgender out of the limelight well before Mustafa or Morina. However, what intrigued me was my aunt's insistence that the story had appeared in the daily *Rilindja*. This conversation encouraged me to dig through the *Rilindja* archives, which date back to 1945 when the paper was founded, where it appeared that Krasnić's story is the earliest recorded account of the transition of a transgender person by Kosovar media.

Published under the title 'He became her – without crossing the rainbow', the *Rilindja* series is written in the manner of a detective story. The journalist jumps through many legal and ethical obstacles in his 'adventure' to uncover the identity of a Kosovar sex-change patient at the Medical Clinical Center in Ljubljana. The story was of public interest because the medical procedure was considered a novel scientific achievement, and there were no legal provisions in Yugoslavia that regulated sex reassignment therapy and intervention. In the article, Sadri Morina, the author (no relation to the trans activist Blert Morina) admits to peering over papers and 'accidentally' seeing Alexandra's name at the Secretariat for Internal Affairs (SIA) in Maribor; getting private information from municipal and education officers in Kosovo; pretending to be Krasnić's brother to find out Alexandra's home address and get into his apartment, where he proceeds to ransack through his things looking for photographs (Morina, 1978b, 1978c, 1978d, 1978e). Describing how he discovers Alexandra's name by accident while snooping through documents, Morina writes 'I knew that what I did was not allowed, even dishonest' (Morina, 1978b). The article prints photos of Krasnić as a boy and at the time of the interview as well as multiple documents, including a photograph of his updated personal ID. In the series, Morina also reveals Krasnić's address (albeit, he does not reveal the city he lives in), his ID number and date of birth, and even quotes his medical diagnosis as a transgender individual extensively (Morina, 1978e; 1978h). In the article itself it was not clear whether the interview was conducted entirely voluntarily and printed with permission. During my interview with Krasnić, he assured me that he had signed off on the quotes and given the journalist permission to print the article after Morina promised to pay him 3,000 Austrian Schillings, which would amount to approximately 700 euros today (MK, 2021). Krasnić says he was never compensated.

The first instalment of the series is an introduction to the phenomenon of sex reassignment and its history, claiming that for the first time such a procedure had been undertaken in Yugoslavia (Morina, 1978a). Contemplating 'modern times' and the demystification of many myths, the author notes that nevertheless '[m]an, has remained the most complicated ... many mysteries remain to be uncovered and especially about oneself' (Morina 1978a). These mysteries include 'the special desires', such as the desire to be 'something else from how nature made one, in short: to change one's gender' (Morina 1978a). Noting that this phenomenon is 'neither rare nor new', Morina goes on to provide data about the population size of transgender people in the world and a historical overview of sex reassignment surgery, which begins with the surgery of an American soldier in Denmark (Morina, 1978a).[9] The article approaches the 'phenomenon of sex-reassignment' with curiosity and open-mindedness but often lacks empathy for its protagonist and treats him with derision. While Morina writes that 'I understood the issue [of sex reassignment] as an epochal achievement of medicine' (1978b), he is flippant about Krasnić's identity. In addition to violating his privacy, he also misgenders Alexandra and in a meta-fictional manner offers a faux apology to the reader, pretending to keep forgetting Alexandra is now a woman (Morina, 1978e).

Interestingly, it is in this first part that the reader is introduced to a new word in Albanian *gjinindërrimi* (literally: gender-change) as the verb for changing one's gender, and *gjinindërrues* (gender-changer) for transgender (Morina, 1978a). This is worth noting because it indicates how the term gender was used to denote sex at the time, and to some degree the lack of distinction between sex and gender persists to this day in Albanian, as is clear by the use of the term gender instead of sex in official documents.

For us researching today, Morina's use of a newly coined term in Albanian that further blurs the sex/gender difference poses difficulties as it hinders us from documenting the exact terminology used by doctors and Krasnić himself. When interviewed in 2021, Krasnić used the term 'transsexual' to describe himself at the time (MK, 2021). Meanwhile, the term *gjinindërrues*, which is more approximate to the term transgender than transsexual, almost sounding ahead of its time today, seems to have been coined by the journalist Morina and is no longer in use today, if it ever caught on.

Morina's quest for Krasnić's identity begins with a reference to a report by the Slovenian daily *Delo*, which he writes had reported that doctors in the medical centre in Ljubljana had successfully reassigned the sex of five patients (Morina, 1978b). However, that seems to have not been entirely true: in the article Krasnić's psychiatrist, Dr Jože Lokar, is quoted as saying 'We just have made the first really successful steps towards changing the sex of those who want to' (Morina, 1978b). In fact, while the article does not specify the medical procedures Krasnić has undergone to become a woman, it depicts Krasnić's transition as complete and even very successful. In the penultimate article in the series Krasnić is depicted in a photograph smiling timidly at the camera, his face framed by mid-length blonde, wavy hair. Underneath the caption reads, 'Alexandra Krasniqi, after the doctors' intervention, now that she's no longer a man, but a woman' (Morina, 1978h). Morina even quotes Dr Lokar as saying that 'the medical intervention [in Alexandra] had the most success from the five', and concludes 'surely her case … will enter the annals of medicine as the most successful until now, not only in our country' (Morina, 1978h). At the time of the interview, Krasnić was undergoing hormonal therapy taking oestrogen and anti-androgen, and identified as 'a transsexual' woman but had not gone through the gender confirmation surgery yet (MK, 2021). He told me that Morina had warned him that he would 'declare' in the story that he had had a surgical intervention, and that he 'shouldn't come to Kosovo before the surgery' (MK, 2021). Krasnić was operated on in 1979 and claims to be the first male-to-female sex reassignment patient in Yugoslavia (MK, 2021).

Alexandra himself and his version of events appear only somewhere in the middle of the article, at the end of the fifth instalment of the series. The journalist, who has pretended to be his brother to lure him into a meeting at a hotel lobby, introduces Alexandra as 'blonde, tall, and pretty' (Morina, 1978e). The serialisation of the story and delay of Alexandra's introduction is no doubt a tabloid technique, and by the time the protagonist is introduced, the reader has 'met' his family, knows Krasnić's father has disowned him after seeing him in women's clothes, and that his mother believes that moving to Slovenia had 'ruined her son' (Morina, 1978d). Nevertheless, Krasnić says that despite the initial negative reactions, eventually his family accepted him as a trans woman and he visited them in Kosovo on multiple occasions, emphasising that he did so only as a guest but never lived with them again (MK, 2021). Krasnić's explanation of his own transition is nuanced, offering some insight into his identification as a 'female' prior to moving to Slovenia. In the article he is quoted as saying:

> Every time we played as children, I liked playing the role of the female. We would play, for example, husband and wife, and I always wanted to be the wife, the bride. I liked it because a female's movements seemed more elegant to me. But, I felt myself as male. Moreover, after I turned fifteen I even liked some girls. I thought of marriage too. Nevertheless, I liked a male friend in my class. I wanted to be a female and to have him as a lover, and then as a husband. But I myself was a man. It wasn't done. (Morina, 1978f)

If this first quote blurs the line between Krasnić's sexual desires and the desire to be a woman, further on, he explains in clearer terms his revelations after he moved to Slovenia: 'On the one hand I was a man, on the other I liked men. There were men who offered me love. But they were homosexuals. I didn't want it that way' (Morina, 1978f). In conversation, Krasnić reveals that he was first introduced to the idea of sex reassignment when he was recovering from hepatitis in a hospital in Slovenia, where a woman had suggested it to him (MK, 2021). 'I didn't even know sex change was possible. When that woman told me, it got into my head,' Krasnić said, adding that he had seen in a magazine article that a German man had become a woman and he became convinced so could he (MK, 2021).

Krasnić was 22 when he was diagnosed as transgender and referred for gender confirmation surgery. 'The consultation with the psychiatrist gave me hope,' Alexandra recounts in *Rilindja* (Morina, 1978f). The team of doctors assembled in Ljubljana to treat such cases, situated their work as a necessity, arising from people either having to seek treatment abroad or worse: 'There have been cases of people who have made attempts to change their sex without professional care ... Thus, it's not a question of a simple "experiment", but an imperative that [our] times demand' (Dr Jože Lokar as quoted in Morina, 1978i). Krasnić's surgeon, Dr Godina, is paraphrased saying that what he does is 'humane work, liberating people from suffering' (Morina, 1978i). At the end of the story, Alexandra lets Morina read his patient card and the diagnosis written by Dr Andrej Veble, in which the doctor alternates between referring to Krasnić as a he and a she:

> She stems from a working class family. Her father is retired. He has 8 children. Misin is the fourth son, ... He rarely communicates with his family, and goes there even less ... He is a *gjinindërrues* [transgender].[10] He once liked a boy and then began feeling himself as a woman. He

is not a homosexual. He often falls in love with men … At work he dresses as a man, outside of work as a woman. His circle knows him at times as a woman, and at times as a man. If he does not change his sex, he can have psychological consequences, to the point of suicide. He is now communicating with a student who thinks he is a woman. So far he has confessed only to a female friend from work … The patient has all the signs of a woman. He is indistinguishable from the way he dresses. His voice is also that of a female. He has a rare intelligence, above average. (Morina, 1978h)

This passage is particularly important as it gives us an insight into the medical discourse used in diagnosing gender dysphoria at the time. Krasnić is reported to feel like a woman and cross-dress; he also has 'a female voice' and 'all the signs' of being a woman, so much so that he is indistinguishable from, presumably, other women, although the diagnosis does not say. Moreover, the emphasis of the diagnosis on what Krasnić *is not* – namely, a homosexual – before adding that he is attracted to men, is indicative just how convoluted the notions of gender identity and sexual preference were (and possibly still are) even for professionals. The reference to Krasnić's 'rare' and 'above average' intelligence, especially considering his ethnic background, might be indicative of power dynamics at play and anti-Gypsyism that could have informed his treatment by Slovenian doctors. Despite progressive policies in Yugoslavia that supported the development of Romani activism and culture (Zahova, 2018), treatment of Romani people was context-specific and varied greatly from one Yugoslav republic to the next with most Roma living in squalid conditions 'from impoverished housing to lower educational standards' (Sardelić, 2016, p 96; 100). As Sardelić shows, in everyday practices, there was an ambivalence to whether Roma were a 'deviant social group' or an 'underclass', and similar arguments to Western cultural racism can be observed in media reports from the Socialist Republic of Slovenia – where Krasnić lived at the time (Sardelić, 2016; Baker, 2018) To the reporter covering the story, however, Krasnić's intelligence represents 'the visa' that opened the door to the treatment 'after which he changed his gender, becoming forever she, comrade Alexandra' (Morina, 1978h).

Formally, Krasnić changed his personal documents to reflect his new gender identity when he was called to complete his military service (Morina, 1978h). The clinical centre in Ljubljana issued a document that Misin Krasnić was now Alexandra Krasnić, 'completing all formalities' and enabling Krasnić to begin his 'life in a dress' (Morina, 1978h). Krasnić said that up to 1990 his name and gender marker changes were recorded in his hometown municipal records (MK, 2021). Krasnić was issued a new ID with his new name, a photograph of which appears in *Rilindja* (Morina, 1978g). This allows us to assume that neither Blert Morina nor M.P. were 'the first' Kosovars to pursue a legal name and gender change, albeit they could be considered as the 'historic firsts' among those who pursued this in post-independent Kosovo – an emphasis of which implicitly reinforces a historical and social distinction between Kosovo during the Yugoslav period and today.

While the reader meets Krasnić as a woman in 1978, and is told that his transition is complete, it seems that Krasnić had been oscillating between gender expressions even before he had started hormonal therapy. In the *Rilindja* article, Krasnić recounts his life in Slovenia when he would present as a man at work but often would go out to dance parties presenting as a woman. Explaining the beginning of his transition, which caused him anguish because of his biological sex, Krasnić recounts:

> Those with whom I worked, would know me at times as a man, at times as a woman. At work I'd go wearing pants, binding and hiding my breasts. I would wear heavy clothes that would cloak the feminine body contours. However at home and in balls, I would take off my mask. This made my life harder. Especially at first … When I danced with men in balls it was the hardest. Bodies would stick together as if they were one, and I was still a man. I would start sweating from the agony. I'd mask as well as I knew. Problems would continue after the balls. I would defend myself from men with different justifications. (Morina, 1978h)

The gender bending was not accepted by his social circle: as Morina writes, 'The physiological changes Misin was going through began to attract negative attention from the people she worked with. … The medical secret was being discovered' (Morina, 1978f). As a result Krasnić had to change multiple jobs and towns, 'Not because they'd find out I changed my sex. Not because they'd gossip. I minded when they sometimes would say something offensive' (Misin Krasnić quoted in Morina, 1978f). In the article, Krasnić also recounts an incident in which he was followed and harassed by two Kosovo Albanians who did not know Alexandra spoke their language and could understand them (Morina, 1978h). At first, the two men start catcalling and attempting to start a conversation; later on they sat in the same train car and started a conversation with him. When one of the men told the other in Albanian 'We'll take [this Slovenian woman] either willingly or against her will. One way is bound to work,' a scared Alexandra got off the train before making it to the intended station (Morina, 1978h).

The last instalment of the series, titled 'Alexandra thinks she will get married', Morina gives the reader and Alexandra a happy ending – bringing us back to the fairy tale narrative I mentioned in the introduction. According to the article, Alexandra is planning to marry a surgeon he met while he was waiting to change his sex (Morina, 1978i). 'Since then, we are always together. She even took on the name [Alexandra] … that I proposed. She's like all other women,' Dr Manfred 'Zilerh' is quoted saying (Morina, 1978i).

While the *Rilindja* story leaves the reader both optimistic about Alexandra's fate and proud of Yugoslavia's medical achievements, I wondered how much of it was accurate. I asked Krasnić about 'Zilerh': at first, he was confused and said he believed the journalist had made up 'the happy ending' to make the story more interesting for his readers, but then he realised the name was misspelled – he had been seeing a doctor Ziherl at the time (MK, 2021). But that too, like many of the details in the *Rilindja* report, was not entirely accurately depicted. Krasnić had been together with Ziherl and had lived with him briefly, but had left him after finding out that Ziherl, a transgender man, was still 'biologically female' (MK, 2021). In conversation with Krasnić, much of the certainty and the finality with which Morina depicts Alexandra's transition to a woman, comes undone. Krasnić, who says he was 'a transsexual' only between 1979–83, experienced a psychotic breakdown and was diagnosed with paranoid psychosis in 1984 after suffering from depression[11] prompted by his gender confirmation surgery (MK, 2021).

Retrospectively, Krasnić is ambivalent about being transgender, and in our conversation referred to himself as a 'former transsexual'. Today, after having detransitioned, and undergone a double mastectomy, Krasnić says that he was 'misdiagnosed' (MK, 2021). 'Transsexuality was not so well known in 1978 and … the psychiatric ward had no experience with transsexuals so they sent me to Jože Lokar, who supposedly had more experience,' Krasnić explained (MK, 2021). When quoting him, I have kept the terminology he uses as it is indicative of the discursive shift that has happened with regards to gender identity since he transitioned. He only used the term *transgender* once, in English, referring to a phase when he no longer felt as a woman but presented as one; otherwise he referred to himself as a homosexual man, or a male-to-female transsexual (MK, 2021). 'Before 1978, I had some kind of feminine feelings, I was shy … but I was not even transsexual but the psychiatrist misunderstood me,' he said at first (MK, 2021). Later on explaining to me how transsexuality is caused by hormonal imbalance he stated:

I was shy, and I had hormonal difficulties. From my hormonal difficulties I was not unhappy that I was a man, but I was shy … In elementary school for example we did not have bathroom stalls for men, and we would pee outdoors, and I would always distance from my class mates because I was embarrassed that I had a male organ, that I was a male … I was a type of a transsexual. … For example my mother's family, each and every one mentions, you were a transsexual. Why? Because I liked women's clothes, *kule, dimitë*, [12] dresses … I liked getting made up, the girls would dress me up with bridal clothes. Yes, I was a type of a transsexual, this must have been transsexuality but from my depression I don't mention that I was really a transsexual. (MK, 2021)

Krasnić was living as a transgender woman in 1978 and had two interventions as part of his sex reassignment in 1979. His surgery was conducted by the Croatian surgeon Marko Godina, who he remembers as having died in a car crash later on. 'I waited for six months in the Ljubljana psychiatric ward for him to come back from his specialization in America,' Krasnić said (MK, 2021). After the surgery, Krasnić, who was self-conscious about the size of his laryngeal prominence and wanted a larger bust abused hormones taking larger doses of both Androcur, an anti-androgen, and Silberstrol, a brand of oestrogen (MK, 2021). He said he used up to ten times more Silberstrol than prescribed by his doctors, without their knowledge (MK, 2021). 'My breasts had grown by the second year … I would even lactate,' he said (MK, 2021).

Krasnić broke the news of his transition to his family with a letter and a picture of himself as Alexandra writing 'You now have one son less, and a daughter more' (Morina, 1978g). Despite Morina's reporting that his father had disowned him, during this time Krasnić went back to his hometown in Kosovo, presenting as a woman (MK, 2021). The publication of the articles in *Rilindja*, however, caused a stir and the relationship with his siblings deteriorated. "My [big] brother could not accept me, 'Because you put yourself on the paper, you accepted [to publish the story],'" Krasnić said, adding that while three of his brothers are still alive, he has no contact with them. "I haven't seen my [older] brother, perhaps in 40 almost 50 years," said Krasnić in a muffled sob (MK, 2021). His paternal cousins too have disowned him, "A few years ago, my uncle's son, he died, he died no more than six months ago … he wrote to me on Facebook directly and said 'Faggot, what do you want? You are dead to us!'" (MK, 2021). His mother's side of the family were more understanding, but his maternal uncle who had accepted him as trans, did not accept him as a homosexual (MK, 2021).

After his surgery, Krasnić had difficulties in keeping jobs as an accounting clerk, despite having a high school degree and being qualified. "[Employers] would initially accept me for a trial period, but then would let me go after 3, 4, 5 months … my gestures were not those of a biological female. I would behave differently with my colleagues, not as a biological female but as a homosexual," Krasnić told me (MK, 2021). When pressed for examples, a mildly agitated Krasnić told me he had affairs with colleagues and that had not been acceptable (MK, 2021). Unable to find a job, Krasnić moved away from Slovenia and was forced to work in night clubs as a showgirl, where he also started to work as a prostitute (MK, 2021). During these years when he considered himself 'a transsexual woman' Krasnić moved around in an unclear timeline between Switzerland, Germany, and Austria getting jobs from an intermediary agency (MK, 2021). He told me that the fact that he was a transsexual often posed a problem for his clients, but they were not aggressive (MK, 2021). It was during this time that he suffered from depression and had a psychotic breakdown. This experience seems to have been deeply enmeshed with his decision to abandon his androgen suppressive therapy and detransition, although from his recounting it is not clear which came first:

> In 1984, after I abandoned my hormonal therapy [oestrogen], I became depressed, I was in Basel, Switzerland, watching homosexual porn on VHS – there were no CDs then, and something depressed me so much in that film that the next morning I realized I was sick ... psychosis. ... In grocery stores I'd see a yoghurt with strawberries and I was scared from the red yoghurt thinking that the Swiss had put human blood in it to try to make me a vampire. (MK, 2021)

After his diagnosis with paranoid psychosis, Krasnić has been hospitalised multiple times in Germany and Austria, and continues treatment today (MK, 2021). In 1986, he was granted a disability pension by Slovenian authorities and has not worked since (MK, 2021). As Krasnić explains, he knew he was no longer a transsexual woman since 1984 and the same year he went back to his hometown Peja in men's clothes (MK, 2021). But this too was not definite, as he went back and forth between presenting as woman and a man:

> By 1984 I was no longer a transsexual. I did not have any feminine feelings, but at the same time I said, the operation is done, it was my bad luck, my *kismet*, so I'm going to live as a woman ... What was helpful was that this way I lost my Adam apple complex, without complexes I'd use women's clothes, but I knew who I was, that I'm not a biological woman. (MK, 2021)

Krasnić refers to this period as being something akin to a transvestite. In 1990, living in Germany, he started androgen hormonal therapy with testosterone, taking T-shots once every three weeks. In 2012, he recounts, he decided that "100 per cent there is no more going back as a transsexual or a woman, no, I'd be] only a man"(MK, 2021). This is also when Krasnić changed his sexual marker in his official documents in Slovenia, adopting his birth name Misin and changing his gender marker to male once again (MK, 2021). Analysing Krasnić's account of how he took this decision, one can notice an interplay of sexism and transphobia that manifests both in his experience of the outside world and in the way he sees himself:

> For a while, when I would go out to have a coffee or eat, old men would come and sit close to me, it would annoy me why men would

disdain me, I am not a biological female to be underrated by an old man … one summer day, I saw an old man with grey hair next to my window and I said to myself "Now I've had enough!" and I opened my closet and all the clothes, all the women's clothes, I took them all and threw them in the garbage bin. And I went to the store, started buying men's clothes, went to the hairdresser, cut my hair, and from that moment I said, and I decided to 100% not play the female role because I was being discriminated by men. (MK, 2021)

In 2013, Krasnić underwent a double mastectomy. Six months before we conducted our interview, he said he stopped his hormonal therapy entirely, complaining he was losing his hair and his bones were becoming heavier (MK, 2021). Today he identifies as a male-to-female transsexual, emphasising that he lives as a homosexual man (MK, 2021).

Krasnić's story offers a unique insight into the history of transgender people in Kosovo as the earliest recorded case of a trans person who has undergone hormonal therapy and surgery. The *Rilindja* articles are a testament to the social context in which Krasnić transitioned, and despite not referencing explicitly his ethnicity, we can still trace the intersectional nature of Krasnić's stigmatisation as a trans Romani woman. Despite the fairy tale ending and the objectification of Krasnić, the series still manages to account Krasnić's experiences of being shunned, harassed, and catcalled, by his family, colleagues, and strangers. Interviewing Krasnić 40 years later provides us with a deeper understanding of that reporting, and at times with alternative facts. His experiences and life after the article's publication in particular offer an insight into the fluidity of gender identity and transitioning as something not necessarily finite. His transition from a man to a woman in 1970s Yugoslavia marks a sharp contrast to the transitions of the two transgender activists, whose accounts I analyse below. His story is also relevant today because it allows us to trace discursive shifts since the 1970s in the language used but also in conceptions of gender identity and sexuality. Such an account does not resolve the tensions between gender identity and sexuality, nor does it presume to do that, but it does allow us to delve into the intersectional nature of trans identity, which is informed by various systems of oppressions depending on race, gender, sexual orientation, class, and disability. This is patent in Krasnić's case whose experience as a Romani person struggling with mental health issues had been markedly different from either Mustafa's or Morina's, both White trans men.

Transitioning in post-war Kosovo

When Lend Mustafa was six, he told his parents that when he grew up, he would become a boy. 'It was just my imagination, it was not because of some information I had. It was only later that I saw that there were transgender people in the world who had their sex reassigned' (Lend Mustafa, personal communication, 29 June 2020a).[13] Mustafa is one of the most prominent LGBTIQ+ activists in Kosovo – one could even go as far as to describe him as a poster boy for the movement. He came out as transgender in a TV documentary titled *Mallkimi LGBT* (The LGBT Curse) broadcast on the national television channel Klan Kosova in 2016 and has not stopped doing media appearances since. In addition to giving countless interviews to raise awareness about the LGBTIQ+ community, Mustafa has been open about his gender identity, transition, and is first to point out how privileged he is as a trans man who has found acceptance from his family. Mustafa, who has spent most of his life in Prishtina, was an LGBTIQ+ activist since he was in high school. At the time, he and his queer friends – he describes them as 'fearless kids' – would attend activities by organisations and do the legwork of distributing posters, flyers, and stickers (LM, 2020a). As one of the most vocal activists, Mustafa led the first Pride Parade held in Prishtina in 2017, giving a speech in front of an exuberant crowd shouting his name (Bulent, 2018, Ep. 4).

Blert Morina, who currently leads CEL – the organisation where Mustafa works – also appeared on *Mallkimi LGBT*, albeit concealed. After the film was broadcast Morina, a transgender man, reached out to Mustafa and established contact (Blert Morina, personal communication, 15 June 2020).[14] Both men were working for LGBTIQ+ organisations at the time: Mustafa was a peer coordinator in QESh; Morina worked in CEL's drop-in centre (LM, 2020a; BM, 2020). Once Morina came out publicly too in an article in *Kosovo 2.0* (Halili, 2017), both became vocal about their identities, trans rights overall, and legal discriminations they faced. This led to a larger public discussion of trans issues in the country: in 2017, the late night show *NIN* hosted a discussion on being transgender in Kosovo (Klan Kosova, 2017), and a year later one of the most popular prime-time political television shows, *Rubikon*, hosted a debate with activists and lawyers (Kohavision, 2018). The same year, a profile of Qerkica, a transgender Ashkali[15] woman from Fushë Kosovë, appeared in a *Kosovo 2.0* exploration of LGBTIQ+ rights in Kosovo (Zhegrova, 2018).[16]

Mustafa and Morina mark a radical departure in both representation of trans people in Kosovo and LGBTIQ+ activism. While both men's stories of coming out are well documented, through in-depth interviews I look at how their personal transition has been intertwined with their work as activists. While they began their transition together and shared many commonalities as professional activists and trans men, their backgrounds differed and they both came to the movement following different paths. They have also chosen different ways to utilise their personal experience for the benefit of other trans people and turn their own transition into either an awareness campaign or a strategic litigation case. Below, I analyse their decision to transition in the public eye as an illustration of turning the personal into political.

Born in 1996 in Germany, Mustafa and his family moved back to Kosovo when he was six after the war ended and when many Kosovars returned (LM, 2020a). Meeting his extended family was a shock – everyone called him a girl and used his full name Lendita (LM, 2020a). He hated it, but it would be years before he would find the language to express how he felt and realise he was transgender (LM, 2020a). Morina, on the other hand, was born in 1990 in Rogova, a village in the municipality of Gjakova – a region hit particularly hard by the Kosovo war. Morina, who was nine during the war and had to flee with his family to Albania, sees himself as one of the children of the war: 'We experienced it more heavily than you [in Prishtina] … maybe we matured ahead of our time' (BM, 2020). As a child, Morina was outgoing and had a special status among his family and friends: he played football on the boys' team and he was known as 'Cufa's son', Cufa being a nickname for his father Jusuf (BM, 2020). This changed when as a teenager Blert moved to Prishtina, to attend high school. From an outgoing person he became 'shy', and resented the fact that he was forced to wear a girl's uniform:

> The fact that I hadn't told anyone during my entire high school [years] lets you understand that time was not the best time in the world. … [If I hadn't gone to Prishtina] maybe at least I wouldn't have that uniform as a reminder every morning that 'Hey, you were born as a girl.' (BM, 2020)

In high school an adolescent Morina had relationships with girls 'which you'd now call heterosexual,' he said, but was not out (BM, 2020). Morina, who was not acquainted with trans terminology at this point, suffered from gender dysphoria but shied away from discussing the matter:

> In my relationships [with girls] we never discussed it. We never could discuss it, never … which was a relief for me. Especially for trans persons, like in my case, I had a lot of problems with dysphoria – when you have a problem to see your body or make that compromise, to accept that this is your body. … And this lack of discussion, I think it gave me the space for empowerment in the sense to not remind me constantly who I was and what my biological sex was. (BM, 2020)

Unlike Morina, who took some comfort in the things that remained unspoken, as a teenager, Mustafa was very curious and impatient to find himself. Mustafa, who was attracted to girls at the time and now identifies as bisexual, was unsure how to define himself. When he was 14 and he made friends with three girls who identified as lesbian and were unapologetic about it, he started opening up:

> We called ourselves lesbian then, because [we wouldn't] now. ... We were all confused if we were transgender, and when I'd tell them, "We're not lesbians, surely we're not lesbians, a lesbian does not want to be a man," they'd tell me "Dude, why are you being so deep?" We lived with our heads in the clouds. (LM, 2020a)

Instead of identifying as a lesbian, Mustafa would simply say he liked girls, skirting the issue of a label altogether (LM, 2020a). He first came out externally, or 'physically' as he puts it: when he was 14 or 15 he cut his hair short and from that moment onwards 'people could no longer see me as female' (LM, 2020a). This is when a friend 'renamed' him Lendi, a masculine version of his feminine name (LM, 2020a). This allowed Mustafa to start dressing up as a boy and he 'felt lighter ... it changed completely how [he] saw [himself] and how others saw [him]' (LM, 2020a). Reading up online, Mustafa also realised that his discomfort stemmed from the way he experienced his gender identity:

> At first I thought there are some lesbians who feel like being men, or that, some lesbians feel it's easier to become a man and live as a man because of society, until I started reading more. ... I had seen [the acronym] LGBT, I knew what LGB was, but I never knew what the T was, and I was curious – OK what is this? And when I started reading the moment that I saw it had to do with gender identity, it *clicked*. And I was so *excited* that I found myself – *this is me* – when you immediately fit with something, when it's right for you. (emphasis added; LM, 2020a)[17]

Most of the information on being trans Mustafa got on his own and online – he had no local references. When he joined LGBTIQ+ organisations as an activist and introduced himself as trans, the people he met there did not know what it meant:

> When I explained, they said, "Nope, most probably this is some kind of a phase and you'll end up a lesbian." This was the extent of lack of information in the LGBTI community. Everybody knew their sexual orientation, but when it came down to gender identity it was something new for the community. I know why this was so: even though I was transgender myself, I thought it was impossible for me to be transgender. (LM, 2020a)

Mustafa's story reveals a generational gap within the LGBTIQ+ community. When Mustafa and his friends started going to drop-in centres and socialising with other LGBTIQ+ individuals who were in their 40s, they realised they had gone through a different experience altogether. Without social media, older queer people had to find each other 'cruising' at the National Library park in Prishtina and would sometimes get beaten up (LM, 2020a). For this generation it was inconceivable to attend marches and parades in public (LM, 2020a). Mustafa is aware how different their worldviews are: 'They were beaten up, some committed suicide … their struggles are not and will never be the struggles of our generation' (LM, 2020a).

Similar to the community which they worked with, LGBTIQ+ activists, who worked as educators and campaigners, had a notion of being transgender, but it was all theoretical (Arbër Nuhiu, personal communication, 14 January 2021). 'Lendi was the first [trans] person I met who came here [at CSGD] and knew exactly what he was,' said Nuhiu, who has been an activist since 2003 (personal communication, 14 January 2021). In the past few years since Mustafa has been an activist, he believes attitudes of the community have changed:

> Now … a number of people from the community who were not accepting towards trans people, many of them are looking into transitioning. Some of them even [said those things] out of their desire, and trying to repress the desire, to transition. It was … perhaps internalized transphobia. (Lendi Mustafa, personal communication 7 August 2020b)[18]

Morina, on the other hand, found the language to define himself quite late. He says he did not know that there was an LGBTIQ+ movement in Kosovo nor what trans meant, but he knew he was a boy (BM, 2020). After enrolling and dropping out of university three years in a row with the hope of going on a Work and Travel program to the United States, Morina finally decided to finish the sociology degree he was enrolled in (BM, 2020). In college he met people that were both open-minded and informed: 'They were the set of people, the Prishtina I dreamt of when I first came here,' he said (BM, 2020). Attending gender studies classes in the first year of his degree was a revelation and inspired Morina to inquire more into his gender identity:

> Although I had met these people seven–eight years after coming to Prishtina … I was so lucky to be surrounded by people who knew these things … and I remember when I came out to one of my classmates, I felt like [until then] I was betraying them because they were so honest with me. I felt like it was a type of betrayal for not sharing. (BM, 2020)

Coming out to his friends and working on papers and research related to LGBTIQ+ issues empowered Morina. It was in this period that he found out there were LGBTIQ+ organisations in Prishtina, and started going to the drop-in centres. When Mustafa and Morina appeared in the documentary film *Mallkimi LGBT*, they identified as trans but neither had begun their transition. At first, neither of them had known gender confirmation surgery was possible. When Mustafa came out to his family as trans at 18, at first, his mother told him that when she was young she had heard of a case in Slovenia, most likely referring to Krasnić, adding, 'But we discovered that it was a lie. These are lies, you can't, it's not possible, you were born this way' (LM, 2020a). At the time of the interview neither Mustafa nor I were aware of Krasnić's existence. It is relevant to note here that Mustafa's mother, who had heard rumours of an individual changing their gender (it is unclear whether she had read the newspaper story), seemed to believe that this was outside of realm of possibility. I bring this up here because it is worth underscoring that trans narratives, even when recorded such as Krasnić's, can still turn into urban myths, their veracity disputed, and their affirmation of trans experience limited.

To a degree, Mustafa's mother was right: none of the medical facilities in Kosovo provide gender confirmation surgery yet, and there is a lack of expertise when it comes to care for transgender people overall. Moreover, when facing the medical institutions transgender people continue to encounter discrimination and stigma. In a 2016 report on social protection and access to healthcare for transgender people in Kosovo, the author found that despite being acquainted with the terminology, medical professionals did not have a positive and inclusive attitude towards trans people (Avdiu, 2016, p 45). Mustafa thought he had to move abroad and 'start a new life' to be able to transition (LM, 2020a). Meeting activists from the region who had transitioned made the possibility tangible, and this is when both he and Morina started looking into their medical options (LM, 2020a). Both men were concerned about the financial burden: neither knew whether they could afford the treatment, especially since the closest available was through the private hospital Acibadem Sistina in Skopje. Krasnić, who underwent his treatment in the Yugoslav public healthcare system, also had enormous expenses: the hormonal therapy alone cost 8,000 Yugoslav dinars a month, only 60 per cent of which were covered by his insurance (Morina, 1978g).[19] Since specialists were not available in Kosovo, Morina and Mustafa had to first travel to a psychiatrist in Montenegro for evaluation, and then to for their hormonal therapy.

Morina began his hormonal therapy in January 2018, while Mustafa started a few months later, in March. The largest expense for Morina and Mustafa constituted their first surgery, the double mastectomy, which costs €3,500–4,000. Morina had it performed in Skopje and took out a loan, which he jokingly told me, he is still paying (BM, 2020). Mustafa organised a crowdfunding campaign for six months to collect the money for his surgery in a private hospital in Belgrade (LM, 2020b). Mustafa told me he would like to do a hysterectomy next but is unsure when he will be able to do it, while Morina is saving for a phalloplasty surgery that will cost around 12,000 euros (BM 2020; LM, 2020b).

Turning transition into a legal battle and a public campaign

While the chronicle of their transition is important in its own right, it is here that I would like to turn the focus to analysing how Morina and Mustafa used their journeys specifically to advocate for trans rights. Already as the two became involved with the LGBTIQ+ organisations, the movement had started reflecting on the needs of trans people. In 2016, the two members of Equal Rights for All Coalition (ERAC), CSGD, and CEL published an extensive report on the state of trans rights titled 'Social Protection and Access to Healthcare for Transgender People in Kosovo' (Avdiu, 2016). Later on, after Morina had assumed a leadership position in CEL, the organisation published a manual for psychological practice with transgender and gender non-conforming (TGNC) individuals, which aims to introduce mental healthcare professionals to the current best practices when dealing with TGNC patients, including transition treatment (Kadriu and Kërqeli, 2019).

From the outset of their transition both Morina and Mustafa were interested in sharing their experience and knowledge with other queer people, and at the same time educate a larger audience. Such a decision had its drawbacks as it drew negative responses and online abuse. In 2017, after Mustafa made a speech in the first Pride Parade in Prishtina, he told me, he had received over 1,500 threats but has never been physically harmed (LM, 2020a). 'I've been coming out all my life and people in comments [on social media] still write to me, "You're gay," "You're a faggot," or as one told me "Don't become a woman because you'd be very ugly,"' Mustafa told me laughing (LM, 2020a).

Mustafa sees himself as close to the community and says that as a visible LGBTIQ+ person he often gets queries from queer people. While he said he had helped multiple individuals in person, he also wanted to help transgender people by chronicling his transition on a YouTube vlog. In his first video, published on 27 March 2018, a few weeks after Mustafa began hormonal therapy, he explains his motives for starting a vlog:

> After coming out publicly, I've received many comments, both negative and positive. I'm starting this vlog for those people who have sent me

positive comments until now, because I want us to be more connected to one another and perhaps because this way it is easier for me to talk directly to the [LGBTIQ+] community. (Mustafa, 2018a)

Between March and July, Mustafa managed to publish four videos in total. In those videos he talks about being an LGBTIQ+ activist, but also shares personal information about how his transition is progressing. In the second video, Mustafa explains what a T-shot is and points out the changes he is experiencing from taking hormones: his facial hair is growing, his voice is changing slowly (Mustafa, 2018b). He also talks openly about his emotional upheavals and how he has suffered from period pain he never before experienced (Mustafa, 2018b). In this video, Mustafa also answers questions that viewers have sent in via YouTube comments from giving out tips on where to get binders, to how to meet up with other queer people. Responding to a question about how much his family has supported him in his decision to transition he says:

> For me it counted as support that they listened and that they did not have a bad reaction. … When I took the decision to transition, and when I talked to my mother about it, she was very scared because she did not know how it works, and obviously, she was scared that I'd regret it. I had to explain it slowly, give examples, and explain all the procedures, until [my family] felt comfortable. (Mustafa, 2018b)

In a way, whether inadvertently or intentionally, with his videos Mustafa is doing the same with his viewers: slowly and in detail, he is introducing the Albanian-speaking queer community and the general audience to how transition works and making them feel more comfortable with the notion. In his third video, published in May, Mustafa talks about managing his emotions, his changing body, and growing taller: "I have so much more energy and force, and I need to balance it constantly … and sometimes anger is very difficult to control" (Mustafa, 2018c). In the video Mustafa recounts how he is still emotionally unstable and some things "seem worse than they are", but he also shares a positive encounter with a doctor in the public healthcare centre (Mustafa, 2018c). Explaining that he needs to get a three-shot prescription for hormones from a local doctor, Mustafa, whose feminine name still appears in his documents, recounts how in the second visit to his doctor, she wrote his adopted name Lendi in the patient file (Mustafa, 2018c). "I didn't even know she could do that, it made me feel so comfortable and happy, it never happened to me before in Kosovo," Mustafa says (2018c).

In the last vlog, published in July 2018, Mustafa addresses explicitly the difficulties of the transition, and the emotional toll it has taken on him:

No matter how much I'm working on myself, it didn't have an effect, I didn't have control over my feelings. I want to share it, I don't want to come [here] only with good news and make it seem like it's easy to go through things. … It hasn't passed yet … but I hope I stabilize soon. (Mustafa, 2018d)

In this last video, after which Mustafa stopped posting on YouTube, he also talks at great length about the movement and activism once again tying his own personal work with what the movement is trying to achieve. Talking about the appearance of informal groups such as Dylberizm and the LGBT Kosovo Facebook page, both of which he applauds, Mustafa decides to address the LGBTIQ+ movement's sectarianism and call for more understanding between activists in and outside of formal organisations (Mustafa, 2018d). "What we're doing, we're all not doing this for ourselves, we are more privileged than others since we can fight … we have to remember we're fighting for the community," he says (Mustafa, 2018d). The video ends with Mustafa urging people to send him questions or comments, before sighing in relief, "Huh, is it done?" Since their posting, the four videos have gathered thousands of views and in the comment section people ask Mustafa for his Instagram or Facebook account to send him questions. Mustafa told me he did not feel emotionally stable to continue with the videos, but he has continued to update his friends on Facebook about his transition.

Morina, too, remembers the beginning of his transition as particularly difficult. He ascribed his stress to the fact he had become executive director of CEL and had more responsibilities. At first, he also decided to document his journey through a film but soon abandoned the idea due to exhaustion from the many commitments (BM, 2020). "One is supposed to enjoy the journey, and for me it became like a nightmare," he said (BM, 2020). One of the major 'commitments' Morina was invested in at the time was the historic lawsuit against the Ministry of Internal Affairs that would confirm his right to change both his gender marker and name as a transgender man. While the case was informed by Morina's visibly changing appearance and the problems this would cause every time he needed to identify himself (Halili, 2018b), it was also a decision of strategic litigation.

It is often noted that Kosovo's legal framework is progressive: the Constitution, ratified in 2008, guarantees human rights and explicitly protects citizens against discrimination on the basis of their gender and sexual orientation. Article 53 of the Constitution explicitly binds Kosovo institutions to interpret human rights and freedoms in line with decisions made by the European Court of Human Rights. Yet, many of the laws in Kosovo are not in the spirit of the Constitution, and they continue to pose obstacles to LGBTIQ+ people enjoying their full rights. For example, the Kosovo Family Law (2004/32) defines marriage as strictly between a man and a woman, while the Law on Civil Status maintains that sex is determined at birth by a medical report (04/L-003). On the other hand, as a result of direct advocacy of human rights activists, the new Law on Protection against Discrimination ratified in 2015, includes protections against discrimination on multiple grounds, including gender identity and sexual orientation (05/L-021). The Law was passed together with the Law on Gender Equality, which defines gender identity as a 'protected characteristic [that] covers the gender-related identity, appearance or other gender-related characteristics of a person (whether by way of medical intervention or not), with or without regard to the person's designated sex at birth' (05/L-020). These legal changes paved the way for activists to problematise the rights of transgender individuals, particularly in Morina's case.

In 2017, Morina was approached by his former high school friend and human rights lawyer Rina Kika, who offered her help if he ever wanted to change his gender marker and name legally (BM, 2020). Morina was not planning on starting a legal battle, since he had prioritised his transition, which he expected to be costly (BM, 2020). Kika took his case pro bono and in April 2018, Morina applied to change the gender marker and name on his personal documents at his local registry office in Gjakova, claiming that the mismatch of his gender identity to his official documents was an obstacle to his social inclusion (Halili, 2018b). The request, based on the existing administrative instruction that delineated conditions and procedures for personal name change and corrections, was denied. Morina and Kika appealed the decision but the Civil Registration Agency (CRA) rejected the request once again in May, stating that Morina had not 'given any evidence, document, note, photography or archive document that shows that Blerta Morina's personal name hinders the person's integration into society' (Halili, 2018b).

What the CRA wanted was additional evidence, such as a medical report proving that Morina was no longer female (Halili, 2018b). If Morina would have simply opted to get his documents quickly, he could have sent in a medical report from his doctors in Skopje: after all, this had worked for Krasnić in 1978, and had worked for Edona James in the 2010s. Both managed to 'correct' their gender markers upon providing medical proof. But this is where the significance of Morina's case lies: Kika and he opted to pursue a strategy referencing the two Laws passed in 2015, according to which gender identity was not tied to a person's biological sex at birth or reassigned by a medical intervention.

To achieve the task of getting the Kosovo state to recognise gender identity as divorced from biological sex, Kika pursued a two-fold approach.

In July 2018, she filed a suit to the Basic Court to annul the CRA decision and a week later submitted a 27-page appeal to the Kosovo Constitutional Court (Halili, 2018b). More importantly Morina and Kika decided to publicise the whole process, with the hope the case would serve as a precedent (BM, 2020). A decision by the Constitutional Court *would* create a precedent to be applied to all similar cases in the future, but one on a lower-level court would not. Over a year later, in September 2019, the Constitutional Court dismissed Morina's request for a constitutional review of the CRA decision saying the suit "was premature," and that "Kosovo's legal system is capable of providing an effective legal remedy to Morina" (Travers, 2019). In October of the same year, days before Morina and others marched in Kosovo's third Pride in Prishtina, Morina's case came before the Basic Court. Two months later, Morina's wish was granted – the court had annulled the decision obligating the civil registry office to change his gender marker and name. The CRA which is overseen by the Ministry of Internal Affairs did not appeal the decision, although they had done so in the case of MP, who had won a similar case in front of the Appeals Court earlier that August (Klan Kosova, 2019). While Morina was exhilarated for himself, he was frustrated that the case did not become a precedent:

> The idea why we went public in the first place so other people wouldn't have to go through this. Otherwise what's the point? ... Moreover, it's such a paradox that you have two cases in which the court says you have a violation of human rights, and obligates them to implement those changes. Why is the Ministry of Internal Affairs not going 'OK, we're in violation, we have two court cases, let's fix those damn procedures.' (BM, 2020)

In 2022, the Ministry of Internal Affairs has yet to change the Law on Civil Status and accompanying administrative instructions and regulations to enable transgender individuals to change their gender marker. While both Mustafa and Morina's attempts to break new ground when it comes to trans rights, either via transitioning in public, or through legal battles, have had limited success, they nevertheless present monumental efforts. Mustafa's coming out single-handedly made way for the inclusion of transgender rights in a national-level public debate. Meanwhile, his video chronicling of his transition provides a nuanced account of transition, that neither pathologises the trans body nor idealises the process of gender confirmation. Morina, on the other hand, while perhaps not the first trans person to change his gender and name officially, has broken new legal ground by forcing Kosovo courts to recognise that gender identity is not inherently linked to the biological sex of the person.

Conclusion

The history of queer people in Kosovo has only begun to be written. As the LGBTIQ+ movement for equal rights solidifies it will also begin producing its own knowledge. It is pertinent that the knowledge production reclaims the ignored and forgotten narratives of queerness that represent an undercurrent in historiography. While we have witnessed a proliferation of television documentaries and media reports about LGBTIQ+ people and activism, there is a lack of research on how narratives on queerness emerge and how they represent queer history. In Kosovo, despite a latent fascination with queerness in folk culture and familiarity with the gender bending of 'sworn virgins', trans people and trans-related issues are introduced perpetually as novel occurrences. This is by no means a problem particular to Kosovo, but rather yet another example of the fragility of queer historiography overall. As Page (2021) writes: "Trans people are in a constant state of being discovered. We have been found for the first time again and again in modern history."

Looking at Kosovo's own modern history, this chapter sought to problematise origin stories and their reliance on erasure. By tracing the earliest report of a transgender person transitioning back to the case of Misin Krasnić in 1978, it destabilises the notion of historic firsts in Kosovar trans narratives. Krasnić's story itself is an example of this "rush for planting the flag of the very first" (Page, 2021) – Morina who had written the report was so bent on *making history* with it, that he had pre-emptively reported that Krasnić had completed his sex reassignment surgery and was one of the first in Ljubljana to do so.

An in-depth analysis of the series in *Rilindja* shows that while sex reassignment was considered a medical achievement to be lauded, the person who was subjected to it, less so. Krasnić's privacy was violated multiple times by the journalist to get to the story, and the issue of consent is questioned by the fact that Morina offered to pay for the interview. Krasnić's own account of events gives us a quite different version of his transition, allowing for an understanding of a more unstable notion of gender identity and the difficulties of being trans in the 20th century.

While perhaps not 'the first' trans people in Kosovo to appear publicly, Mustafa and Morina who are featured in the final part of this chapter, both represent a radical departure in queer representation and activism in Kosovo. Unlike Krasnić, who was not an activist, they have weaponised their identity to advocate for equal rights for LGBTIQ+ people through public campaigning and legal action. The difference is not simply generational and it requires a deeper analysis of the intersectional nature of their experiences as well as a historicisation of their socio-economic context. The leap between Krasnić and Mustafa and Morina in that sense is colossal, and not only temporally. Within that jump, and even before it, there is a vast territory of queerness that has yet to be mapped out and unearthed. This chapter is a step towards that historical work.

Acknowledgements

The author would like to thank Lend Mustafa, Blert Morina, and Misin Krasnić for being generous with their time and stories. The author would also like to note that this chapter would have been impossible to complete without the help of Myzafere Limani, Hazbije Krasniqi, and Shkumbin Brestovci who helped with archival research and contacts.

Notes

[1] Kosovo official documents are issued in three languages: Albanian, Serbian, and English. The term 'gender' is used in Albanian and Serbian to denote the document holder's sex. As a result, this chapter refers to the sex signifier in documents as a 'gender marker', denoting how in the local context sex and gender are often conflated even in legal discourse.

[2] As a site of articulating and negotiating nation-branding and statehood, NEWBORN has either been interpreted as symbol of the desire to reinvent Kosovar society (Ströhle, 2012, p 228); or as monument that conveys different messages to different audiences – reiterating both the 'newborn narrative' to an international audience, and 'keeping the past alive' for the local Albanian audience (Boguslaw, 2020, p 85). For a more recent analysis of how practices around repainting the monument, and who has the right to do so, could be interpreted as practices in sovereignty see: Boguslaw, A. (2020) Almost sovereign: Kosovo's NEWBORN sculpture and the indeterminacy of the state. *Nations and Nationalism*, *2021*, 1–16.

[3] Even the origin of this quote, by now a cliché, is disputed, indicative of just how slippery the game of 'firsts' is. While most commonly attributed to *The Washington Post* publisher Philip Graham, Jack Shafer has managed to trace the phrase's first use in an editorial by Alan Barth published in 1943 (Shafer, 2010).

[4] The 2007 film *Beyond the Rainbow*, directed by Ismet Sijarina and produced by Elysium CSGD, employs the tale as a metaphor for the journey of LGBTIQ+ people in general.

[5] *Rilindja* refers to Krasnić, whose surname has a Serbian spelling, as Krasniqi since in Albanian orthography proper names are written as they are pronounced. I have opted to use the legal spelling of their surname.

[6] *Rilindja* did not report on Krasnić's ethnic background, but Morina describes meeting his family in the Roma neighbourhood (1978a). Krasnić told me he identifies as Roma (personal communication, 1 February 2021).

[7] A note on the use of pronouns: in this chapter I refer to Krasnić as he/him since he identifies as a man today and told me he had been 'a transsexual for only three–four years of his life' (MK, 2021). At the time of the publication of the *Rilindja* article, Krasnić identified as a woman and the article predominantly uses feminine pronouns. When citing the article directly, I've left the original pronouns used in the newspaper.

[8] Henceforth, personal communication with Misin Krasnić on February 1, 2021 will be referenced as (MK, 2021). After finding the *Rilindja* report, I searched for Alexandra Krasniqi online before finding Misin Krasnić on Facebook. This interview was conducted through a Facebook video call.

[9] Morina does not reference Christine Jorgensen, an American transgender woman who became prominent for her gender reassignment surgery in the 1952, by name. While Jorgensen's case was spectacularly covered and has held sway in the popular imagination as

'the first sex-change surgery', as Page notes, the first documented case of male-to-female sex change is considered to be that of Dora Richter from 1931 (Stryker, 2017).

[10] It is not clear which term was used in the original Slovenian, so I have kept here the original in Albanian that was used by Morina. The term *gjinindërrues* can literally be translated as gender-changer but could have been a translation of transsexual.

[11] Krasnić uses the Albanian term *dëshpërim*, which translates to both depression and disappointment. My understanding was that he used it in the former sense.

[12] Traditional balloon pants worn by women.

[13] Henceforth personal communication with Lend Mustafa on 29 June 2020 will be referenced as (LM, 2020a).

[14] Henceforth the personal communication with Blert Morina on 15 June 2020 will be referred to as (BM, 2020).

[15] Ashkali are an ethnic minority, commonly understood as one of the related groups falling underneath the umbrella term Roma, as defined by the Council of Europe (2012, p 4). Ashkali people, who speak the Albanian language, are recognised as a distinct ethnic minority in Kosovo.

[16] Multiple activists I interviewed for this chapter referred me to Qerkica, who is in her 40s, as one of the oldest trans women they knew; Qerkica declined to be interviewed for this chapter.

[17] I have italicised the words he said in English in the original, although the interview was conducted in Albanian. Mustafa, like many young people in Kosovo, speaks a blend of Albanian and English. I will mark the words he used in English in the original as it shows how the language used to identify oneself today, especially as a queer person, borrows heavily from the English terminology that has become staple worldwide.

[18] Henceforth the personal communication Lend Mustafa on 7 August 2020 will be referred to as LM, 2020b.

[19] If adjusted for inflation through the Bank of England inflation calculator, the sum amounts to the value of £7,500 today.

References

Ahmeti, A. (2017, 12 October) Police investigate two incidents related to Kosovo Pride. *Prishtina Insight.* Retrieved on 29 September 2021 from https://prishtinainsight.com/police-investigate-two-incidents-related-kosovo-pride

Avdiu, N. (2016) Social protection and access to healthcare for transgender people in Kosovo: The Equal Rights for All Coalition ERAC. Retrieved on 29 September 2021 from https://www.lgbti-era.org/one-stop-shop/social-protection-and-access-healthcare-transgender-people-kosovo

Baker, C. (2018) *Race and the Yugoslav region: Postsocialist, post-conflict, postcolonial.* Manchester: Manchester University Press.

Bilefsky, D. (2008, 23 June) Sworn to virginity and living as men in Albania. *The New York Times.* Retrieved on 29 September 2021 from https://www.nytimes.com/2008/06/23/world/europe/23iht-virgins.4.13927949.html

Blert, M. (2019, December 31) @rinekika @cel_kosova. Retrieved on 29 September 2021 from https://www.instagram.com/p/B6vIBoBlwIK4 QyqiU0bNKUoLua2QtHyWQhpYK00/?igshid=1c8qk8ung78cx&fbc lid=IwAR0RphyhmBf7r4g53wI3sD6vEzeeT07c6WPuKkMH5i26H6- 0NCGhHPuQjvM

Boguslaw, A. (2020) Kosovo's NEWBORN monument: Persuasion, contestation, and the narrative construction of past and future. In J. Apsel and A. Sodaro (eds) *Museums and sites of persuasion: Politics, memory and human rights* (pp 74–88). New York: Routledge.

Breue, R. (2020, 20 June) LGBT artists still fighting for Pride. Deutsche Welle. Retrieved on 29 September 2021 from https://www.dw.com/en/ balkan-lgbt-artists-still-fighting-for-pride/a-53842909

Bulent, M. (2018) The sky is turning. [Documentary film]. Retrieved on 29 September 2021 from https://kosovotwopointzero.com/en/the-sky- is-turning/

CEL. (2019, 15 April) Hyn në fuqi kodi penal me mbrotje ligjore edhe për personat LGBTI. Center for Equality and Liberty. Retrieved on 29 September 2021 from https://cel-ks.org/hyn-ne-fuqi-kodi-penal-me- mbrojtje-ligjore-edhe-per-personat-lgbti/

Civil Rights Defenders. (2012, 20 December) Kosovo police must investigate hate crime attacks. *Civil Rights Defenders*. Retrieved on 29 September 2021 https://crd.org/2012/12/20/kosovo-police-must-investigate-hate- crime-attacks

Council of Europe. (2012, 18 May) Council of Europe Descriptive Glossary of terms relating to Roma issues. Retrieved on 30 January 2022 from http://a.cs.coe.int/team20/cahrom/documents/Glossary%20Roma%20 EN%20version%2018%20May%202012.pdf

Demolli, D. (2012, 17 December) Attack on Kosovo 2.0 widely condemned. *Balkan Insight*. Retrieved on 29 September 2021 from https://balkaninsi ght.com/2012/12/17/attack-on-kosovo-2-0-widely-condemned/

Dickemann, M. (1997) The Balkan sworn virgin: A cross-gendered female role. In S.O. Murray and W. Roscoe (eds) *Islamic homosexualities: Culture, history, and literature* (pp 197–203). New York: New York University Press.

Duffy, N. (2018, 11 October) Kosovo Pride takes place despite calls to ban it. *Pink News*. Retrieved on 29 September 2021 from https://www.pinkn ews.co.uk/2018/10/11/kosovo-pride-2018-photos-ban/

Durham, E. (2013) *Shqipëria e Epërme, një udhëtim në Shqipërinë e Veriut të vitit 1908*. Tiranë: IDK.

Dylberizm. (2019, 24 August) Vallja e bukur ritual: Kalimi i Ylberit. Retrieved on 29 September 2021 from https://www.facebook.com/ watch/?v=455235595062521

Fricker, M. (2011) *Epistemic injustice: Power and the ethics of knowing*. Oxford: Oxford University Press.

Gashi, P. and Travers, E-A. (2018, 10 October) Kosovars celebrate country's second Pride Parade. *Prishtina Insight.* Retrieved on 29 September 2021 from https://prishtinainsight.com/gallery-kosovars-celebrate-countrys-second-pride-parade-mag/

Halili, D. (2017, 10 October) Stepping into your true body. Kosovo 2.0. Retrieved on 29 September 2021 from https://kosovotwopointzero.com/en/stepping-true-body/

Halili, D. (2018a, 17 May) Landmark request to change name and sex marker denied. Kosovo 2.0. Retrieved on 29 September 2021 from https://kosovotwopointzero.com/en/landmark-request-to-change-name-and-sex-marker-denied/

Halili, D. (2018b, 31 July) Transgender case taken to Kosovo's highest legal institution. *Kosovo 2.0.* Retrieved on 29 September 2021 from https://kosovotwopointzero.com/en/transgender-case-taken-to-kosovos-highest-legal-institution/

Halili, D. (2020b, 17 May) How IDAHOBIT came to Kosovo. *Kosovo 2.0.* Retrieved on 29 September 2021 from https://kosovotwopointzero.com/en/how-idahobit-came-to-kosovo/

Kadriu, F. and Kërqeli, A. (2019) Manual for psychological practice: With transgender and gender nonconforming individuals. Prishtinë: Centre for Equality and Liberty of the LGBT Community in Kosova (CEL) Retrieved on 29 September 2021 from https://cel-ks.org/wp-content/uploads/Manual%20for%20Psychological%20Practice%20with%20transgender%20and%20gender-nonconforming%20individuals.pdf

Klan Kosova. (2014, 22 March) *Edona James – shqiptari që kaloi ylberin.* Privé [Video file] Retrieved on 29 September 2021 from https://www.youtube.com/watch?v=Z1RiygMjYyA&t=139s

Klan Kosova. (2016, 29 May) *Mallkimi LGBT.* Zona Express. [Video file] Retrieved on 29 September 2021 from https://www.youtube.com/watch?v=Y3dC5CqkXus

Klan Kosova. (2017, 19 June) *Transgjinorët kosovarë rrëfejnë përvojat e tyre.* NIN. [Video file] Retrieved on 29 September 2021 from https://www.youtube.com/watch?v=HvrKbkhNFos

Klan Kosova. (2019, 21 August) *Historike: Gjykata kosovare për here të pare lejon nderrimin e gjinisë.* [Video file] Retrieved on 29 September 2021 from https://www.youtube.com/watch?v=cFvnlDUUTXQ&feature=emb_title

Kohavision. (2018, 29 May) A mund të ndërrosh gjininë në Kosovë? Rubikon. Retrieved on 29 September 2021 from https://www.youtube.com/watch?v=wrhsCSp8JUc

Law No.2004/32 Family Law of Kosovo. (2004) Assembly of the Republic of Kosovo. *Official Gazette.*

Law No.04/L-003on Civil Status. (2011) Assembly of the Republic of Kosovo. *Official Gazette.*

Law No. 05/L-020 On Gender Equality. (2015) Assembly of the Republic of Kosovo. *Official Gazette.*

Law No.05/L-021 on the Protection from Discrimination. (2015) Assembly of the Republic of Kosovo. *Official Gazette.*

LGBTI ERA. (2019, 22 July) New criminal code in Kosovo strengthens protections for LGBTI persons. LGBTI ERA. Retrieved on 29 September 2021 from https://www.lgbti-era.org/news/new-criminal-code-kosovo-strengthens-protections-lgbti-persons

Morina, B. (2019, December 31) @rinekika @cel_kosova. Retrieved on 29 September 2021 from https://www.instagram.com/p/B6vIBoBlwIK4 QyqiU0bNKUoLua2QtHyWQhpYK00/?igshid=1c8qk8ung78cx&fbc lid=IwAR0RphyhmBf7r4g53wI3sD6vEzeeT07c6WPuKkMH5i26H6-0NCGhHPuQjvM

Morina, S. (1978a, 2 November) Ai u bë ajo – pa e kaluar ylberin: Legjenda u bë njëmendësi. *Rilindja*, p 9.

Morina, S. (1978b, 3 November) Ai u bë ajo – pa e kaluar ylberin: Pikënisja nga hiçgjë. *Rilindja*, p 8.

Morina, S. (1978c, 4 November) Ai u bë ajo – pa e kaluar ylberin: Mos është gabim i oficarit? *Rilindja*, p 9.

Morina, S. (1978d, 5 November) Ai u bë ajo – pa e kaluar ylberin: Unë linda djalë, e tash … *Rilindja*, p 9.

Morina, S. (1978e, 6 November) Ai u bë ajo – pa e kaluar ylberin: Më në fund me adresë në xhep. *Rilindja*, p 9.

Morina, S. (1978f, 7 November) Ai u bë ajo – pa e kaluar ylberin: Më pëlqente të isha vajzë. *Rilindja*, p 8.

Morina, S. (1978g, 8 November) Ai u bë ajo – pa e kaluar ylberin: Fotografia e grisur. *Rilindja*, p 8.

Morina, S. (1978h, 9 November) Ai u bë ajo – pa e kaluar ylberin: Më njihnin here femër, here mashkull. *Rilindja*, p 9.

Morina, S. (1978i, 10 November) Ai u bë ajo – pa e kaluar ylberin: Alexandra mendon të martohet. *Rilindja*, p 8.

Mustafa, L. (2018a, 27 March) I'm starting a VLOG (introduction). Retrieved on 29 September 2021 from https://www.youtube.com/watch?v=pXFzzA2uF2Q

Mustafa, L. (2018b, 21 April) 6 java n'Testosteron (ndryshimet, sfidat, pyetjet). Retrieved on 29 September 2021 from https://www.youtube.com/watch?v=ISEfYImYOVY&t=511s

Mustafa, L. (2018c, 22 May) Menaxhimi i emocioneve (2 muj e gjyse ne T). Retrieved on 29 September 2021 from https://www.youtube.com/watch?v=zL4dCTcy4g4&t=241s

Mustafa, L. (2018d, 17 July) Tranzicioni dhe ndryshimet ne levizje VLOG#4. Retrieved on 29 September 2021 from https://www.youtube.com/watch?v=WbrfhzrtKUs

National Democratic Institute. (2015, 28 October) NDI poll on LGBTI issues in the Balkans is a call to action. NDI. Retrieved on 29 September 2021 from https://www.ndi.org/LGBTI_Balkans_poll

Page, M.M. (2021, 19 January) Never be new again. Valley of the D – Substack. Retrieved from September 29, 2021 from https://valleyofthed.substack.com/p/never-be-new-again

Privé (2014, March 22) Edona James – shqiptari që kaloi ylberin. Klan Kosova. Retrieved on 29 September 2021 from https://www.youtube.com/watch?v=Z1RiygMjYyA&t=139s

Qendra për Barazi dhe Liri (2017) Lëvizja LGBT. Prishtinë: Qendra për Barazi dhe Liri.

Rexhepi, P. (2016) EUrientation anxieties: Islamic sexualities and the construction of Europeanness. In Z. Krajina, and N. Blanuša (eds) *EU, Europe unfinished: Mediating Europe and the Balkans in a time of crisis* (pp 145–61). London and New York: Rowman & Littlefield.

Rexhepi, P. (2017) The politics of (post)socialist sexuality: American foreign policy in Bosnia and Kosovo. In D. Jelača, M. Kolanović, and D. Lugarić (eds) *The cultural life of capitalism in Yugoslavia* (pp 243–60). London: Palgrave Macmillan.

Sardelić, J. (2016) Roma between ethnic group and an 'underclass' as portrayed through newspaper discourses in socialist Slovenia. In R. Archer, I. Duda and P. Stubbs (eds) *Social inequalities and discontent in Yugoslav socialism* (pp 95–111). London and New York: Routledge.

Shafer, J. (2010, 30 August) Who said it first? Journalism is the 'first rough draft of history'. Slate. Retrieved on 29 September 2021 from https://slate.com/news-and-politics/2010/08/on-the-trail-of-the-question-who-first-said-or-wrote-that-journalism-is-the-first-rough-draft-of-history.html

Stryker, S. (2017) *Transgender history: The roots of today's revolution.* Berkeley: Seal Press.

Ströhle, I. (2012) Reinventing Kosovo: Newborn and the young Europeans. In D. Šuber and S. Karamanic (eds) *Retracing images: Visual culture after Yugoslavia* (pp 223–250). Balkan Studies Library, 4. Leiden, NL: Brill.

Tarifa, F. (2007) Balkan Societies of 'social men': Transcending gender boundaries. *Societies Without Borders*, 2(1), 75–92.

Travers, E-A. (2019, 9 October) The good, the bad and the unconstitutional: Transgender rights before the courts. *Prishtina Insight*. Retrieved on 29 September 2021 from https://prishtinainsight.com/the-good-the-bad-and-the-unconstitutional-transgender-rights-before-the-courts-mag/

Wood, V. (2019, 8 September) Bosnian capital holds first Pride parade amiounter protests and a backdrop of violent opposition. *The Independent*. Retrieved on 29 September 2021 from https://www.independent.co.uk/news/world/europe/sarajevo-pride-first-bosnia-herzegovina-lgbt-protests-a9096631.html

Young, A. (2000) *Women who become men: Albanian sworn virgins*. Oxford: Berg.

Zahova, S. (2018) Romani writers and the legacies of Yugoslavia. *Baltic Worlds*, *11*(2–3), 25–33.

Zhegrova, D. (2018, 12 December) A place to call home: Kosovo 2.0. Retrieved on 29 September 2021 from https://kosovotwopointzero.com/en/a-place-to-call-home/

5

Tortuous paths towards trans futures: the trans movement in Slovenia

Martin Gramc

In November 2014, a group of transgender people met in Ljubljana at the first *TransMisija*, which would become the most important trans-related annual gathering in Slovenia. This was a crucial moment in the national history of transgender organising as it brought together actors that would shape the politics of the movement in the forthcoming years. The energy of the new initiative and the desire of its people to question the established gender norms were palpable and it looked like a change was within our reach. However, the initial enthusiasm soon started to dissipate through tensions that enveloped the movement with a growing rate. Painful disagreements about representation quickly arose among us making many of my colleagues and fellow activists decide to go their own ways. The impact of these divergences still reverberates in my activist engagement to the extent that has even led me to question whether I am the right person to write this text. Trying not to succumb to the powerful forces that truncate our sense of agency when we find ourselves in marginalised and precarious communities, I realised that my insecurity could also constitute a productive starting point.

This chapter provides an account of the development of the Slovenian transgender movement paying particular attention to its internal conflicts and their political/personal implications. These conflicts stem from differences in understanding activism as well as diverse geographical locations and their contrasting political realities. In this regard, I am especially concerned about overly constrictive identitarian boundaries of what it means to be a trans activist imposed by some activists and their wish to delimit the perimeter of activist legitimacy. I consider this an authoritarian and patriarchal practice, which not only depreciates certain identities among the movement subgroups but ends up reproducing wider social patterns about who can count as a legitimate gendered subject. Such tensions also point to the difficulties with which some activists come in contact with their own involvement in perpetuating gender oppression. Moments of contention lead to repeated failures of coalitional politics that would consider everyday experience as the foundation block of queer/trans emancipation and give people affected by transphobia and heterosexism precedence over rigid identitarian boundaries or unending theoretical discussions.

My text relies upon the queer of colour critique (Muñoz, Lorde, Lugones) to theorise the conditions for trans activism in Slovenia as these authors provide tools to unearth how race and ethnicity intersect with gender and class within the Slovenian trans movement (Crenshaw, 1991). In this regard, I touch upon the too often neglected category of race in the post-Yugoslav space – discussion foreclosed due to the seemingly coterminous identification of ethnicity with race and exemption of this space from global racial relations (Baker, 2018; Bjelić, 2018).

With this in mind, the first part of the chapter brings a historical account of the movement pointing to some of the most important episodes in its development. I show that the movement has relied on the already existing activist infrastructure provided by the gay and lesbian mobilisations even though these alliances have also varied in terms of strength and durability. After this, I briefly review the literature that has examined 'internal mechanisms' of the LGBT movement operation showing how supposedly emancipatory initiatives often have a hard time problematising patriarchal norms that they purport to challenge. I then draw upon my own empirical corpus, which consists of interviews with activists to engage more closely with the tensions within the Slovenian transgender movement. I focus on the main issues of contention underlying their potential to push the movement forward without, however, ignoring their sometimes high emotional costs. I finish by looking at the geographical aspects of trans organising both in terms of urban–rural tensions in a highly centralised state which hinders the outreach of trans people in rural areas (like in Serbia) as well as in terms of the activists' shifting allegiances towards Europe, on the one hand, and 'the Balkans', on the other. Taken together these elements offer an insider's insight into the most relevant endeavours that strive to improve the status of transgender people in the Slovenian political context.

The movement and its people

The transgender movement as a new political actor emerged shortly after the 2012–13 anti-corruption protests that stirred up the political scene. The demonstrations, which started in Maribor and spread around the country, demanded resignations of the corrupt politicians and included a wide range of social groups that could not come up with a more coherent programme (Kirn, 2013). These protests, which also witnessed substantial LGBT participation, to a great extent coincided with the rising visibility of transgender activist initiatives on the global scale. They thus offered a platform upon which Slovenian transgender activists came together to address transgender issues, make trans people assume a more prominent place in the public arena, and shed new light on those who were known to be trans in the past, but were erased from the LGBT history as such.

Up to that point the public representation of transgender people (for example, Salome) had been sensationalist and mostly based on personal stories. Transgender women were depicted in a fashion similar to the one that used to be reserved for homosexuals: they were sexualised, medicalised, and presented as something rare and mysterious (Kuhar, 2003). Such a tokenistic and reductionist portrayal could be challenged in the new circumstances in which trans activists like Filip Vurnik and Adam Julian (Mrevlje, 2019) made ever more courageous incursions into the national media landscape by making visible trans and non-binary identities that defied gender binary. Like this, the transgender movement had already gained a certain momentum by the time Pia Filipčič,[1] a trans woman, won *Big Brother* in 2015, where she was exposed to a lot of transphobic comments. Her participation in the show served as a reminder that the lives of transgender people were not changing for the better as fast as activists had expected (Koletnik, 2015).

A couple of years prior to Pia Filipčič's appearance, transgender people met in support groups hosted firstly by *Legebitra* and facilitated by Linn Koletnik. This was an opportunity for many transgender persons to create a safe space, build a community, and engage with activism in a more decisive way. However, during the sessions a disagreement arose between transgender and transsexual people as the latter claimed they were 'really' trans because they transitioned medically and aligned both their appearance and identity with the gender binary. This strand advocated in favour of transnormativity, the idea that gender reassignment surgeries constitute the only acceptable way of being transgender (Vipond, 2015). The differences within the group around this question became so pronounced that it had to split.

Legebitra was not the only organisation that at the time provided a safe space for gender non-conforming people. There were also *Društvo Kvartir*, established in 2010, and *Društvo Appareo*, established in 2013 (Blažič, 2018). Both organisations worked intersectionally: while the former focused on bisexual and transgender issues, the latter had a broader approach. Along with *TransAkcija*, the two organisations were a source of new non-normative politics – critiquing the established gay and lesbian agendas that to some extent became normative, making transgender issues more visible, demanding systemic change, advocating for coalitional practices grounded in everyday experiences, and moving towards more queer approaches as a critique of the identity-oriented logic of the gay and lesbian movement (Perger, 2014).

A breakthrough for the transgender movement was the launch of the already mentioned *TransMisija* – a yearly meeting dedicated to transgender issues and providing a platform upon which different actors in the field of transgender human rights could converge: activists, doctors, lawyers, government representatives, public officials, transgender people, and all other interested parties (Koletnik, 2014a, 2014b). The claims and problems expressed during *TransMisija* highlighted all of the main issues of the movement: raising awareness about transphobia, safe treatment of transgender people in the process of medical transition in accordance with the World Health Organization standards, legal gender recognition based on self-identification, depathologisation of transgender people and use of gender-inclusive language.[2]

TransMisija and media outlets brought attention to transgender people as the movement slowly started to consolidate its program and identity. The first yearly meeting was followed by the increasing appearance of transgender activists in liberal and leftist mainstream media (*Delo, Dnevnik, Mladina*). Unlike the gay and lesbian initiatives, our claims and grievances were not only limited to alternative or community platforms (Blažič, 2018) but quickly found their way towards more mainstream channels. Ever since 1984, community media have been an important vehicle for the promotion of sexual and gender rights and legitimation of non-normative identities (Blažič, 2018). By the time the transgender movement emerged, the mainstream media had already to some extent adopted the approach of community media but kept focusing on surgical transition without challenging the gender binary (Blažič, 2018). In spite of growing presence, the public was not confronted with a diverse image of transgender people as only a part of the community was visible, namely transmasculine young people who have internet access, use social networks, and are included in the broader LGBT movement.

Moreover, the Trans March that took place in the Autumn of 2018 marked a new milestone in the development of the movement. It appropriated the logo and the ideas of the 2010 Ljubljana Pride Parade *Enough Waiting!* (Dovolj čakanja). The Trans March as a transgender intervention into the gender binary was inspired by the gay, lesbian, and other antifascist activists' 'occupation' of Metelkova[3] within which there was also a space for gender non-conforming people (Velikonja, 1999; Mozetič, 2014). The protesters passed by the Ministry of Interior and the Ministry of Health where they demanded a change of policies towards transgender people, namely legal gender recognition and transition. The March was to date the most explicit public gesture done by the movement.

However, the emergence of the transgender movement was accompanied by a right-wing backlash and an anti-gender campaign fighting for traditional values (Kuhar, 2017). Since the 2010s, the Slovenian LGBT movement was no longer at the forefront of advocacy and emancipatory change in the post-Yugoslav region (Antić Gaber and Kuhar, 2019) as it faced an anti-same-sex marriage mobilisation organised under the auspices of the Roman-Catholic Church. The first same-sex marriage referendum was followed by another one in 2015, when the transgender movement gained its momentum. This time anti-gender activists were led by Aleš Primc who in 2001 had already won the referendum that banned biomedical artificial insemination of single women (Greif, 2016). In 2015 Primc reappeared along with anti-gender activists Metka Zevnik and Vesna Vilčnik attacking transgender activists and claiming that they promoted 'gender ideology'. It is not unimportant that Primc is well connected to transnational anti-gender politics as he espoused the same rhetoric as French, Italian, and Croatian anti-LGBT campaigners (Kuhar, 2017) and supported Croatian anti-gender and anti-LGBT activist Željka Markić during an anti-marriage equality campaign in Croatia in 2013 (Primc, 2013).

Explicitly transphobic statements were uttered during a television debate on the Slovenian public broadcasting service when Primc, while conflating transgender people with non-heterosexual people, accused LGBT activists of wanting to redefine the legal definition of marriage and by doing so turn children into gays and transgenders (Perger and Muršec, 2018). Another transphobic strategy of the anti-gender campaigners was insisting on the idea that 'gender ideology' effectively means that children could change their gender on a daily basis (Kuhar, 2017). Unlike in 2012, when there was still no sign of transgender movement in the public, in 2015 the anti-gender activists seized the opportunity to instrumentalise the transgender movement and its progressive politics against marriage equality by conflating transgender people with gay and lesbian who seek to impose non-traditional gender notions on children and their parents under the pretext of marriage equality bill. The 2015 marriage equality mobilisation was based on portrayals of lesbian and gay people as nice and kind, similar to heterosexual and cisnormative people and therefore deserving of marriage rights. That initiative did not dispel homophobic, biphobic, and transphobic fabrications, which many LGBT activists, including myself, saw as harmful for our community. Such a 'soft' approach was detrimental to the transgender movement because the LGBT campaigners did not prove anti-gender campaigners wrong in their attempts to vilify transgender people as dangerous to children. Instead of actively refuting anti-gender statements, gay and lesbian campaigners left these issues unaddressed for the sake of achieving marriage equality. There was a tacit agreement that problematising anti-gender statements could lead to a loss of potential supporters. On the other hand, there were many transgender people in the marriage equality campaign who supported the cause even though gay and lesbian activists did not stand up for us.

In this way, the LGBT movement lost not only the campaign and the opportunity to broaden the range of LGBT public representations but also induced fissures in the already fragile alliance between the transgender movement and the gay and lesbian movement. The campaign deepened the division between the liberal strand of the gay movement and the radical strand of the transgender movement. The former sees the transgender movement as detrimental to the prime gay agenda – marriage equality – because transgender activists (allegedly) 'stole' the gay movement by gaining visibility in the media and establishing themselves as an important actor within the LGBT community. There are, nevertheless, some 'dissident voices' within the gay movement that express support and solidarity with the transgender movement. Among the most visible is Mitja Blažič who during the second *TransMisija*, just a month before the referendum in 2015, stated that he found solidarities within the LGBT community important (Sešek, 2015).

Unlike those with the gay movement, the alliances between the transgender and lesbian feminist movements are less turbulent. Both have, for example, found inspiration in the writer Ljuba Prenner[4] for his gender non-conforming stance. Many lesbian feminist events are inclusive of transgender people, first and foremost the ones hosted by radical lesbians. Trans people are welcome and active at Lesbian-feminist university (Lezbično-feministična univerza) and the Red Dawns festival (Rdeče zore) as performers, organisers, and sometimes – still – as seekers of shelter (Oblak and Pan, 2019). Feminist events at Red Dawns are open for transgender people as the organisers aim to problematise (cis)sexism, misogyny, and transmisogyny (Dobnikar and Grobler, 2015).

Intractable oppression: tensions *within* LGBT movements

In their account about the development of the transgender movement in Croatia, Hodžić, Poštić, and Kajtezović (2016) show how transphobia within some parts of the LGBT (activist) 'community' forced trans activism to evolve from the practically invisible T inside the LGBT initiatives to autonomous trans-led activist enterprises and networks. While this evolutionary pattern can apply to many transgender activist initiatives around the globe, what is perhaps less noticeable – and therefore more prone to escaping researchers' attention – are tensions within the transgender movement itself, which can have profound political and personal consequences. This is mostly related to the fact that activists who gather around certain sexual or gender identities tend to operate in difficult circumstances, be dispersed, and often represent points around which societal oppression (for example, homophobia or transphobia) crystalises in threats, harassment, violence, and a general sense of personal insecurity.

When reflecting upon intra-movement relations, Muñoz (1999, p 8) argued that 'minority identifications are often neglectful or antagonistic to other minoritarian positionalities'. In this regard, activist groups operating in straitened circumstances should not be imagined as spaces of democracy, consensus, or coordinated action given that they can also be – and often are – highly hierarchised settings within which people can get objectivised, denigrated, and oppressed. The spaces outside established social order (or as Nataša Velikonja (1995, p 78) calls them 'hollow spaces of civilization') are not *per se* particularly nurturing for subjects who are pushed out of or cannot find their place within the dominant public (Muñoz, 1999). Correspondingly, minority subjects experience further marginalisation within already oppressed social groups. It is crucial to focus on multiply oppressed members of a marginalised group to examine their specific position, which is too often neglected when examined by the dominant anti-discrimination approach, and to obtain the full scope of intersecting oppressions, which are more than the sum of separate forms of oppression (Crenshaw 1989).

Essentialist activism and community building can surely provide a sense of belonging, give power, pride, and resources to marginalised identities (Gamson, 1997), but can also contain and operate multiple mechanisms of oppression (Gamson, 1995; Nagoshi and Brzuzy, 2010). Those activists who are White, ethnically Slovenian, more educated, living in urban areas, better networked, and closer to political sources of power can use these positionalities to push for their ends within the marginalised group they belong to.

In addition, those who are more privileged, especially more educated, can use that knowledge to perpetuate marginalisation instead of doing away with the sources of oppression (Lorde, 1993). However, the distribution of resources and privileges is only one part of the marginalisation of the marginalised. The other one has to do with the way in which some communities imagine themselves as 'ideal' on the basis of their tendency to homogenise experiences and erase differences among their own members (Young, 1986). Activist communities are especially inclined to this type of organising because they need to establish themselves as coherent and visible political actors (Bilić, 2012a) and by doing so may end up excluding dissenting voices (Young, 1986). Such exclusions taking place within already marginalised groups beg the question as to how it is possible that those who are already disposed of social power perpetuate oppressive social practices through an imposition of restrictive identitarian boundaries.

The experience of marginalisation within the dominant public sphere does not always render social agents able to eliminate dispossession of power and oppression from their own activist praxis. This led me to draw upon conceptualisation of division between oppression and emancipation by chicana feminist Maria Lugones (2000, p 468):

> The distinction between oppressive and resistant/emancipatory constructions of reality is an abstract distinction. The distinction does not map out onto social reality in such a way that particularly located people function within or with one logic exclusive of the

other. Most particular subjects work with both logics. All subjects can be understood as active contributors to, collaborators in, creators of oppressive or resistant practices even when the logics of oppression constitute some subjects as passive. That is, resistance and oppression vie as constructions of everyday life. One way of putting the point is to think of particular subjects as oppress-*ing* (or collaborat-*ing*) or be-*ing* oppressed and as resist-*ing*.

I keep this risk of oppression in mind as I explore the ways in which Slovenian trans activists talk about their experiences with the mobilisations for the improvement of their own social status. The strenuous and often hurtful patriarchal practices within the wider LGBT community where transgender people face misgendering, misrecognition, and denigration have been, to a certain extent, examined (Gramc, 2018; Hodžić et al, 2016; Perger, 2019). However, while these few analyses tackled the topic of exclusionary and prescriptive identities among the non-heterosexual and transgender 'alphabetic soup', the internal operation of the transgender movement in Slovenia has not up to now been analytically approached.

Method

To start filling this lacuna, I have conducted ten semi-structured interviews with transgender activists. My empirical corpus arose through my conversations with respondents who are young, highly educated, and living in Ljubljana. The interviews were conducted in Slovenian in February and March 2020 in public spaces and cafes throughout the Slovenian capital (and completed before the onset of the pandemic). Prior to the interview the respondents were acquainted with the purpose of the project and informed about how the data would be managed and used. The accounts of interviewees are anonymised due to negative experiences of the fellow trans activists within the trans movement with some of the activists mentioned in the chapter. All of the interviews started with a broader question regarding the respondents' biographical episodes associated with their activist engagements and continued with more specific questions. These mostly pertained to the politics that fuelled their activist endeavours as well as to the ways in which they thought about their positions within the trans/ LGBT movement in Slovenia and in the broader post-Yugoslav space. The interviews were transcribed and analysed using inductive thematic analysis with a view to identifying the major themes in the dataset. In spite of my efforts, I did not manage to interview all of the most visible actors as some of them declined my invitation making me yet again aware of the depth and relevance of the movement fissures.

Of origins, initiatives, and connections

In this section I draw upon my empirical corpus to explore three interrelated dimensions of the Slovenian trans movement, namely: motivations, frictions, and locations.

Motivations

Over the last years, Slovenian trans activists have created a new social movement with its own symbolic logic, which draws upon the support and resources of the lesbian and gay as well as feminist movements. Mapping out the issues and systemic oppression of transgender people (as was also the case for gay and lesbian people) was inextricably connected to personal encounters and facing systemic obstacles with medical–administrative institutions. The transgender movement is thereby defined by those who have most knowledge and access to medical–administrative institutions and community care/building as Ana and Bran stated:

> I understand trans activism from very different perspectives. One is that what I do. I work in a client-activist and system-activist way. Something else is everyday activism done by transgender people and by us who support trans people. Generally, I understand systemic activism as those of us who work in organisations or who are in privileged positions, still in a position of power, and somehow we try to change the system so that it is more just for trans people, we try to make it non-exclusionary and non-discriminatory. (Ana, personal communication, February 2020)

> For me trans activism has more levels. One, what I started with, is purely community care. You share information that you otherwise cannot get within the health care system, concerning transition, concerning some procedures, talks, experiences, purely these things. Then there is an entirely systemic level, this system is very neoliberal and NGO-oriented. (Bran, personal communication, February 2020)

It is clear from many of my interviews that the access to medical–administrative institutions influences the fight of transgender activists in the broader social-political landscape, whereas community building is less concerned with that aspect and it builds on empowering and giving sense of belonging. These two areas represent the main challenges for the transgender movement, but each has its own relatively autonomous sub-field.

Medical–administrative institutions are only one of the most important loci of the transgender movement; the focus is on medical transition and legal gender recognition, both based on self-identification and in accordance with standards of the World Health Organization pointed out by Carl: 'I think the main challenges are definitely systemic: legal gender recognition, regulation of medical transition and then if we go through everyday life, definitely a legitimization, recognition that goes hand in hand with the destabilization of gender binary as we experience it and gender roles and gender expressions' (Carl, personal communication, February 2020).

His and other answers by the respondents show how community building represents the most important and at the same time the most difficult process shaping the movement. Coming together was important for trans people because it gave us a chance to share experiences of isolation and lack of recognition. It is no wonder then that Črt along with other respondents pointed to the importance of socialising which validates identity and gives us a sense of community:

> Trans community exists in socialising, organized by *Kvartir*. Then some individuals have connected themselves and have a circle outside these meetings. I also must mention *TransAkcija*. Because it is important. So, I think the there are three transgender circles. There may be more, but I know only three. (Črt, personal communication, March 2020)

Frictions

This quote leads me to the question of community fragmentation that is associated with different needs of transgender people living in the world that ostracises and renders us vulnerable. In relation to the Slovenian context, Ana stated:

> Trans community exists, but it is not equal as/to LGBT+ community. I think it is very fragmented. Non-homogenous. I understand trans community as many little trans groups, that are arising within the frame of different organisations, different social settings or whatever. We can say that there is a community but from my point of view I cannot say that it is representative or that it includes everything. (Ana, personal communication, February 2020)

The formation of transgender non-governmental organisations confers more power to people who are part of an organisation because they have more access to finances, media, governmental bodies, and other important socio-political actors. This process is not necessarily visible to those who benefit from it. Oppressed transgender activists perpetuate oppression by having more social power, which intentionally or unintentionally silences other voices within the movement, succinctly stressed by Dominik:

> I don't know, I think that people who are in the position of power in these organisations, especially in *TransAkcija*, and possibly somewhere else, should overcome their ego and reflect on things and come together and decide or at least clearly admit: Yes, we do it for ourselves, for systemic changes, or we do it to empower trans people, especially people who do not live in Ljubljana maybe, who live all over Slovenia, somehow hidden. (Dominik, personal communication, February 2020)

In other words, there is a hierarchy that fuels conflict within the transgender movement and which revolves around the issue of what kind of subject is the most appropriate for public visibility. This hierarchy is twofold: on the one hand, there is a transnormative strand that strives to fit into normative gender roles and is problematised by some transgender activists as too narrow but still perceived as a legitimate part of the movement. As in the words of Dominik:

> You have to empower people who want to live gender stereotypes, let's say that this is a conflict maybe, but I think that it is very important, because I think that even if a person considers their gender stereotypically, this is valid, because if there were no gender stereotypes, we would say it is valid. (Dominik, personal communication, February 2020)

The transnormativity within the trans community and trans movement is part of the greater division within the transgender movement. This division is gendered, and it affords greater visibility to non-binary and transmasculine people giving them more power within the movement. Even when gender non-binary people present themselves as not fitting into the gender binary, the neutral or subversive gender expression are often read as masculine in the patriarchal culture, especially when gender non-binary people position themselves somewhere on the masculine gender spectrum and were assigned female at birth according to Črt:

> Yes, speaking of trans women. Lea from *TransAkcija* is French, Ve from *Kvartir* is English, Salome is Croatian. I think I am the only trans woman who is a part of an organisation, but I do not appear publicly, I did not transition medically. Why is there nobody else to do it? Considering there are very strong actors on the masculine side, who expose themselves and do not feel bad about it. Sorry, but in Slovenia

they are mainly assigned female at birth. (Črt, personal communication, February 2020)

The activists who advocate in favour of transnormativity strive to maximise their symbolic capital by appropriating and fitting into the existing gender binary order and the non-normative side fights back. On the other hand, another strand of the transgender movement strives to be hypercritical and deems more oppressed trans people and activists as more legitimate. This strand can be understood as another kind of 'transnormativity' – one that employs *intersectionality as a discursive tool* in the struggle over symbolic as well as social and financial capital leaving race and ethnicity unaddressed. Race is never addressed within the movement, which is surprising given the fact that Slovenian trans activists largely draw upon the digital Anglophone activist sphere where race plays an important role. On the one hand, the invisibility of race echoes the racialisation processes of Slovenian/Balkan/ Eastern European national projects based upon unspoken Whiteness and hence Europeanness (Imre, 2006). On the other hand, invisibility of ethnicity is even more striking since the leftist activist circles in Slovenia were quite vocal about the rising ethnocentrism in the wake of Yugoslavia (Jalušič, 2002), but it seems that strong ethnic homogenisation (paralleled by the process of self-racialisation [Bjelić, 2018]) unavoidably left its mark on the Slovenian transgender community.

Rather than focusing on working with and for particularly precarious individuals in the community, some strands of the movement engage in theoretical examination of different forms of oppression and thereby deem people who are not well versed in theoretical issues as less legitimate trans people and activists or excludes them from discussions and community activities. This demand for the 'right' trans person is advocated by *TransAkcija* and represents the conflict over who counts as trans person and is part of transgender community and movement. It has divided the community and the movement as Dominik pointed out:

Because the problem is – I am going to directly name some names – *Transakcija* works for itself and not for the trans community. ... I think, it shows, that this is for somebody's own ego or something. For something which is not intended for the community or some people who just need a proof that they are ok and valid. But you need to be extremely cognizant, to reflect on everything, which *TransAkcija* also does not do, but ok, you are just not good enough to be a part of it. (Dominik, personal communication, February 2020)

The interviewees almost unequivocally referred to how the fight for symbolic capital and financial resources leaves many people within the community hurt. This is not much different from broader social context in which marginalisation and oppression are part of everyday life. The struggle for clear divisions may not even be known to all those involved. I was certainly not aware of it as I, like many other fellow activists, felt that the progressive politics of the movement and the fight against oppression should be put before personal disagreements. As many colleagues a few years ago stopped collaborating with *TransAkcija* because they did not agree with its understanding of transgender identity and politics, it became clear that we had found ourselves entwined in that intricate interplay of oppression and emancipation. As Enja pointed out:

> I think when you come from a marginalized group, you come from a marginalized background, abuse is part of your existence and I think that's maybe why it's been difficult to create a healthy community in Slovenia. … Yeah, I mean there still is a lot of harm. I think Slovenia's trans community is traumatized by Slovenia's trans community. I think it's really been an unhealthy painful journey these first years of (real) trans activism. (Enja, personal communication, March 2020)

The answer by Enja highlighted how the power struggle not only includes who can speak for other transgender people and what is represented in the public but also what it means to be a trans person: 'How things should be is often put before what a user or a trans person needs and feels and then it is somehow put in the first place how things should be. Yes, somebody defines what is truly trans, what is trans enough' (Carl, personal communication, February 2020).

The struggle for symbolic boundaries of collective identity is gendered and it happens between subgroups who fight for legitimacy in the socio–political system that demands an individual to represent a minority and bestows more power to masculine gendered individual. This frame, which reveals that protection against oppression runs the risk of transforming itself into violence, is eerily exposed in Bran's words: 'That I knew how to recognize violence that was at times creepily similar to violence I experienced within my own family. Which is disputable on so many levels that I won't even begin with. But for me personally that was the breaking point' (Bran, personal communication, February 2020).

The imperative of intellectual correctness, which is related to the abovementioned tension over what it means to be the 'right trans person', is often translated into calling people out – a term associated with Anglophone digital spaces that has been adopted by Slovenian transgender activists whose activism was in the beginning online oriented. This is another mechanism of constituting movement boundaries that at the same time includes the fight for more symbolic and social power summed up by Enja:

I think it's a call out culture. If people cared more about academia it might be better but there is like pretension to it in a way and there is this idea that you have to be the right kind of, like you have to be the best trans, or the best queer. … Here specifically in Ljubljana it is influenced by who is in a position of social power to make people feel like shit. (Enja, personal communication, March 2020)

Locations

The dynamics of the movement cannot be understood without appreciating its spatial dimension. Transgender activism has developed in the same places and spaces that witnessed the evolution of the gay and lesbian movement. The urban centres, first and foremost Ljubljana as the biggest city and capital, provide the spaces where communities and sexually and gender non-normative individuals can organise in activist groups. The autonomous city zone Metelkova was squatted in the 1990s by gay and lesbian activists and it would later provide space for many transgender people and events. Transgender activism is based in Ljubljana and it is centred mainly around transgender youth and a few transgender and LGBT organisations. That leaves many older, poor, geographically remote transgender people out, who cannot meet in person, attend different activities. In the words of Carl: 'Big problem is centralization, as I see it, predominantly, when a lot of young people because of studies and later on because of work move to Ljubljana' (Carl, personal communication, February 2020).

Carl's statement points out how activist centralisation in the capital city cannot be separated from class issues and funding, which is centralised in a few organisations there. On the one hand, already established lesbian and gay organisations in Ljubljana have better chances of finding finances for transgender-related topics by applying for projects on a national or municipal level because they have better access to information than those in more rural areas (see also Butterfield, 2018). On the other hand, established connections between transgender organisations and other important actors in the field of queer politics ease funding opportunities. The third contributing factor to activist centralisation is the fact that the Slovenian capital is also an educational centre, which attracts and provides chances for many trans people, especially for those who come from a middle class background or elite, to learn about gender issues and engage with activism. This thereby drains the Slovenian periphery of educated, critical thinking trans people.

The question of centralisation of finances is entangled with who counts as part of the movement. Connections within the transgender movement and other social movements are based on personal contacts and are barely formalised. As Bran states, the transgender movement is primarily organised around LGBT organisations:

We also do things because of the non-governmental sector that serves itself and does not meet the needs of community. You actually have to apply for a call to get finances and then you have to write a report and a lot of times you do not respond to the concrete needs of the community and that is also a big problem we are faced with. Not to mention competition when it comes to calls. I mean, we self-sabotage ourselves and give each other mean looks. I mean, that is really not in my interest. (Bran, personal communication, February 2020)

Bran's opinion is not an anomaly as several other respondents also mentioned how the fight for resources, the smallness of the physical space, and the community itself can negatively impact the development of the movement because it precludes more organic and official collaborations as many individuals do not want to work with others because of personal grudges or fight for resources or the combination of both. Nevertheless, personal interactions and relationships certainly contribute to intersectional entanglement of activist thinking and action, primarily between lesbian–queer feminists and transgender people. Individual engagement of transgender activists is also present in labour movement, but it is not systemic and continual, as Črt stated: 'Certain people from *Kvartir* are part of *Red Dawns* or other organisations. In *Zborke* or something. But even if there were no *Kvartir*, the connection would come about. I think that a lot of bisexual people are transgender and I think this is an intersection' (Črt, personal communication, March 2020).

Several other respondents did not forget to mention that while the bulk of work and activities takes place in Ljubljana, this does not mean that nothing is done in the rural areas. *Kvartir* invites people from all over Slovenia to write for their zines, whereas *TransAkcija* reached out via the internet to invite transgender people to participate in the making of a documentary. It is not only transgender organisations who reach out to transgender people in the rural areas or vice versa, but local human rights non-governmental organisations and youth centres also invite transgender activists and facilitators to raise awareness, such as Ana:

In principle all the support groups that I facilitate are in youth centres, at the same [time] we also offer workshops and education, different forms of support. For example, I and two co-workers always respond if there is a need to professionally educate in any way. We are always ready to go in the field and train people if there is a need or wish for knowledge. The need is always there, but the problem is that the wish is not present, e.g. it is not recognized that there is a lack of knowledge. (Ana, personal communication, February 2020)

More internationally oriented trans activists also mentioned the connections among transgender organisations and individuals outside the confines of national borders. The connections among trans movements in the region reveal the shared political–social past in general but also draw from the alliances of feminist and gay and lesbian movements in the last decade of Yugoslavia. The transgender movement integrated itself in the lineage of the regional activist solidarity, which came into being right in the beginning of the Yugoslav wars as many organisations and individuals from Slovenia in the recent years established connections with other transgender organisations in the former Yugoslav republics. The transnational alliances of transgender activists from Slovenia are not merely occasional and do not pertain only to pride parades in the post-Yugoslav space but they are growing stronger and more concrete as Bran highlighted: 'Well, I have been collaborating a lot in the Balkan region for the past two years. Maybe more intensely for the last year. Purely because of *Transpozijum*,[5] that I attended, and I think it is a fantastic project' (Bran, personal communication, February 2020).

Some of the respondents also commented that the leaning toward 'Europe' was recognisable in the guests invited to participate in the first *TransMisijas*. The international participants were all coming from Western European countries and organisations such as Transgender Europe (TGEU) – Noah Keuzenkamp (TGEU) or Broden Giambrone (Transgender Equality Network Ireland). Establishing ties with organisations in the former Yugoslav republics came into play later when the alliances between activists and organisations from the former Yugoslav countries, for example Trans Network Balkan (Trans Mreža Balkan), *Transpozijum*, and the Slovenian transgender movement were established. The movement remembered its socio-political past, which continually leads to questioning of the country and its people whether we/they belong to Western Europe or are there still some ties with Yugoslavia and its socialist past, summed up in Dominik's words:

> I think that Slovenia is a funny case because, on the one hand, it can be very close to the ex-Yugoslav countries, on the other, it is much more Western, but then again totally unrelatable with other parts of Europe, especially with Western Europe. Probably because of the history and everything, we can connect better with the ex-Yugoslav countries, especially with Croatia because it is close. Serbia as well, I guess. (Dominik, personal communication, February 2020)

Conclusion

This chapter has offered an account of the internal dynamics of the Slovenian transgender movement focusing on tensions that have developed along a few axes of differentiation. I have particularly engaged with the conflicts stemming from the constrictive identitarian logic operating within the movement as well as with the political consequences of this process. On the one hand, the challenges that the Slovenian trans movement has faced over the last two decades include social institutions affecting the everyday life of transgender people. On the other hand, there is the process of community building, politics of mobilisation, and the conflicts that arise with these. Over the years, activists changed the media representation of transgender people not only in community media but in mainstream media as well during time when trans activism gained transnational visibility. The activists introduced new gender–queer politics and gave the LGBT movement a new momentum. One of the major struggles of the transgender movement is connected to changing systemic obstacles within medical–administrative institutions and building coalitions within other LGB(T)I+ agents. Similarly, the transgender activists built coalitions outside the country on the European and especially ex-Yugoslav level. Thereby they drew upon decades-long connections between feminist, gay, and lesbian circles. However, establishing ties within the movement was a difficult, at times even hurtful process for many fellow transgender activists. This has been the most difficult process not only because the needs of transgender people are different but because it entails delimiting the symbolic and identity boundaries of the movement.

Frictions within the movement stem from restrictive notions of gender identity imposed by some activists. I have approached this imposition, which led to the questioning of activist legitimacy, as an authoritarian practice that denigrates certain identities, silences dissenting voices, and reproduces patriarchal social patterns about who counts as a legitimate gendered subject. These tensions point to the abstract thin line between emancipation and oppression (Lugones, 2000). This line is invisible to some activists who perpetuate gender oppression in the process of defining commonalities because they either cannot or do not want to reflect upon their own behaviour or because they wish to impose their personal ends on the movement. Another reason lies in the entanglement of friendships with political goals within the movement. This often translates political disagreements into friendship feuds and vice versa deflecting energy from the movement (Young 1986).

The intertwinement of personal and professional engagement in political groups is especially difficult to escape in such a small country like Slovenia where one quicky becomes acquainted with all the major figures in the given social setting and can easily form a clique. In such small social and political groups people who have the most resources, connections, and privileges easily wield this power to endorse their own goals by positioning themselves as leaders who dictate what is the right political strategy at the same time instrumentalising personal ties and friendships within these cliques, which makes emancipatory and critical action difficult. In this sense, one could say that the transgender movement did not leave the Yugoslav past behind: the patriarchal practices of transgender activists are entangled with the authoritarian notions of leadership and ostracisation of dissident voices which in the post-Yugoslav space have been present even among anti-war and human right activists (Bilić, 2012b).

Moreover, the imperative to be extremely critical by using intersectionality as a discursive tool and a symbol of knowledge rather than as an actual activist practice was inherited from the gay and lesbian (to a lesser extent feminist) movement. Hill Collins and Bilge (2016) point out that conflating critical and progressive perspectives can lead to dogmatism which borders on policing ideas. This has brought two different results within the field of the transgender movement. One strand is reflexive of social gender norms as a way to gain recognition, to break the symbolic power of the gender binary system, and achieve more equality within the medical–administrative institutions while empowering the community. The other part appropriated radical reflexivity to strengthen its symbolic and consequently material position within the movement and thereby oppressed other transgender people by silencing or calling us out when we used 'inappropriate' words or when we simply expressed disagreement. The movement thus provides an example of how radical reflexivity can be (ab)used to continue with oppressive practices when people are not self-reflexive about their own behaviour within a system based on unequal distribution of resources.

Another aspect of internationalisation of the movement is visible in its wavering alliance between Western Europe and former Yugoslav republics. The Slovenian gay and lesbian movement and the LGBT festival are 'European' and thereby distant from the supposedly backward Balkans, yet at the same time they insist upon their support of queer politics and the fact that the Festival is the oldest such manifestation in Europe, with its beginnings in the socialist period. This framing then also challenges the notion of Western LGBT activisms and culture as trailblazing (Kajinić, 2016) and paves the way which other non-Western LGBT human rights organisations may follow. Haunted by its Balkan/Yugoslav heritage, Slovenia is trying to be seen as part of Western Europe and hence as White. Yet, it cannot smoothly fit into the Western political and cultural frame and sever its multiple ties with former Yugoslav republics meaning that it is never really White enough (Mills, 1997).

Finally, many aspects of the movement operation have not been addressed in this chapter and can constitute productive lines of enquiry in the future. Among these are the role that masculinity and femininity play within the movement as well as the relevance of class relations in activist endeavours.

Considering the Yugoslav past and the multi-ethnic character of Slovenia, it would be also useful to explore how ethnicity figures within the transgender activist initiatives as residents and migrants from former Yugoslav countries represent the biggest ethnic minority in Slovenia. This is reflected in the transgender movement, which is predominantly White and Slovenian in ethnic terms, and there is little discussion on why ethnic others – Serbs, Croats, Bosnians, Kosovars – are excluded or not visible within the movement. Ethnicity and race are only seemingly invisible in trans activism while intersecting axes of class and gender are more visible. This is because the distancing of Slovenia from the Yugoslav space and insisting on being European relies on the unspoken Whiteness of the Slovenian nation-state project whose ideology the Slovenian transgender movement silently adopted. Another big issue worth exploring would be class distinction as Slovenia is still one of the countries in which income and wealth are more equally distributed, but the inequalities in terms of class are displayed through the educational system, rural–urban tensions, access to cultural events, and networking with important interest groups. In spite of the problematic aspects of the movement and many unsuccessful attempts at community building, new coalitions seem to be emerging on the basis of more inclusive and horizontal transgender politics – these surely deserve scholarly attention.

Notes

[1] Pia Filipčič, the winner of *Big Brother* in 2015, who did not want to be associated with the transgender movement and issues even though she came out during the show as a trans woman. Filipčič's reluctance to be associated with the transgender movement as a trans woman is on one hand indicative of how transgender women in Slovenia are invisible within transgender activism and also in the public space. On the other hand, Filipčič's distancing from trans activism as an openly trans celebrity operates within the broader production of (trans) celebrities who are detached from the social groups with which they are in a similar gender, class, sexuality, and race/ethnicity position, the most prominent example being Caitlyn Jenner.

[2] The Slovenian language is gender binary (even verbs are gendered) and the neutral version, like the English they or Swedish hir, does not exist. Transgender activists and some linguists fight for the use of the underline (_) to include all genders. For example: ljubimec_ke (lover).

[3] Metelkova is the only autonomous alternative space in Ljubljana that hosts numerous progressive social movements and related events.

[4] Ljuba Prenner was a lawyer and writer who was dressing in male clothing from a young age, wrote his first crime novel in the Slovenian language, and was using male pronouns in his private life (Mozetič, 2014). Ljuba Prenner became widely known in the beginning of his career due to cases he took and was revered by the public but was also in dispute with the League of Communists of Yugoslavia, which suspended his working licence several times due to his gender expression and critical attitudes.

[5] Transpozijum is a yearly conference/seminar hosted by Trans Mreža Balkan for connecting transgender people from the former Yugoslav republics and every year takes place in one of these.

References

Antić Gaber, M. and Kuhar, R. (2019) Identitetna gibanja in politike spola v Sloveniji. In R. Kuhar (ed) *Identitete na presečišču kriz* (pp 101–23). Ljubljana: Znanstvena založba Filozofske fakultete Univerze v Ljubljani.

Baker, C. (2018) *Race and the Yugoslav region: Postsocialist, post-conflict, postcolonial.* Manchester: Manchester University Press.

Bilić, B. (2012a) Not in our name: Collective identity of the Serbian Women in Black. *Nationalities Papers*, *40*(4), 607–23.

Bilić, B. (2012b) *We were gasping for air: (Post-)Yugoslav anti-war activism and its legacy.* Baden-Baden: Nomos.

Bjelić, D.I. (2018) Toward a genealogy of the Balkan discourses on race. *Interventions*, *20*(6), 906–29.

Blažič, M. (2018) *Razvoj in artikulacija prizadevanj za človekove pravice lezbijk, gejev, biseksualnih in transspolnih oseb v tiskanih LGBT-skupnostnih medijih v Sloveniji* [Unpublished bachelor's thesis]. University of Ljubljana.

Butterfield, N. (2018) Imagined rural/regional spaces: Non-normative sexualities in small towns and rural communities in Croatia. *Journal of Homosexuality*, *65*(13), 1709–33.

Crenshaw, K. (1989) Demarginalizing the intersection of race and sex: A Black feminist critique of antidiscrimination doctrine, feminist theory and antiracist politics. *University of Chicago Legal Forum*, *1989*(1), 139–67.

Crenshaw, K. (1991) Mapping the margins: Intersectionality, identity politics, and violence against women of color. *Stanford Law Review*, *43*(6), 1241–99.

Dobnikar, M. and Grobler, A. (2015) Feminističke bake, majke, kćerke ... u promišljanju. *Treća*, *27*(1–2), 75–87.

Gamson, J. (1995) Must identity movements self-destruct? A queer dilemma. *Social Problems*, *42*(3), 390–407.

Gamson, J. (1997) Messages of exclusion: Gender, movements, and symbolic boundaries. *Gender and Society*, *11*(2), 178–99.

Gramc, M. (2018) *Seksizmi v LGBT+ skupnosti.* [Unpublished Master's thesis]. University of Ljubljana.

Greif, T. (2016) Patologija cerkveno-političnega diskurza o pravici do istospolne zakonske zveze in vloga medijev. *Časopis za kritiko znanosti*, *266*(44), 145–62.

Hill Collins, P. and Bilge, S. (2016) *Intersectionality: Key concepts.* Cambridge: Polity Press.

Hodžić A., Poštić, J., and Kajtezović A. (2016) The (in)visible T: Trans activism in Croatia (2004–2014). In B. Bilić and S. Kajinić (eds) *Intersectionality and LGBT activist politics: Multiple others in Croatia and Serbia* (pp 33–55). London: Palgrave Macmillan.

Imre, A. (2006) Global entertainment and the European 'Roma problem'. *Third Text*, *20*(6), 659–70.

Jalušič, V. (2002) *Kako smo hodile v feministično gimnazijo*. Ljubljana: cf*.

Kajinić, S. (2016) The first European festival of lesbian and gay film was Yugoslav: Dismantling the geotemporality of Europeanisation in Slovenia. In B. Bilić (ed) *LGBT activism and Europeanisation in the post-Yugoslav space: On the rainbow way to Europe* (pp 63–85). London: Palgrave Macmillan.

Kirn, G. (2013, 26 February) The Slovenian popular uprising within the European crisis. Retrieved on 29 September 2021 from http://critcom. councilforeuropeanstudies.org/the-slovenian-popular-uprising-within-the-european-crisis/

Kuhar, R. (2003) *Medijske podobe homoseksualnosti*. Ljubljana: Mirovni inštitut. Retrieved on 29 September 2021 from http://mediawatch.miro vni-institut.si/edicija/seznam/14/mediawatch14.pdf

Kuhar, R. (2017) Changing gender several times a day: The anti-gender movement in Slovenia. In R. Kuhar and D. Patternote (eds) *Anti-gender campaigns in Europe: Mobilizing against equality* (pp 215–33). London: Rowman & Littlefield.

Koletnik, A. (2014a) Cisseksizem ni feminizem. *Spol.si*. Retrieved on 29 September 2021 from https://spol.si/blog/2014/11/13/cisseksizem-ni-feminizem/

Koletnik, A. (2014b) Strokovno srečanje TransMisija. *Spol.si*. Retrieved on 29 September 2021 from http://spol.si/blog/2014/11/30/strokovno-sreca nje-transmisija/

Koletnik, A. (2015) 1 September Transspolna življenja so legitimna. Torek ob petih. Retrieved 29 September 2021 from http://torekobpetih.si/ komentar/transspolna-zivljenja-so-legitimna/

Lorde, A. (1993) The master's tools will never dismantle master's house. In C. Morraga and G. Anzaldua (eds) *This bridge called my back: Writings by radical women of color* (pp 98–107). New York: Kitchen Table: Women of Color Press.

Lugones, M. (2000) Community. In A.M. Jaggar and I.M. Young (eds) *A companion to feminist philosophy* (pp 466–75). Oxford: Blackwell Publishing.

Mills, C. (1997) *The racial contract*. Ithaca: Cornell University Press.

Mozetič, B. (2014) *Grmade, parade in molk: Prispevki k neheteroseksualni zgodovini na Slovenskem*. Ljubljana: ŠKUC.

Mrevlje, N. (2019, January 1) Življenjska zgodba: s spremembo oznake spola končno vidi in čuti sebe. *Siol.net*. Retrieved on 29 September 2021 from https://siol.net/trendi/odnosi/zivljenjska-zgodba-s-spremembo-spola-kon cno-vidi-in-cuti-sebe-intervju-485984?fbclid=IwAR2rHOklpw7YZsJPK oHBr7YJ7W2DR3DsKiZ5tGGeycdIa0PoLH1G7K1SrUo

Muñoz, E.J. (1999) *Disidentifications: Queers of color and the performance of politics*. Minneapolis: University of Minnesota Press.

Nagoshi, J.L., and Brzuzy, S. (2010) Transgender theory: Embodying research and practice. *Affilia: Journal of Women and Social Work*, 25(4), 431–43.

Oblak, T. and Pan, M. (2019) Yearning for space, pleasure, and knowledge: Autonomous lesbian and queer feminist organising in Ljubljana. In B. Bilić and M. Radoman (eds) *Lesbian activism in the (post-)Yugoslav space: Sisterhood and unity* (pp 27–61). London: Palgrave MacMillan.

Perger, N. (2014) Med queer teorijami, queer gibanji in gejevsko-lezbičnimi gibanji. *Družboslovne razprave, 30*(77), 71–89.

Perger, N. and Muršec, S. (2018) Seksualno nebinarne osebe in nekatere dimenzije njihovega vsakdanjega življenja. *Časopis za kritiko znanosti, 47*(275), 30–44.

Perger, N. (2019) *Vsakdanje življenje oseb z nebinarnimi spolnimi in seksualnimi identitetami* [Unpublished doctoral dissertation]. University of Ljubljana.

Primc, A. (2013, 28 December) Čestitke ob rezultatih referenduma na Hrvaškem. Družina. Retrieved on 28 December 2021 from https://www.druzina.si/clanek/62-52-cestitke-ob-rezultatih-referenduma-na-hrvaskem

Sešek, K. (2015, 24 November) Spolov je nešteto, tudi v Sloveniji. Torek ob petih. Retrieved 29 September 2021 from http://torekobpetih.si/tema/9049/

Velikonja, N. (1995) Homoseksualnost in politika. *Časopis za kritiko znanosti, 23*(117), 75–88.

Velikonja, N. (1999) Narod, nacionalna država in homoseksualnost. *Časopis za kritiko znanosti, 27*(195/196), 137–51.

Vipond, E. (2015) Resisting transnormativity: Challenging the medicalization and regulation of trans bodies. *Theory in Action, 8*(2), 21–44.

Young, I.M. (1986) The ideal of community and the politics of difference. *Social Theory and Practice, 12*(1), 1–26.

6

(Post)socialist gender troubles: transphobia in Serbian leftist activism

Bojan Bilić

Towards the end of September 2020, as the world was bracing for the second wave of the COVID-19 pandemic, I received a Facebook notification that invited me to like the freshly established Lesbian and Gay Solidarity Network (Lezbejska i gej solidarna mreža, LGSM), a leftist initiative stemming from the need for 'radically different forms of LGB organising'[1] in Serbia. In spite of a conspicuous shortening of the acronym that had finally, after decades-long struggles, started doing justice to all of its four commonly used letters, I was curious about this new arrival to the often obscure and conflict-ridden domain of Serbian activist politics. As I plunged into the group's 'manifesto', I quickly found myself agreeing with the wish to resurrect the importance of class in our social analyses, emphasise women's liberation, permeate engagement with feminist principles, and rescue non-heterosexual emancipation from the jaws of elitism and hegemonic impositions. Alas, my enthusiasm began to subside as I read that gays and lesbians are a 'minority' whose right to 'same-sex attraction' should have precedence over sexual practices or fetishes of any kind. Queerness, which I thought could serve as an antidote to the painful legacy of the region's reified identities, was not spared either: instead of being seen as a tool devised with the promise of giving us access to badly needed breathing space, of loosening the identitarian noose around our non-normative lives, it was condemned as a means for 'justifying rotten coalitions with heterosexuals' and a 'fiction' to be banished from the knowledge that nourishes our mobilisations. By the end of the collective's programmatic statement I could not help feeling a sense of both disappointment and frustration as I learned that 'social pressure to engage with persons of the opposite sex' and hormonal and surgical interventions which 'aim at "correcting" the body' are little more than 'new and perfidious forms of old conversion therapy'. It took me a bit of time to get my head around such a discursive manoeuvre that did not only relegate trans[2] people (the missing T!) to a pseudoscientific practice, but also drove yet another, particularly destructive, stake through our already fragile coalitional hearts and endeavours.

The LGSM 'manifesto' constitutes the tip of the transphobic iceberg that has been floating through a great deal of Serbian leftist (and feminist) activism in recent years. LGSM is an offshoot of Marks21 (M21), an organisation founded in Belgrade in 2008 with the aim of offering a version of Marxism that could respond to the challenges posed by the 21st century. Determined not to surrender politics into the unreliable hands of the ruling class, these contemporary Marxists pledge to contribute to the empowerment of workers and all of those suffering under oppression. They refer to themselves as a group of revolutionary socialists dedicated to developing Marxism as a 'live theory' that would inform everyday practice and eventually reinstate workers as sole owners of the means of production (Marks21, n.d./a). Even though Serbia, a protractedly impoverished, disillusioned, and captured state, indeed is in urgent need of policies that would protect it from capitalist onslaughts, in the 13 years of its existence, M21 does not seem to have replenished the depleted reservoirs of proletarian potential. Quite the contrary, the group has become notorious for the tenacity with which some of its current and former members pursue the transphobic cause repeatedly bringing it into the centre of their attention and engaging in an obsessive assault against one of the most marginalised segments of the population.

While at first sight such perseverance may appear surprising for a collective that promises to (help) humanise the world, a more detailed look into both its operation and antecedents reveals strong patriarchal and neocolonial currents that, when combined, subvert progressive values in a way that makes declared socialists come dangerously close to their reactionary opponents. In this chapter I draw upon semi-structured interviews with trans and feminist activists to explore why it is that some strands of Serbian leftist activism – which has had a hard time recovering from the 1990s' nationalist blow – mark gender difference in such a rigid way that 'what is socially peripheral' becomes symbolically central (Hall, 1997) to the point of exclusion, discrimination, and verbal violence. While I focus empirically on the polemics surrounding M21, whose most visible male members have been particularly vocal about the risks that trans (women's) emancipation allegedly poses for the precarious achievements of the leftist and feminist movements, I juxtapose it with Praxis, an older Yugoslav Marxist initiative that can hardly boast about its feminist record. Within such an analytical frame (which tends to foreground structural aspects and subdue personal tensions and preferences that are, nevertheless, far from negligible in the functioning of small collectives), I argue that the capacity of the 'trans question' to split the already minuscule left side of the political spectrum is reflective of the long-term conservative and neocolonial dimensions of the Yugoslav/Serbian Left. This 'question' points to the global neocolonial entanglements of local activist knowledge production or, rather, uncritical knowledge appropriation which can have potentially oppressive consequences.

With this in mind, I am not primarily interested in regurgitating the often malevolent and transnationally similar 'theories' of essentialised sex difference that tend to dismiss at a stroke years of feminist scholarship. I am rather led by the question as to how it is at all possible that a destructive discourse of discrimination has escalated in an activist community within which trans people might reasonably expect to find shelter, solidarity, and support. In the first part of the text I set the background for my analysis by outlining the contours of the debate, mostly led in the United Kingdom and the wider Anglo-Saxon world, that has constructed trans women and non-binary people as a threat to cis women. In the second introductory section, I take a look at some of the most important features of autonomous Marxist organising in socialist Yugoslavia, namely *Praxis*, which purported to offer a 'relentless critique of all existing conditions' (Vodovnik, 2012) and thus serve as a leftist corrective of the socialist regime. Engaging with the literature which has approached that collective from a sociological and ethnographic perspective, I underline the less frequently discussed patriarchal and neocolonial features of its operation. My analysis then shows how the M21's 'denial of [trans] authenticity' (Bettcher, 2006, p 204) builds upon this largely unproblematised conservative legacy ending up in rigid identity politics that dehumanises vulnerable social groups.

In this regard, I argue that (at least some of the) recently expanding trans-exclusionary attitudes stem from the intersection of the mounting pressures to deal with sexism within the organisation of M21 itself, and the uncritical translation of the 'trans rights' controversy from the United Kingdom into the highly sensitive and radically different arena of Serbian activist politics. Like this, rather than being an emancipatory avant-garde that would produce a plausible alternative to the ever more powerful neo-fascist forces in the country, M21 becomes a proponent of 'pre-emptive conservatism' that produces political/personal damage by attacking a straw man of trans menace. Such a practice cannot be separated from the repatriarchalisation impulses and the 'hardening' of the line between 'men' and 'women' that have been brought about by the ascendancy of neoliberal capitalism in the region alongside conservative nationalist religious ideologies. In this way – and perhaps paradoxically – transphobia becomes an indicator of the extent to which the capitalist logic, based upon gender hierarchies, has pervaded (even) what seems to be offered as a response to the devastating effect that logic has had on Serbia's post-socialist social life.

Colonial dimensions of trans-exclusionary politics

On 8 July 2018, *Pride in London*, a voluntary collective that organises Pride parades in the UK capital, published a statement apologising for the incident in which a group of lesbian activists, known as *Get the L Out*, 'forced their way to the front of the parade' (*PrideinLondon*, 2018, online) demanding to march behind the rainbow flag. They argued that the trans movement, which according to them also includes 'males who identify as lesbians ... enforcing heterosexuality' on them, was a manifestation of the pervasive 'rape culture' that oppresses (lesbian) women. This unfortunate episode gained international visibility providing unmediated access to the dispute around trans identities and experiences that has been ravaging British feminism over the last two decades. Anti-trans politics took a particularly sharp turn in 2017 when Prime Minister Theresa May announced plans to reform the 2004 Gender Recognition Act that would allow trans people to change their birth certificates through self-determination. This announcement led to an upsurge in anti-trans sentiment based on the idea that *sex* markers cannot be changed because they constitute a biological/material reality distinct from *gender* as an expression of social role or ideology. In other words, such essentialising positions assume that sex is an immutable property according to which trans women should be marked as 'male' and trans men as 'female'. If this 'biological' order of things were to be disrupted via trans and gender non-binary identities, 'men' could bring women in danger by ending up in women-only spaces. Advocates of this view are labelled as 'TERFs'[3] (trans-exclusionary radical feminists) by trans people and their sympathisers because they act in favour of *excluding* trans women and girls from the domain of legitimate womanhood (Pearce et al, 2020).

Even though TERFism was largely 'imported' in the UK from the US feminist circles throughout the 1970s, it is in the British public discourse that it found especially fertile soil becoming a 'respectable bigotry, shared by parts of the left as well as the right' (Jacques, 2020, online). 'TERF wars' are embedded in broader transnational right-wing and anti-feminist developments underscoring not only the co-constitutive nature of sex and gender but also their intricate entanglements with racialised identifications. The persistence of trans hostility in the UK can hardly be detached from the mechanisms through which British feminism has interacted with colonialism and empire (Lewis, 2019). Imperial policies were to a great extent concerned with enforcing heterosexuality through criminalisation of homosexual practices (Akintola, 2017) as well as with strengthening the gender binary. One aspect of colonial racialisation process was not only that the racial 'other' was a potential sexual threat but that Black women and non-binary people were perceived as dangerously masculine, never really reaching the standard of White women's supposedly 'natural' femininity (McClintock, 2013; Pearce et al, 2020). That (White) cis women can nowadays present themselves as *vulnerable* While depicting trans women as perilous is an expression of power that these women have over trans women or racialised others of any gender (Pearce et al, 2020). The combined effect of Whiteness and gender normativity can be so strong as to occlude the fact that it is trans women and non-binary people of colour – and not cis women – who are at a disproportionately high risk of gender-based violence (Hasenbush et al, 2019).

However, even though the TERF argument has lost a lot of its destructive force in the US, it has taken deep roots in the UK because British feminism has not been exposed to Black and indigenous feminist politics to the extent to which this happened with its American counterpart (Lewis, 2019). Lewis (2019) argues that mass mobilisations, which have occurred between the 1990s and 2010s in many parts of the world, including the US, have produced a rising awareness of the interactions between race, gender, and class. Given that the space for such rearticulations of the major operators of power has been much more constricted in the UK over the last decades, middle- and upper-class White feminists have preserved their agenda-setting influence. This has provided a framework for trans rights discussion in a way that has not only led to a 'bitter left-on-left conflict' (Kearns, 2018, p 25) within the UK but far and wide beyond the borders of the UK.

In this regard, the LGB Alliance, a British activist organisation that 'advances the interests of LGB people', has recently announced a worldwide network of anti-trans LGB collectives – the so-called LGBInternational – also hailing the accession of the abovementioned Serbian LGSM to the initiative. Examining the membership of these groups, which have – like the Serbian one – been established around September and October 2020 from Ireland to Australia and from Norway to Brazil, Paisley (2020) has shown that their followers on social networks are almost entirely a subset of the British *LGB Alliance* followers. The Irish group, for example, has more followers in the UK than in Ireland whereas the Welsh group has more followers in England than in Wales. On the basis of this analysis, Paisley concludes that rather than being an international movement, the LGBInternational is an astroturf campaign that harms the LGBT community across the globe by explicitly excluding trans people from it and undermining decades of activist work. In a similar vein in which homophobia was an imperial export that still makes it hard to abolish anti-LGBT legislation in many former British colonies (Akintola, 2017), trans hostility is being propelled by powerful media and activist organisations. The question then arises as to how this movement hybridises with transphobic sentiment, patriarchal legacies, and colonial dispositions in non-UK social and cultural contexts.

Patriarco-neocolonial entanglements of Yugoslav Marxist organising

'Yugoslav philosophy in the Sixties and the beginning of the Seventies has been a curious social phenomenon' (Marković, 1976, p 63). The renowned (and eventually also inglorious) Yugoslav/Serbian Marxist philosopher

Mihailo Marković could have hardly anticipated all of the contradictory connotations that his 1976 statement would acquire over the forthcoming decades. Marković was one of the central figures of the Marxist humanist movement that developed in the Socialist Federal Republic of Yugoslavia and from 1964 to 1974 published *Praxis*, one of the leading international journals dedicated to Marxist thought. The so-called Praxis School included philosophers and social scientists mostly from the Universities of Belgrade and Zagreb who, while not having a homogenous philosophical orientation, gathered around their repudiation of Stalinist dogmatism and the dissatisfaction with the course that Yugoslav socialism was taking in the mid-1960s. Engaging in a new reading of the 'young Marx', *Praxis* took 'the risk of complete freedom in analysing the present-day world and its own society' (Marković, 1976, p 63) and articulated a critical discourse that took issue with the resilience of class distinction, party bureaucracy, and economic inefficiency that were afflicting Yugoslavia at the time. The reinterpretation of Marxist philosophy that the group offered positioned *humanism* at the heart of political engagement, which should lead towards novel forms of critical subjectivity striking a final blow to the remnants of alienation that the Yugoslav self-management socialism inherited from its capitalist antecedents (Vodovnik, 2012).

However, the political project that extolled human creativity and invoked a new kind of personhood commensurate with an authentically socialist community was an overwhelmingly men's endeavour. Not only were all of the central *Praxis* theorists from both Belgrade (with the exception of Zagorka Golubović) and Zagreb men, but one would have a hard time finding more than ten women (for example, Blaženka Despot, Nadežda Čačinovič-Puhovski, and Agnes Heller) in the list of 224 scholars (praxis. memory of the world, n.d.) that ever took part in the Korčula Summer School where members of the group gathered annually in the company of their illustrious – mostly Western – international colleagues. Such an unbalanced gender distribution notwithstanding, some *Praxis* members (Ivan Kuvačić, Gajo Petrović, and Rudi Supek) were praised by pioneering feminist activists of the time (for example, Vesna Kesić, Slavenka Drakulić, and Biljana Kašić) for their readiness to support the nascent mobilisation by, for example, allowing a session on feminism to take place within their research group at the University of Zagreb (Lóránd, 2018). Nevertheless, there was a general feeling that feminism was not a matter of major importance and that 'leftist ideas [were] lacking a feminist angle' (Lóránd, 2018, p 48): for example, Biljana Kašić (Lóránd, 2018, p 32) stated that 'the Praxis philosophers did not take feminism seriously, and at the meetings women did not comment much'. Similarly, Vesna Kesić (Lóránd, 2018, p 32) had an unpleasant encounter with the abovementioned Mihailo Marković 'who said it is ok that we come and talk about feminism, but asked us: could you please look more feminine?' *Praxis* obviously could not establish productive affinities with the ever more intense feminist engagement that started developing within a political system in which the declared equality between men and women was enveloped in thick patriarchal layers. Not favourably looked at by the socialist regime and not finding its place within (the leftist) alternatives to it, Yugoslav feminist activism would achieve its heyday throughout the 1970s and 1980s, in the wake of *Praxis* demise (Bonfiglioli, 2008).

Moreover, *Praxis*' masculinist character did not reflect only its patriarchal dimensions but also its perhaps somewhat more subdued colonial undertones. Approaching the collective through a decolonial lens, Karkov and Valiavicharska (2018, p 17) demonstrate that, in spite of all its theoretical novelty, *Praxis* 'operated with a colonial definition of the human whose purported universality rested on a highly exclusionary foundation. The Yugoslav conception of 'socialist man' was but another version of (Western) man *over-representing* itself as if it were the human, at the expense of various non/sub-human others.'

These authors argue that the group's articulation of Marxist humanism had Western colonial underpinnings and was complicit in the logic of Western coloniality by means of a Eurocentric ethnohumanist perspective with supposedly universal applicability. Through a close reading of many of the most visible *Praxis* members (Marković, Životić, Vranicki, Supek), Karkov and Valiavicharska (2018) identify pervasive racialising binary distinctions (for example, Serbian nationalists vs Ottoman Turks, civilised men dedicated to praxical activity vs primitive people, ethnocentrism and savage habits vs truly human universal culture) which those scholars mobilised to account for the obstacles that socialism was facing on the way towards its full emancipatory realisation (also hindered in the view of Životić by the multi-ethnic composition of the Yugoslav federation; Karkov and Valiavicharska, 2018). On the one hand, invocations of the new socialist person to a great extent glossed over the deep fissures of 'race'/ethnicity (Albanians, Muslims, Roma), gender (women), class, and geographical location (urbanity) that consistently punctured Yugoslav socialist reality. On the other hand, even though perfectly positioned for such an endeavour in a country that was a founding member of the Non-Aligned Movement, *Praxis* scholars did not establish discursive links with the Global South and its rich legacy of Black people's decolonial struggles (Stubbs, 2020).

Such a theoretical omission constituted a 'colonial myopia' (Karkov, 2015; Karkov and Valiavicharska, 2018, p 15), which led some members of the collective to start 'replicating strategies of internal colonialism with highly repressive consequences for vulnerable populations' (Karkov and Valiavicharska, 2018, p 24).[4] The dissolution of the broader socialist frame towards the end of the 1980s and throughout the 1990s both domestically and internationally, allowed the patriarchal and the colonial dispositions to merge in a particularly destructive manner. In Serbia, Slobodan Milošević's Socialist Party was systematically corrupting and hijacking the Left on behalf of an ethnonationalist project accompanied by an intense repatriarchalisation that started erasing feminist achievements. Within this process, there were apparently surprising political transformations: for example, Mihailo Marković, once a staunch socialist, became the main ideologue of Milošević's regime employing racist discourses that were fanning the flames of ethnic hatred (Jakišić, 2011; Fuchs, 2017). While the complexity of *Praxis* cannot be reduced to the personal destinies of any of its members, it does testify to the degenerative potential of leftist politics characterised by serious patriarchal and colonial 'blind spots'.

Method

Similarly to its much more widely known predecessor, M21 (a group of around 30 members) is committed to a revolutionary intervention that would establish a classless society. Within this overarching goal, the collective claims to be engaged in two major struggles: the first one is 'against any kind of oppression since it is impossible to be in favour of a socialist revolution if we do not actively fight for the liberation of women and LGBTTIQA+ population', while the second is turned against 'the interference of the imperialist forces of the West and the East and their local nationalist clients from the ranks of the ruling classes who have been the major obstacle to a peaceful cohabitation of the Balkan peoples through the entire history of our region' (Marks21, n.d./b, online). In the light of its recent trans-exclusionary campaign, I draw upon 15 semi-structured interviews to explore how former members of the collective (including trans persons) as well as trans and feminist activists who followed its operation discuss the extent to which M21 had stuck to these two declared principles.

The interviews were organised in two rounds: the first round (eight interviews) was conducted in December 2019 in the framework of my broader research project about the development of trans-related politics in Serbia. There my questions revolved around motivations for activist engagement and an articulation of activist strategies, more generally. At the beginning of every interview, the interviewees had a chance to talk about their involvement in trans initiatives. This was then examined in further detail on the basis of an interview guide. Given that transphobic sentiment in leftist and feminist organising figured prominently in those interviews and the debate around it intensified in the meantime, a second interview round (seven interviews) was done in December 2020. At that point the interviews focused on the internal gender-related dynamics of M21 and the status of women and trans persons within the collective. One former M21 member, who is also a trans activist, was interviewed in both rounds, whereas another former member was approached in the second round.

The participants included women, men, trans women, trans men, and one non-binary person aged between 23 and 40. They were recruited through snowball sampling and interviewed in Serbia either in a bar (first round) or over the phone (second round). The interviews lasted between 45 minutes and two hours and were recorded with an mp3 voice recorder. All of the interviewees received verbal information concerning the design and procedure of the study and gave their informed consent. The interviews were subsequently transcribed and analysed using inductive thematic analysis with the view of identifying patterns pertaining to the two abovementioned aspects of the collective's operation.

Results

On the basis of my empirical corpus, I explore three interrelated elements of M21 operation: (1) patriarchy and sexism, (2) TERFism, and (3) uncritical translations.

Patriarchy and sexism

When it appeared in 2008, M21 promised to offer a new answer to the question as to how feminist and leftist strands could converge in the work of one activist organisation. This meant creating a wide front of action that would mark itself off through the participation and engagement of those living under oppression, including women and LGBT people. In the words of one interviewee:

> When I joined, quite early on, it looked to me that the collective was not just an empty story, but that they were actually trying to do something substantial ... there was more room for women there than in other leftist initiatives ... they had some principles, quite unlike some other leftist organisations that do not deal with feminism ... at that time, M21 was considered a group that was not only sticking to economic issues, but was trying to have a bigger picture and pay attention to gender and sexuality. (Personal communication, December 2019)

In spite of its emancipatory orientation, gender hierarchies have followed the collective from its very beginnings. This was obvious, for example, in the manner in which new women members were treated:

> I did notice, especially in the case of one female comrade, that women were pandered much less than men ... when they (women) joined

the organisation without knowing enough or if they had some slight liberal leanings, they would be instantly even ridiculed ... I have in mind one woman specifically, well a man now, but then he took part in a discussion as a woman ... after her intervention in a contentious matter, one man said: 'and if you asked her what those tensions were all about, she would not be able to say' ... one could feel a sort of scorn. (Personal communication, December 2019)

Such gender-related distinctions were also reflected in the way in which activities were distributed among the collective members:

very often women would get to do note-taking duties or translation or some kind of more passive activities ... most of the women in the group were there for all the technical and non-technical matters, while the men were saying 'I'm going to write', 'I'm going to speak' ... it looked like they concerened themselves with theory and speaking much more often than women ... When it comes to discussions at the meetings, they were mostly dominated by men ... I'm not saying that men didn't do practical things altogether, but somehow there was a division of labour which was clearly marked by gender ... as time went by these issues became more serious. (Personal communication, December 2020)

The interviewees who either participated in or followed the development of the group state that members were aware of the recurrently emerging sexist attitudes but that there was never enough readiness to address them in a more resolute fashion:

most of the time feminist topics remained in the background even when serious things were at stake ... they were not really handled ... not that the group didn't work on sexism ... they just never worked thoroughly, they were mostly interested in preventing some overt incidents, but the power relationships remained intact ... something would get resolved along the way, but was not part of the 'central program' so to say ... things were criticized throughout the year and it constantly looked like efforts were made to overcome them, but new problems arose again and again ... we had several men in the group who showed critical behaviours over the years, one of them was expelled, but a statement about it was never published ... it seemed that if we worked hard enough, we could overcome the problems, at least to a certain extent, at least some of them ... however, things remained pretty much the same and new issues kept appearing that were toxic. (Personal communication, December 2019)

TERFism

Given its interest in LGBT politics, the collective followed the development of LGBT activism in the country, especially in the most contentious moments surrounding the organisation of Pride parades. As its objective was to see how LGBT mobilisations could acquire a stronger leftist/class dimension, in 2015 – a few years before the transphobic wave – it published two texts by the trans activist Sonja Sajzor. As one of my interviewees stated:

> M21 was the only leftist group where there were more people who were not straight … some came out as trans after leaving the group though … M21 was actively following what was happening at Pride and participated here and there in some smaller actions … there was always an idea that we needed a queer organisation on the left, but it was never really encouraged … I remember that there was a debate before one pride and that we concluded that it should have some form of leftist protest … Because of that in 2015 we asked Sonja Sajzor to publish some of her texts that criticized the way in which Pride was organized … this was possible because the position of the group towards the trans question was different back then. (Personal communication, December 2020)

However, as the collective was increasingly plagued by patriarchal patterns that threatened to divide it, the intensification of trans activism and the accompanying TERF[5] narrative over the last few years were perceived by some members as an opportunity to strengthen the feminist course. TERFism offered a straightforward argument that allowed many members of the group not only to circumvent complex gender-related debates but also to present themselves as people who have women's emancipation at heart. In the words of one interviewee:

> TERFism appeared as a way of marginalising the sexism problem, of covering it up … Regardless of one particularly vocal woman, the primary source of transphobia were indeed men … it looked like they adopted the TERF argumentation because it turned out easier for them to deal with feminism in such a way … They make use of radical feminism as an alternative to thoroughly dealing with feminism … this has to do with the fact that through TERF they started drawing some parallels between sex and class, so they tried to push the complexity of gender issues into their readings of classical Marxism. But, none of them is really familiar with the topic to the point of being able to talk about it meaningfully … it is easier for them to simply not enter into it … truth be told, their interpretation is correct in certain aspects, but the problem is far more complicated … they neglect the part that does

not fit into the story they are insisting on. (Personal communication, December 2019)

More specifically, while trans-exclusionary sentiment started taking root in the collective in the spring of 2018, the speed with which it spread among the membership was surprising for many of my interviewees. In an attempt to account for it, one of them associates this profound change in the politics of the group with the idea that transphobia began to be promoted by the most prominent members:

In the summer of 2018 we had a congress where trans was not a topic at all … what was a topic was our code[6] of conduct and I participated in its writing … ironically, that code still exists on their website and speaks about LGBTQ people … in the meantime, they changed their attitudes, changed their practice, and left the code there … I couldn't explain it to myself for a long time after leaving the group … I thought if we gathered on the left because we thought people were equal regardless of sex, gender, religion, etc … how then can you advocate a practice that is completely inconsistent with that, how can you not see that what you are doing directly endangers people's lives, and the struggle you say you stand for … Later on, I thought that there was a pressure from the loudest people within the group who started sharing a bunch of problematic texts, so it was easy for such beliefs to gain ground … In the beginning, those people who held TERF views were not numerous, but the thing is that they were more experienced and, so to say, senior activists … even if you don't look at them in such a way that you believe every word they say, you do, nevertheless, tend to perceive them as role models. (Personal communication, December 2020)

In this process, the position of the informal leader of the collective was particularly important as he himself started employing trans-exclusionary rhetoric to divert attention away from the mounting sexism accusations. Once friends with the abovementioned Sonja Sajzor and quite favourable to the improvement of trans people's social status, he went through a striking political transformation in an effort to preserve his feminist reputation.

[H]e slowly started losing legitimacy because of the way he treated women both in and out of the group … in the beginning he was actually quite supportive of the trans cause … he did not agree with his girlfriend at the time who was TERF but as time went by and as he was facing more and more criticism, he was slowly switching to the other side … he found support among some TERF women and continued acting as a great feminist, he was proud of what a feminist he was ... so, at one point he came to the position of the most criticized man within the organisation and took over the TERF narrative to become the greatest feminist again, a 'protector of women' ... he played a knight on a white horse for some women within the organisation ... during one period he constantly threw out posts on trans topics, it was a complete obsession ... he adopted TERFism at the moment when he thought it would suit him ... one could see that as his position within the organisation weakened, his TERFism argument became more pronounced. (Personal communication, December 2020)

Such a strategic choice of the group's leader had a long-lasting effect on the collective's membership cementing its trans-exclusionary perspective and rendering it rather impermeable to trans knowledge and lived experience.

At the moment when he started being openly TERF, the collective still did not have a clear stance ... apart from two more visible male members who held those positions and one or two radical feminists, the majority of the membership was still closer to a pro-trans orientation ... then he decided single-handedly to attend an event where the status of trans women was discussed ... there he expressed a TERF stance disregarding the collective, criticising the panellists ... and he was just one step away from an expulsion already at that point ... I thought the organisation would use that occasion to put a cap on such behaviour and part ways with that patriarchal praxis ... I remember having a strong impression that if they do not throw him out, the whole group will go into that story ... and that's exactly what happened ... some more TERF people joined, even those who used to say 'we are not sufficiently informed' ... even those with whom I was on good terms never asked me for any source or conversation to get information about trans issues ... an echo chamber had already been formed ... a very typical story in which they covered up their internal problems by finding an external enemy – trans women. (Personal communication, December 2020)

Although the leader and one of the founders of the collective managed to garner support around trans hostility, that was not sufficient to keep it together. In August 2020 he was expelled and left the collective along with five other members. The official statement read that 'his very personal approach in the more recent phases of the M21 development turned out to be an obstacle for further growth and effective political work of the organisation' (M21, 2020, online). One of my interviewees makes this more explicit:

The fissure that recently happened within the group does not have anything to do with transphobia, because both sides are transphobic … but it does have to do with sexism … the person who used to be recognized as the leader expressed so much sexism that it was too much even for them to swallow … there were privileges with speaking, with taking space … some macho moments, even physical threats … they were really always ready to defend him publicly, but just too many things accumulated. (Personal communication, December 2020)

Uncritical translations

The issue regarding the status of the trans population could not have acquired such an affective charge without being nourished by information from a space in which it had a much stronger polarisation potential. In this regard, it is relevant that M21 was associated with the UK-based Socialist Workers' Party since its earliest years. The collective thus had a first-hand view of the topics discussed at the British Left.[7] In the words of one (former) activist:

M21 is so British-oriented that British sources were followed more than our local ones … as a matter of fact, those sources framed the way in which the group later approached the trans question … M21 had links with the UK Socialist Workers' Party, a part of the International Socialist Tendency which has its strongest presence in Britain … Towards the end of 2012, we decided to secede as a crisis arose in the Socialist Workers' Party over allegations of rape … I know that we then decided to cut our links with them and made a special issue about it … at that point some members turned more towards *Counterfire*, another leftist organisation from Britain. (Personal communication, December 2020)

Given that there was no particularly visible pro-trans activist mobilisation or a debate regarding trans persons in the Serbian media, the M21's transphobic discourse was mostly imported from the British and wider Anglo-Saxon context through their links with the British leftist scene. As one trans activist states:

pretty much all of their examples come from the UK and have almost nothing to do with our own situation here … in their recent letter of protest on the occasion of the screening of the movie *Little Girl*, they talk about a BBC Newsnight report, discuss the operation of the NHS …[8] in his presentation at the conference *Feminism and the Left* that took place in Belgrade in November 2019, the leader of the group disregarded the local context and talked about the Vancouver Rape

Relief Centre, the British organisation *Mermaids*, and relied upon the New Zealand-based author Renee Gerlich ...[9] even the name of that recently launched offshoot initiative *Gay and Lesbian Solidarity Network* is supposed to be reminiscent of the support given by lesbians and gays to the British miners in 1984 and 1985 ... on their page they talk about the case of Keira Bell from Cambridge who decided to detransition ... it looks like they are now a part of the alleged *LGBInternational* that is based in England. (Personal communication, December 2020)

The influence that the British trans debate has on the way in which M21 articulates the issue and imports it into the local political milieu is also strengthened by the fact that one of the most prominent members and a co-founder of the collective lives in the UK. In the words of one interviewee:

> he started that story quite subtly, mostly through individual conversations ... I remember I was sitting with him at one point and he started talking about the 'toilet argument' or whatever ... I remember there being a nasty comment ... I then underlined that I could not speak on behalf of England, because first, it was sure that he had much more information than me, but second, and more importantly, I thought we could not simply compare Britain and Serbia as these are completely different levels of marginalisation of the trans population ... let alone could one just copy and paste such things ... it looked absurd to me to equate those scales given that we are here at a miserably low level of political organisation or any kind of solidarity and support. (Personal communication, December 2020)

Conclusion

In this chapter I have engaged with the question as to how it is possible that in an inimical social climate of unbridled corruption, pervasive poverty, and a constant threat of fascist incursions in public life, an allegedly leftist collective launches a war against trans people, and especially trans women, as one of the most marginalised social groups. I have positioned the recent upsurge in anti-trans sentiment in a longer-term analytical framework pointing towards resilient patriarco-colonial currents that were present also within *Praxis*, an internationally known instance of Yugoslav/Serbian leftist organising. I have argued that trans hostility that nowadays hails from the Marxist activist group M21 and its offshoot organisation LGSM has at least two intertwined dimensions: first, it appears as a strategy that helps the prominent male members of the collective to preserve their ever more fragile feminist reputation; second, it arises as a result of patriarco-colonial entanglements produced through an uncritical translation of TERF attitudes ('just copy and paste', as quoted above) from the middle-class-oriented British feminist and leftist engagement.

More specifically, *Praxis*, which operated in the context of state socialism with a relatively marginal feminist mobilisation, was more openly patriarchal having, in spite of all of its progressive theorising, a (White) *Western man* in the centre of its *Weltanschauung* (Karkov and Valiavicharska, 2018). On the other hand, in much more unfavourable capitalist circumstances, marked by political correctness within which liberal feminist claims cannot be easily ignored, M21's argumentation revolves around a (White) *Western woman* whose painfully won rights are to be protected from the purportedly omnipresent threat of trans incursion. Inheriting pervasive sexism (further amplified throughout the 1990s) from some of their Yugoslav predecessors, the most prominent M21 members take recourse to transphobic stances in order to divert attention from its recurrent eruptions and present themselves, instead, as guardians of the feminist cause. In such a way, transphobia is employed as a patriarchal instrument that sacrifices a highly marginalised group of people for the sake of demonstrating one's supposed commitment to women's emancipation.

The fact that Yugoslav/Serbian Marxist 'humanism' has championed both Western *White man* (*Praxis*, Karkov and Valiavicharska, 2018) and *White woman* (M21) in their sex-based, patriarchal representations, testifies to its distinctly heteronormative (*Praxis*) and increasingly also homonormative (M21) character. The hardships of supporting gender and sexual subjectivity that would go beyond binary oppositions immersed in power differentials is reflective of the tenacity with which this kind of activist engagement has resisted any substantial and politically relevant queer permeation. *Woman* is here a subject of those feminist strands that reify the gender binary and construct her primarily as a victim who should be vigilant of her painfully won rights (Vilenca, 2019). In this regard, M21's trans hostility, rather than helping them achieve their declared objectives, uncovers the counter-revolutionary nature of the post-Yugoslav 'transition', which keeps the region in the 'second feminist wave': the *woman* at the centre of the collective today is not a supposedly universal, biologically based reality but precisely the *political subject* that could have figured more prominently (or at least more synergically) in the operation of *Praxis* almost five decades ago.

That an allegedly leftist collective has found itself advocating in favour of a rigid gender distinction in 2020 shows the extent to which the Serbian Left has been in the meantime embraced by imperio-capitalist expansionism that put an end to the socialist world. By adopting such an approach M21 is not only out of sync with the most progressive currents of transnational gender emancipation, but it is also missing an opportunity to build upon the legacy of Yugoslav socialism, which tried to destabilise the gender binary through (at least) constitutionally equalising the political, social, and economic status of men and women, an issue that many capitalist countries still struggle with today. Neoliberal capitalist domination in the Yugoslav space has been over the last decades accompanied by strong repatriarchalisation processes that have hardened the line between 'men' and 'women' and worked towards entrenching traditional gender roles. This would not have happened had a reified gender binary not been essential for the way in which capitalism organises division of labour in the postsocialist semi-periphery (Blagojević, 2009): it strives to reduce labour costs by systematically reproducing patriarchy and downgrading the rights of workers, women, and especially trans people who have a hard time joining the labour force (Gonan and Gonan, 2018; Jandrić, 2018).

Therefore, the post-Cold War incorporation of Serbia and the wider Yugoslav region in global geographies of neocolonial capitalism, which has occurred at enormous social costs, has implications for the organisation of leftist collectives. Deprived of its vocabulary through racist/nationalist 'socialists', the Serbian Left has been wounded by prolonged international isolation, erasures of socialist feminist knowledge, and a general impoverishment of intellectual potentialities brought about by a systematic destruction of scientific standards (Blagojević, 2009). Actively dispersed and purged of emancipatory substance, the Left has become increasingly exposed to the risks of 'uncritically' importing Western feminist debates. In the absence of a socialist-feminist 'critical mass' that would constructively 'translate' them (Clarke et al, 2015), such imports are given free rein to hybridise with local patriarchal traditions in a way that produces significant political-personal damage. Through this process, M21 is not only complicit in – rather than resistant to – the neocolonial logic that peripheralises and impoverishes the region, but it offers a 'preemptive' conservative response to the imagined trans menace that is, according to them, expected to emerge in the years to come. Thus, the collective's transphobic sentiment shows how backlash is not to be understood as a development that merely gives precedence to (once defeated) conservative elements, but rather as a force that envelops the entire political field enabling surprising alliances[10] and shifting the perimeters of political struggle towards the right.

With this in mind, this text points to one dimension of an affective reconfiguration that has been taking place after the wars of the Yugoslav succession which were supposedly waged in the name of the Yugoslav constitutive nations' desire to live in their *own* (nation-)states. While such state-building processes continue to serve as sources of tension, the ethnic fragmentation of the Yugoslav space has made the hostility 'reserved' for *ethnic others* retreat in front of intolerance of *sexual and gender others* (Bilić and Radoman, 2019; Bilić, 2016, 2020). For example, Bosnia and Herzegovina, where ethnic belonging figures as a major criterion of political life, witnessed its first Pride parade only in 2019, whereas such events have unfolded in the much more ethnically homogenous Slovenia from 2001. This shows the capacity of ethnic issues to seize the political agenda and override, degrade, or dismiss any (trans)gender- and (non-hetero-)sexuality-related grievance. However, once the 'ethnically different' enemy is held 'in check', non-normative genders and sexualities are moved into the foreground of conservative politics. Divisory lines get to be redrawn *within* national communities not only enabling certain segments of both the left and the right to converge around an attempt to re-establish the patriarchal gender norm on essentialist grounds but also changing the frontiers of transregional alliances along new ruptures.

Such processes, embedded in highly polarising and affectively charged circumstances of regional politics, unfold in the atmosphere of rapidly growing trans knowledge. In spite of the fact that Belgrade is internationally recognised for gender confirmation surgeries (Nord, 2019) and therefore a site in which medical expertise about trans bodies has accumulated over the last decades, the social and political aspects of the ongoing 'trans revolution' are to a great extent still a *terra incognita* in the post-Yugoslav space. However, leftist groups have not so far framed trans-related issues as a domain of intersectionally sensitive *learning* that could benefit from an embodied trans experience and appreciate how 'race', class, gender, and sexuality interact within a constraining neocolonial arrangement of their own social context. The 'preemptive' hegemony of the Anglo-Saxon narrative of 'trans threat' forecloses discursive spaces and obstructs a linguistic evolution that would more precisely voice local lives and let them into the public space on an equal footing. One possible way of allowing this new 'language' to appear would be to diverge 'from conventional Western modes of knowing' (Escobar, 1995, p 216) towards the more pluralist, decolonial conceptions of the human offered by Black feminism and the Global South (Karkov, 2015). If it was hard for *Praxis*, coming from one of the centres of the Non-Aligned Movement to establish discursive links with that emancipatory legacy, the endeavour is both harder and more necessary for contemporary leftist organising that occurs in the world stripped of any meaningful socialist 'dams' to neocolonial/ capitalist expansion. Both *Praxis* and M21 can serve as a warning about how an intrusion of racist thinking into supposedly leftist circles can make emancipatory struggles degenerate into oppression and dehumanisation.

Finally, an account that juxtaposes two Marxist initiatives from two quite different time periods – Yugoslav socialism and post-Yugoslav/ Serbian neoliberal capitalism – cannot do justice to the full scope of recent transphobic mobilisations. Although they are hard to disentangle due to overlapping membership, regional leftist and feminist/women's/lesbian organisations have their own developmental routes and the hostility that some may be showing towards trans and gender non-binary persons may be emanating from them for ideologically different but complementary reasons (see, for example, Bakić, 2020). A more detailed look should be taken at the dynamics through which parts of regional feminist organising have been abandoning their socialist heritage in recent years and hardening the line between men and women. For example, the 2015 Belgrade Lesbian March organisers insisted that it be a *women-only* event explicitly excluding men from participation in a protest unfolding in *public* space (Bilić, 2020). Such a strategic choice, similar to the Marxist predicaments outlined above, points to the combined effect of capitalism and repatriarchalisation: it reifies the gender binary through reproducing the patriarchal pattern of exclusion and sharing the capitalist desire to privatise the common good. While trans liberation is still to face challenges in the forthcoming decade, it can hardly gain the upper hand as long as discriminatory attitudes towards women, men, and other genders stem from those who should act as its major proponents.

Notes

[1] LGSM was founded in Belgrade in September 2020 by lesbian and gay members of M21. It has recently concentrated its activities on helping gay, lesbian, and bisexual people who face the threat of homelessness and/or violence. The 'manifesto' of the initiative is available online here: https://lgsolidarnamreza.org/about/

[2] I use 'trans' as an abbreviation of 'transgender' and an umbrella term referring to people whose gender identity or expression differs from the one assigned at birth. In addition to trans men and trans women, this term includes those who are non-binary or genderqueer.

[3] While 'TERF' is widely used by trans supporters, it is perceived as a misogynist offence by trans-exclusionary activists.

[4] Similarly, Baker (2018, p 111) argues that Yugoslavia's identification with the global anti-colonial struggle was often 'race-blind', whereas Subotić and Vučetić (2019) claim that although declaratively anti-colonialist, the Yugoslav socialist regime did not sufficiently appreciate the racialised structure of global society.

[5] The term 'TERF' has also been imported into the Serbian language along with the wider trans-related debates and is now commonly used by trans activists and their supporters. On the other hand, similarly to other members of their international network, M21 and LGSM activists consider that word problematic and point to its local pejorative versions, namely *terfulja* and *terfača*.

[6] Available online here: https://marks21.info/kodeks-ponasanja/

[7] Some British anti-trans feminists have backgrounds in the social history of working-class women and the labour movement. See, for example, the controversy surrounding the historian Selina Todd (Woolcock, 2020).

[8] Available online here: https://marks21.info/otvoreno-pismo-festivalu-slobodna-zona-povodom-prikazivanja-dokumentarnog-filma-mala-devojcica-stop-transovanju-dece/

[9] Available online here: http://theinnerscar.blogspot.com/2019/11/feminizam-i-levica-panel-rod-i-pol.html

[10] In this regard, one could take a look at the polemics that developed around an issue (vol. LV, no. 3) of the sociological journal *Sociološki pregled*, which under the guise of scientific freedom brought a series of highly problematic, both homo- (for example, Šuvaković, 2021) and trans-phobic (Vuković, 2021), 'contributions' to the current (homo)sexuality and (trans)gender-related debate in the Serbian public sphere. This issue (also in English available here: http://www.socioloskipregled.org.rs/2021/10/25/socioloski-pregled-vol-lv-2021-no-3/) stimulated 'one part of the Serbian sociological community' to organise a

petition in support of same-sex partnerships and LGBT people, more generally. In their reaction to the petition (available here: https://lgsolidarnamreza.org/2021/11/02/odgo vor-socioloskoj-i-naucnoj-zajednici/), LGSM restricted itself to disagreeing with certain homophobic claims including Šuvaković's (2021, p 747) idea that same-sex unions 'have no social function except for satisfying their own [that is, lesbian and gay people's, BB] sexual needs'. While failing to problematise the transphobic sentiment of the issue, LGSM called upon an open exchange of empirically substantiated findings as if this were a matter of course in a profoundly polarised society.

References

Akintola H.E. (2017) Britain can't just reverse the homophobia it exported during the empire. Retrieved on 29 September 2021 from www.theguard ian.com/commentisfree/2017/jul/28/britain-reverse-homophobia-emp ire-criminlisation-homosexuality-colonies

Baker, C. (2018) *Race and the Yugoslav region: Postsocialist, post-conflict, postcolonial?* Manchester: University Press.

Bakić, A. (2020) TERF: Radikalna desnica u feminističkom ruhu. Retrieved on 29 September 2021 from https://voxfeminae.net/pravednost/terf-radika lna-desnica-u-feministickom-ruhu/

Bettcher, T.M. (2006) Understanding transphobia: Authenticity and sexual violence. In K. Scott-Dixon (ed) *Transforming feminisms: Transfeminist voices speak out* (pp 203–10). Toronto: Sumach Press.

Bilić, B. (ed) (2016) *LGBT activism and Europeanisation in the post-Yugoslav space.* London: Palgrave Macmillan.

Bilić, B. (2020) *Trauma, violence, and lesbian agency in Croatia and Serbia: Building better times.* London: Palgrave Macmillan.

Bilić, B. and Radoman, M. (eds) (2019) *Sisterhood and unity: Lesbian activism in the (post-)Yugoslav space.* London: Palgrave Macmillan.

Blagojević, M. (2009) *Knowledge production at the semiperiphery: A gender perspective.* Belgrade: Institut za kriminološka i sociološka istraživanja.

Bonfiglioli, C. (2008) Belgrade 1978 remembering the conference 'Drugarica zena. Zensko pitanje – novi pristup?' 'Comrade woman. The women's question: A new approach?' Thirty years after. [Unpublished master's thesis]. University of Utrecht.

Clarke, J., Bainton, D., Lendvai, N., and Stubbs, P. (2015) *Making policy move: Towards a politics of translation and assemblage.* Bristol: Policy Press.

Escobar, A. (1995) *Encountering development.* Princeton: Princeton University Press.

Fuchs, C. (2017) The Praxis school Marxist humanism and Mihailo Marković's theory of communication. *Critique: Journal of Socialist Theory,* 45(1–2), 159–82.

Gonan, L. and Gonan, M. (2018) Transfobija i ljevica. Retrieved on 29 September 2021 from http://slobodnifilozofski.com/2018/12/transfob ija-i-ljevica.html

Hall, S. (1997) The spectacle of the 'other'. In S. Hall (ed) *Representation: Cultural representations and signifying practices*. Milton Keynes: The Open University.

Hasenbush, A., Flores, A.R., and Herman, J.L. (2019) Gender identity nondiscrimination laws in public accommodations: A review of evidence regarding safety and privacy in public restrooms, locker rooms, and changing rooms. *Sexuality Research and Social Policy*, *16*(1), 70–83.

Jacques, J. (2020) Transphobia is everywhere in Britain. *The New York Times*. Retrieved on 29 September 2021 from www.nytimes.com/2020/03/09/opinion/britain-transphobia-labour-party.html

Jakšić, B. (2011) Nacionalističke kritike *Praxisa*. *Filozofija i društvo*, *22*(2), 77–104.

Jandrić, I. (2018) Institucionalni patrijarhat kao zakonitost kapitalizma. Retrieved on 29 September 2021 from http://slobodnifilozofski.com/2018/12/institucionalni-patrijarhat-zakonitost.html

Karkov, N.R. (2015) Decolonizing *Praxis* in Eastern Europe: Towards a south-to-south dialogue. *Comparative & Continental Philosophy*, 7(2), 180–200.

Karkov, N.R. and Valiavicharska, Z. (2018) Rethinking East-European socialism: Notes toward an anti-capitalist decolonial methodology. *Interventions: International Journal of Postcolonial Studies*, *20*(6), 785–813.

Kearns, M. (2018) TERF wars. *National Review*, 25–6.

Lewis, S. (2019) How British feminism became anti-trans. *New York Times*. Retrieved on 29 September 2021 from www.nytimes.com/2019/02/07/opinion/terf-trans-women-britain.html

Lóránd, Z. (2018) *The feminist challenge to the socialist state in Yugoslavia*. London: Palgrave Macmillan.

Marković, M. (1976) Marxist philosophy in Yugoslavia: The *Praxis* group. *Marxism and Religion in Eastern Europe*, 63–89.

Marks21. (2020) Izveštaj s osmog kongresa. Retrieved on 29 September 2021 from https://marks21.info/izvestaj-s-osmog-kongresa-marks21/

Marks21. (n.d./a) O nama. Retrieved on 29 September 2021 from https://marks21.info/o-nama/

Marks21. (n.d./b) Kodeks ponašanja. Retrieved on 29 September 2021 from https://marks21.info/kodeks-ponasanja/

McClintock, A. (2013) *Imperial leather: Race, gender and sexuality in the colonial conquest*. London: Routledge.

Nord, I. (2019) Routes to gender-affirming surgeries: Navigation and negotiation in times of biomedicalization. In G. Griffin and M. Jordal (eds) *Body, migration, re/constructive surgeries* (pp 209–24). London and New York: Routledge.

Paisley, D. (2020) LGB Alliance. Retrieved on 29 September 2021 from https://twitter.com/davidpaisley/status/1330480707043471360?s=25&fbc lid=IwAR2rBA7MCRNVNdAfVZFSWOgjFdpRqIBq-7om9-7c69iy WbRi8twycYB3ISI

Pearce, R., Erikainen, S., and Vincent, B. (2020) TERF wars: An introduction. *The Sociological Review Monographs*, *68*(4), 677–98.

Praxis.memory of the world. (n.d.) Učesnici Korčulanske ljetnje škole – popis. Retrieved on 29 September 2021 from https://praxis.memoryoft heworld.org/#/book/3c821ef4-1336-42d0-a846-f21d650d71bc

Pride in London. (2018) Statement from Pride in London regarding the 2018 protest group. Retrieved on 29 September 2021 from https://pridei nlondon.org/news-and-views/statement-from-pride-in-london-regard ing-the-2018-protest-group/

Stubbs, P. (2020) Socialist Yugoslavia, the Global South and the non-aligned movement: the limits of Yugocentrism. Retrieved on 29 September 2021 from https://www.youtube.com/watch?v=s94vaVINHoA&list=UUwM 2JKE3w1-sv-3pqaHheKw

Subotić, J. and Vučetić, S. (2019) Performing solidarity: Whiteness and status-seeking in the non-aligned world. *Journal of International Relations and Development*, *22*(5), 722–43.

Šuvaković, U. (2021) A contribution to the debate about social recognition of marriage-like and family-like social phenomena. *Sociološki pregled*, *55*(3), 731–50.

Vilenica, A. (2019) Tri pravca rodnog abolicionizma. Retrieved on 29 September 2021 from https://www.bilten.org/?p=28496

Vodovnik, Ž. (2012) Democracy as a verb: Meditations on the Yugoslav Praxis philosophy. *Journal of Balkan and Near Eastern Studies*, *14*(4), 433–52.

Vuković, A. (2021) Circulus vitiosus of the sex/gender dichotomy: Feminist polemics with trans activism. *Sociološki pregled*, *55*(3), 660–70.

Woolcock, N. (2020) Selina Todd: Feminism professor in trans row defended by free-speech activists. *The Times*. Retrieved on 30 December 2021 from https://www.thetimes.co.uk/article/professor-selina-todd-barred-from-event-celebrating-womens-lib-is-backed-by-free-speech-campa ign-7r98m5j9p

PART III

Culture

7

Trans artivism in the post-Yugoslav space: resistance and inclusion strategies in action

Aleksa Milanović

My first appearance with members and allies of the trans community in a street protest happened after a whole decade of my activist engagement in the regional trans community. Before that, I participated in numerous anti-fascist and LGBT protests in Belgrade, but this was my first participation in a street action organised by the local trans community to step out and gain visibility in public space as well as to fight for the rights of trans, intersex, and gender-variant people (TIGV). My involvement in this particular action was motivated, first, by the desire for the Serbian trans community to experience this type of activism, and, second, by my wish to analyse it for the purposes of this text. Almost six months before this event I wrote an abstract for this chapter announcing that I would write about trans artivism as a form of social intervention in the post-Yugoslav space. I was interested in writing about one specific event – a street performance named *Masks*, which at that time had already been performed twice in Montenegro and once in Croatia. I realised that it would be useful for my research to suggest organisation of the same performance in Serbia given that I could take part in it both as a participant and a researcher. When I came up with that idea at a meeting of the trans self-support group, the group coordinators told me that they had already considered performing such an action to mark the Trans Day of Remembrance. The members of the group were enthusiastic about the initiative and the performance took place on 20 November 2019.

On that day, the activists held banners with one side coloured in black and the other in white. The text on the black surface indicated a problem that trans people face due to transphobia while the text on the white surface carried a positive and affirmative message of resistance to transphobia. The scenario for this performance implied that each activist was to take one banner and mask, then all of them were to form a circle in a public space and hold a negative message for 30 minutes, after that they were to take off masks and turn the banner to hold a positive message for the next 30 minutes (taking the mask off is not mandatory, and people who are not comfortable with doing that are allowed to keep it). Unfortunately, I was unable to be part of the whole process of preparing that event, but I was there as a participant on the day of the performance. When I got there I chose the banner that suited me, and I stood in the circle with other people. This was the fourth edition of *Masks* in 12 months, in three different countries and with the involvement of three different activist groups. Those four events differed from each other in various ways, but regardless of that, they pointed to the connection between trans communities in the post-Yugoslav space, which could be seen as a shared artivist space. That connection constitutes a great advantage, which could be used for achieving local activist goals, but in order to use the full potential of this connection, the TIGV communities in the mentioned shared space should be organised along similar lines.

In this chapter I discuss the possibilities of taking over the representation of trans and gender variant persons by the trans and gender variant persons themselves and their communities. To do that I focus on a recent example of the performance *Masks* and engage with the ways in which art is used as an activist tool across trans communities in the post-Yugoslav space. My argument is twofold: first, I claim that artivism is a powerful way for the TIGV community to achieve self-representation and be recognised and visible in the public space and the media; second, I show that artivism can serve as a form of social action with a potential to enable and support social and political mechanisms of change. In this regard, I argue that the TIGV community has to achieve a certain level of structural development if its artivist events are to exert a social impact.

Art and activism

Representation of social phenomena often stands out as one of the most important functions of art. Thinking about the relationship between art and trans and gender variant identities, one needs to engage with the politics of representation, that is, the ways in which trans and gender variant persons are represented (or not represented at all) in different arts. Within art as a field of representation, the concept of gender is construed and developed as a specific phenomenon and due to the influence of norms some gender identities are revealed, presented, thematised, and intensively represented, while some are left aside or moved to the field of the marginal Other. Gender identities or expressions designated as Other are most frequently represented as deviant, dangerous, absurd, awkward, tragic, or funny (Uzel, 2014). We should be aware of the significance and the power that such representations have because those who are in a position to represent exercise power over their (passive) objects of representation. Therefore, trans and gender variant people should not stay in the passive position. In order to change this position, we have to take over and use representation as active agents. 'Put simply, if we do not attend to representation and work collectively to bring new visual grammars into existence (while remembering and unearthing suppressed one), then we will remain caught in the traps of the past' (Gosset, Stanley, and Burton, 2017, p xviii). So, if we take into account the fact that art can be a powerful political tool, taking over representation and its use in activism lead us to another important function of art, namely social change.

The appearance of trans people in public discourse in the post-Yugoslav space comes down to sporadic media appearances of individuals in interviews, which means that the visibility of our community is quite limited. Besides that, media representations of trans people and media articles about trans topics are mostly sensationalist and limited to stories connected to medical procedures, personal struggle with gender identity, local cases of violence towards TIGV people, and world news from tabloids about TIGV people. The language that reporters use in their articles about TIGV people is mostly offensive and pathologising. In order to change that, some activist organisations created and published manuals for reporting on TIGV topics and shared it with the local media so they can familiarise themselves with acceptable terminology (Gayten-LGBT, 2016; Asocijacija Spektra, 2019; Trans Aid, 2019). But even if media reporters read and implement some of those suggestions, the question remains as to which stories and issues the media will report. If they continue to report about the same stories as before, then our community will perhaps be represented with improved terminology but in the same context. One of the possible solutions to this problem is the production of stories through various activist events and actions. This means increased visibility, creating opportunities for the emergence of a different kind of representation and at the same time inclusion of TIGV people as subjects instead of objects of local news.

The performance *Masks* was one of those occasions through which people from the local TIGV community could access the media, increase visibility, and represent themselves in a public space. It is also a story about how art can be put in the service of activism and how different outcomes could emerge depending on the way the community was engaged, involved, and invested in this story. People who created and performed this performance were not professional artists – instead, they were amateurs not interested in creating an artwork but in achieving their goals with an artwork. They appeared in a public space in order to perform a political rather than an artistic act.

One of the possible forms of activist reaction and political action are artistic practices that perform a critique of everyday life and problematise social reality. Such artistic practices are one possible form of resistance to the dominant discourse of power, and they usually occur as an effect wherever power emerges. Thus, similarly to activism, art can also be focused on different types of analysis, problematisation, and re-examination of everyday life and social problems, or on performing an intervention in a particular social space. However, if one considers social functions that these artistic practices perform, one can see the differences between them. American art critic and activist Lucy Lippard (1984) made a distinction between political art and activist art, and that distinction is based on the tendencies of artistic activity. She defined political art as an artistic activity that deals with social topics but only at the level of analysis and criticism, while activist art, in addition to analysis and criticism, tends to be directly involved in the topics it deals with by intervening in order to bring or initiate social change. This means that activist art goes beyond the framework of political art and enters the sphere of active political engagement (Aladro Vico et al, 2018). Therefore, if artists perceive and create their artwork as a means of achieving political and social change, that practice could be defined as a specific hybrid form of artistic socio-political engagement known as *artivism*.[1] It is important to note that artivism should not be perceived as a new type of artistic practice or a new form of artistic expression but as a new type of political action and a new method of advocacy (Novović, 2021). Artivsm is therefore a political strategy that could be implemented through informal education of artists in order to stimulate their interest in socio-political problems or through empowering and encouraging people from marginalised social groups to engage in artistic work that would reflect the state of a given community and increase its visibility.

Trans artivism

Stephen Duncombe (2016), one of the founders of the Centre for Artistic Activism in New York, identified the main goals of artivism, which almost entirely coincide with the general aims of TIGV activism in our region. In order to point out their primary functions, I will sort these complementary aims on the basis of their main orientation, namely the one toward community or the public. Community-oriented goals include community building, inviting participation, providing useful tools, encouraging experimentation, and inspiring visions of a better world. Public-oriented goals include fostering dialogue, raising awareness, and altering perceptions about important issues. They also include disrupting the dominant and general opinions and views, making cultural shifts, and impacting and making immediate and long-term cultural and structural changes. There are two goals on Duncombe's list that I define as equally oriented to community and the public. They include making space for creative work and transforming the environment and experience.

The first group, that is, community-oriented goals, implies communication within the community and focuses on community members and their wellbeing, needs, and empowerment. Due to the high level of transphobia in the post-Yugoslav countries and the fact that TIGV communities are relatively young,[2] community building is among the most important activist aims. Accordingly, artivist work, which implies joint activities to get to know each other better, socialising, peer support, education, and empowerment, are essential for local communities. Since most trans people in this region are eager to enter the medical process of transition, many of them, after they finish all medical procedures, leave the community and blend in with the general population (Zulević, 2012). Due to such tendencies, it is crucial to motivate people to keep connections with the community and do any activist work to widen the community and empower young and new community members.

The second group, that is, the public-oriented goals, focuses on communication between the community and the public. That communication aims to inform the general population about TIGV-related issues, initiate a conversation with others to raise awareness, break stereotypes and prejudices about TIGV people and our community, and start a conversation that will challenge general social attitudes on this issue. Most of the communication with people outside the community is done by representatives of non-governmental organisations through advocacy and lobbying. They speak on behalf of the whole community in front of government institutions and media, so they are often the only ones who can be heard. If the community is detached or insufficiently connected with people who work for those NGOs they cannot adequately inform and influence others to change policies, legislations, and public opinion. This is how artivism can contribute to developing different approaches of addressing issues and creating opportunities for community members to speak for themselves.

The remaining two goals that I mentioned above are applied to safe space and public space issues. The exclusion of TIGV people from domains of public life is directly connected to transphobia. To solve this problem and gain the right to be visible in public space, we have to be empowered as individuals and as a community. Creating a safe space for dialogue with people outside the community is the first step. It could be a gallery or cultural centre where TIGV people could exhibit their works to the general public and meet people interested in seeing those works and talking with authors. The second step could be going out in open public spaces, like streets and public squares in urban areas where the TIGV community could encounter casual passers-by. 'A need for visibility as well as the rejection to hide one's identity in public space represents direct opposition to mechanisms of disciplinary power and an attempt at remaking the space in order for it to be open and available for everybody' (Milanović, 2017, p 119). Through artivist intervention, the TIGV community could transform and reorganise public space in a political sense and disrupt its homogeneity. Such actions produce a new public discourse by pointing out injustice, discrimination, everyday problems, and life experiences of the TIGV community to their neighbours, fellow citizens, and all the people who share this common public space. These are the main reasons why this type of goal could be perceived as oriented towards the TIGV community who are banned from public space and at the same time towards the broader public.

Before entering a stage where TIGV communities could use art for activist purposes, they must pass through a few formative stages. The first stage is forming a community which implies communication and gathering people who share the same or similar identity positions. In most of the ex-Yugoslav republics that process started with the formation of self-support groups (Hodžić et al, 2016; Milanović, 2020b; Milikj, 2020; Ulićević, 2020). The next stage usually is work on empowerment of the formed community, which eventually should lead to building capacities for activist work. Initially, during self-support group meetings, community members share problems and slowly become involved in finding solutions for everyday problems they cope with within a specific social context. When the community becomes empowered enough, their members decide to publicly announce problems such as discrimination and transphobia to the outside world. One of the ways to do that is through creative activist action, which includes different artistic projects.

Only well-organised and empowered communities manage to come to that stage. Usually, instead of coming to that stage, the local community occasionally gathers around an activist non-governmental organisation. That organisation does all the activist work while most community members stay passive and only use that organisation's services such as self-support groups, workshops, or psycho-social and legal support. The degree of activist engagement of members who belong to a particular community does not depend on how long that community has existed or how many members it has. However, it depends on how that community is organised and how empowered it is. Activist work performed by organisations isolated from the community is generally not oriented toward developing creative and artistic practices that involve community members' teamwork. I argue that this kind of activist work can be important for community members but not in building community or its development, growth, and solidarity among their members.

An example of this can be seen if we compare trans activism in Serbia and Montenegro. The self-support group for trans people in Serbia was founded in 2006 (Vidić and Bilić, this volume), which could be considered as the starting point of trans activism in the country. In Montenegro, the first self-support group was founded in 2013, seven years later than in Serbia. Despite that, the TIGV community in Montenegro is more visible. It has done more creative activities that brought them more visibility through public appearances and media coverage in the last five years (Milanović, 2020a). Three years since its foundation, Association Spektra, as the only organisation in Montenegro that deals specifically with the protection and promotion of the human rights of TIGV people, has tripled its membership, which is involved in strategic decision-making, various actions, and community activities (Ulićević, 2020).

Meanwhile, the TIGV community in Serbia has been incoherent, unorganised, and invisible to the public. Also, only a small number of TIGV people in Serbia are engaged in TIGV activism because there is a lack of motivated community members for activist work. All of this results in the absence of organised social events, safe spaces, workshops, lectures, panel discussions, artivist projects, and other community activities. The lack of these needs and activities prevents the Serbian TIGV community from becoming more empowered, visible, diverse, organised, educated, and capable of taking self-representation into its own hands.

In the following section, I will analyse the *Masks* performance to compare these two communities' development and provide insight into their similarities and differences. The very fact that the same performance was staged in Montenegro, Croatia, and Serbia – in a short period – indicates that the post-Yugoslav space can function as a single activist space. However, the way *Masks* was prepared and performed in Serbia and Montenegro, and the results and outcomes of this activist action in those two countries indicates that their TIGV communities are not at the same development stage and that they have a different structure.

The performance of *Masks* in Montenegro

This performance was designed and presented for the first time in 2018 in Podgorica, capital of Montenegro, by activists from the non-governmental organisation Association Spektra. That was the first public performance and the first public gathering of TIGV people in Podgorica as well as in Montenegro (Ulićević, 2020). In order to explain how they got there, I will briefly present a history of the development of trans activism in Montenegro. Gathering of TIGV people in Montenegro started in the beginning of 2013 when a self-support group for transgender persons was created and operated as a part of the organisation Queer Montenegro. In the beginning, this group had only two members and one of them was the group founder and facilitator, Jovan Ulićević Džoli. During the next two years more people joined the group and at the end of 2015, the group had ten members. Those people decided to create an informal trans activist group and they named it Transians. Two years later, Association Spektra grew out of this informal group and was registered in 2017 as the first trans activist organisation in Montenegro. Spektra was founded by six transgender and non-binary people, and now it has 17 active members, all involved in strategic decision-making, different actions and activities (Ulićević, 2020).

The people gathered around the self-support group and later around the informal group Transians were working on self-empowerment and empowerment, and thanks to that in a few years they were ready to form Association Spektra as a result. The first public action of the trans community in Montenegro was done in 2016 by Transians and this action included making posters with educative and creative messages, which were spread throughout Podgorica. The action was called 'Let's go under the rainbow together', and the main goal of that action was raising visibility by sharing personal messages and stories about TIGV persons. In the same year Transians organised one more visibility action, which included making posters. This time the posters with educative messages were shared not only with the general public but also with various institutions and the academic and scientific public. This action was titled 'Celebrating Human Diversity'. The next level in gaining more visibility for the TIGV community in Montenegro was the public coming out of some members of Spektra and sharing their personal stories with the local media. At that moment they became ready for their first public gathering as a community. In 2018 they decided to mark the Transgender Day of Remembrance with a public performance and for the first time to step out together in public space with the intention of showing 'rebellion against the system that does not recognise their existence' (PR Centar, 2018).

The performance was prepared and staged by the activists of Association Spektra (see Ulićević and Brković, this volume). They bought all the necessary materials for making masks and banners, wrote a scenario, took all precautions in case of incidents, and devised a support system for activists who would stood in the circle with banners on the Podgorica's central square. The masks were hand-made of plaster and gauze rolls applied directly to the face over plastic foil, so the mask's shape was adapted to each participant's face. Masks were made at least a day before the performance. Banners were made from cardboard and painted on both sides. One side was painted in black and there was a 'negative' message on it that is, a short sentence about discrimination or violence towards trans and non-binary people. The other side was white and it carried a 'positive' message that is, encouraging words that were a response to the negative message from the other side of the banner. Here are some examples.

On the black side:
Because of the violence I suffered, I had to drop out of school.
On the white side of the same banner:
Despite everything, I live freely.

On the black side:
From October 2017 to September this year, 368 trans people were killed.
On the white side of the same banner:
Ten living proud trans people are in this square today.

On the black side:
In order to change the sex mark in documents, I had to be sterilized.
On the white side of the same banner:
I stand here proud to be here and to refuse to bow my head.

On the black side:
The guy from my class threw a chair at me.
I did not report him out of fear.
On the white side of the same banner:
Fear will never paralyze me again.

The description of the performance preparations shows that the community had to spend some time working together to design, find, and buy supplies and finally make masks and banners. The concept of this performance implied standing together in a formed circle outside a safe space for one hour and being exposed to the public, which could be unpleasant, even dangerous if there were provocations or assaults. Consequently, actions like this must be designed, organised, and performed by people who share the same values and goals and who get along, encourage, and trust each other. Artivist goals oriented towards the community could be easily accomplished with this kind of joint work on projects such as *Masks*.

As for the social impact, the joint activist intervention in public space certainly impacted casual passers-by, but this activist group also had other strategies for influencing the public. Sharing information and sending invitations on social media platforms, and calling media reporters to be present and report about the event were recognised by activists as the most important impact-related objectives of the performance. It should be noted that at least six online media in Montenegro (*Vijesti*, RTCG, FOS, Dan, Antena M, CdM) published texts about this event, of which one was the Radio and Television of Montenegro public service broadcaster with a national reach. Media reports, which considerably increased the visibility of the trans population, consisted of photos, videos, explanations of this event, and statements that the executive director of Spektra Jovan Ulićević and an activist Hana Konatar gave after the performance. Both of them sent similar messages to the public. They stated that the trans community decided to show that their lives and freedom are the most important, that the trans community was ready to stand up for their rights, and that violence and oppression would not prevent them from showing that they were ready to confront the transphobic pressures (PR Centar, 2018).

Apart from Podgorica, activists of Association Spektra performed *Masks* in another Montenegrian town, Kolašin (see our volume cover). They decided to respond to the violence perpetrated against a trans person in Kolašin, which happened at the end of August 2019. The performance was held on 16 September and the media announced it as the first public gathering of trans people in Kolašin. Most of the media in Montenegro published texts about this event, which included statements of three activists from Association Spektra: Hana Konatar, Marija Jovanović, and Nikola Ilić. This is significant because it indicates the empowerment of new community members who are willing to speak publicly and communicate with the media. Their statements were similar to those from Podgorica. Marija Jovanović pointed out that the primary goal of this performance, and all their activist actions, was to send the message that the trans community existed in Montenegro and it would not give up the fight for their human rights or tolerate the violence. Nikola Ilić stated 'that the citizens of Kolašin were not interested in reading what was written on the banners' and that in Podgorica, 'they had a greater degree of people's attention' (PR Centar, 2019). The same as in Podgorica, the primary strategy for achieving visibility with this performance included calling media reporters. Even some of the most widely read online media in Serbia wrote about this event, focusing on the fact that it was the first gathering of trans people in Kolašin.

In a patriarchal and transphobic society such as Montenegro, public appearance and public protest of TIGV people can happen only when the TIGV community is strong enough to resist fear and stand up for their civil rights. They choose artivism as a tool of self-representation and expressing rebellion in the hope that this is the most accessible and effective way to communicate with the media and the public at large. Media reports about the TIGV population in the Balkans are mostly focused on sensationalist articles about the medical process of transition or on reports about violence or negative aspects of life of TIGV people. In order to change that some of activist organisations regularly inform local media about their activities and events that they organise. Consequently, public artivist actions or artistic events could be a good source for reporting about TIGV issues. The trans community in Montenegro recognised the potential of artivism and decided to use this strategy to gain more space in media. In 2019 Association Spektra organised two public performances in Montenegro, its activist Marija Jovanović authored two photo exhibitions in Podgorica, and Association Spektra with Queer Montenegro hosted a photo exhibition, *Trans Balkan*, authored by the Belgrade-based photographer Aleksandar Crnogorac. Each of these events was reported in the local media. According to Milanović (2020), in the six monitored online media portals, 45 per cent of texts that deal with trans issues were reports about activist and artivist events and interviews with TIGV activists. Even though those media reports had a mostly neutral tone, that kind of publicity can be considered positive for the TIGV community. One of the activist goals is educating media workers about TIGV issues and teaching them how to avoid negative practices of reporting, sensationalist, and unethical approaches or use of negative labelling and discriminating language when it comes to TIGV-related topics. Another goal of activism is to provide material for journalists and to gain space in media in order to be visible and recognised as a community that belongs to that society. Activists in Montenegro have decided to address these goals and to put a lot of attention on the media, which they identified as a possible ally in the fight for civil rights and as an instrument for establishing communication with institutions and the public, more generally.

Masks in Croatia and Serbia

In 2019 the *Masks* performance was held in Zagreb (Croatia) in March and in Belgrade (Serbia) in November, but the media did not cover those events, neither did the organisers of those events have the same plan and strategy for using this event for visibility purposes as was the case in Montenegro. The reason for performing *Masks* in Zagreb was the first Balkan Trans Intersex March, which was held on 30 March. The organisers of that event were Association Spektra from Montenegro, Trans Aid from Croatia, and Trans Network Balkan as a regional organisation. Their idea was to use the performance to promote and announce the Balkan Trans Intersex March as a more significant event. The performance was held a few days before March, in the city centre while activists shared leaflets with invitations to the March and information about trans issues. Activists from Association Spektra brought masks made by the trans community in Podgorica, while performers made banners in Zagreb. There were six performers in the circle: three persons from Montenegro, two from Croatia, and one from North Macedonia. They had three drummers from *Drum 'n' bijes* collective (Drum 'n' rage) as support. Trans Aid organised the filming of preparing banners, going together to the public square, and of the performance itself. From that video material, they made a two-minute video for social networks. Since several different organisations organised *Masks* in Zagreb intending to promote the regional gathering, this action cannot be analysed as the work of local activists and the TIGV community from Croatia. When it comes to organising and staging this performance in Serbia, the situation is different than in Croatia because in Serbia, as in Montenegro, this event was used for marking the Trans Day of Remembrance. For that reason, I will analyse and compare the staging of the performance of *Masks* only in Montenegro and Serbia to compare these two communities' development and their capacities for using art as an activist tool.

The trans community in Serbia has existed for a longer period than the trans community in Montenegro. Given that the population of Serbia is 11 times bigger, there are many more trans people in Serbia than in Montenegro. Despite this, trans activism is at a higher level of development in Montenegro than in Serbia. The gathering of TIGV people in Serbia started in 2006 when a self-support group for transgender persons was created as a part of the organisation Geten (formerly Gayten-LGBT). In the beginning, the group consisted of four people, but in the following years, that number increased. Many trans people from Serbia were members of the self-support group, but those people only used Geten's services and were not included in activist work. There were no community-building programs or organised community activities and programs for empowering trans people for activist work. That resulted in an unorganised and incoherent community, the absence of community activities except meetings of the self-support group, and a low degree of visibility of trans people in the public discourse.

In the introduction of this text, I described when and how the Serbian TIGV community decided to perform *Masks*. That plan was put into action and in November 2019 the *Masks* performance was held in the centre of Belgrade on the occasion of the Trans Day of Remembrance. It was organised by two facilitators of a self-support group and sponsored by the organisation Geten. One of the self-support group coordinators, Saša Lazić, contacted Marija Jovanović, an activist from Association Spektra. Marija sent him detailed instructions on finding materials for masks and banners, explaining how to make masks and how to prepare banners, and instructed him on how to stage the performance. She also included tips for finding a location, security precautions, organising community and allies support, and a strategy for promotion and communication with media representatives.

However, the Serbian TIGV community had the capacity to follow and fulfil only part of those suggestions due to a lack of people interested in activism and a lack of available community space needed to prepare materials. Plastic masks were purchased in a costume party shop and the banners were made by people from the self-support group. All of us gathered in the main square in the city centre a few minutes before 7 pm, and everyone chose a banner that suited them. Here are some examples.

On the black side:
I don't feel safe even at home.
On the white side of the same banner:
I will never stop fighting for my rights.

On the black side:
My mother told me that no one would love me.
On the white side of the same banner:
Trans people bravely remain what they are.

On the black side:
Invisibility kills me.
On the white side of the same banner:
Non-binary persons exist.

There were 15 members of the self-support group and their friends with masks and banners who formed the circle. The gathered group decided that the performance should be shorter than anticipated in the original scenario. Instead of an hour, we stood for less than a half an hour – about ten minutes showing the black side of the banner and about ten minutes showing the white side of the banner. Non-uniformed police officers who were present all the time imperceptibly moved us towards one corner of the square, which reduced the radius of the circle we formed. There were about 20 of our allies standing on the square who came to support us. Casual passers-by generally paused briefly in front of us and then continued to walk. It was a windy and chilly November evening, and there were not many people in the square. After the performance, we lit candles in memory of the trans people murdered in the past year and left the square. This event was not covered by the Serbian (or any other) online media, nor was the Trans Day of Remembrance marked in the local media. For such actions to be able to fulfil their full potential and reach as many people as possible, it is necessary to invite media representatives on the spot and talk with them about the event. With media coverage such events would be more visible to the general population but also to members of the TIGV community throughout Serbia.

The Serbian trans community did not have a strategy or a plan for preparing and staging the performance. Their only goal was to perform *Masks* as a single action of public appearance. It looked more like a flash mob action isolated from any context and purpose. We did not achieve visibility in the media with this performance, nor did we achieve community empowerment that could motivate community members to perform new similar actions or do joint activist projects. The reasons for this are numerous. For artivism to be used as a tool that yields results, the community must have the conditions to implement it in activist work. First of all, community members must have a safe space to exchange ideas and to create artivist actions. Also, they must be empowered enough to perform those actions publicly. The Serbian TIGV community has no material conditions and is not sufficiently empowered or connected to exploit the potential of artivism. This activist action indicated that there are TIGV people in Serbia who are interested in engaging in activism and who can be easily mobilised for actions of this type. Trans issues are occasionally discussed in Serbian feminist and leftist circles and generally in public discourse. Due to the strengthening of the trans exclusionary movement in Serbia, that topic has become more frequent lately and because of that there will always be TIRV or LGBT people who are ready to support trans activist initiative and to engage in occasional endeavours such as this performance. However, to achieve change, it is not enough to mobilise people from time to time. In order to use the activist potential that these people can provide, it is necessary to organise them into a strong, connected, and empowered TIGV community that shares the same values and principles and forms activist goals based on them.

Conclusion

In this chapter I presented a performance that was held in four different social contexts: in capital cities of three different countries and one town. Organisers and participants of those artivist events were activists and people from three different countries. They are connected thanks to the activist networking that is being developed in this area by the Trans Network Balkan – a regional organisation for trans, intersex, and gender variant people, which operates in eight countries (Bosnia and Herzegovina, Croatia, Montenegro, Serbia, Kosovo, North Macedonia, Slovenia, and Albania). Those three communities are in different stages of development and have different resources for practising activism, which was reflected in the organisation and staging of the *Masks* performance. In relation to each other their choice of artivistic strategy was different. Activists from Montenegro were focused on community building, media coverage of that event, and communication with the public; activists in Croatia wanted to invite more people to participate in the event, while activists in Serbia wanted to appear in the public space and express protest in the name of all TIGV people exposed to transphobia. All three performances point to the connection and cooperation that exists between local TIGV communities in the post-Yugoslav space, but also to the numerous differences between these communities.

Through a comparative analysis of the preparation and staging of the *Masks* performance in Montenegro and Serbia, I claimed that the TIGV community using artivism can achieve a certain degree of visibility and provide resistance but also that artivism requires a developed community and material resources.

For the Serbian community these two necessary components are not difficult to provide due to existing connections and cooperation between regional communities and activists. Our advantage lies in the fact that we have the opportunity to learn from other communities' experiences and to see their good results. That provides us not only with new necessary knowledge but also with the motivation to engage in activist work. Confirmation of that statement can be found in recent developments in the field of TIGV activism in Serbia. In February 2020, several trans and non-binary people from Serbia participated in community organising training in Podgorica. The training was held by activists from Trans Network Balkan and Association Spektra and was intended for TIGV people living in the territory of North Macedonia, Serbia, Albania, and Montenegro. Following this event, two participants from Serbia showed the initiative to get involved in activist work, and soon they started to gather people in Serbia and to form an informal activist group by the name TOTA – Trans Organization of Trans Activists (Milanović, 2020b). By the end of 2020, at the suggestion of the TIGV community in Serbia, the name TOTA was replaced by the name *Talas* (Wave). In 2021 that informal group with the help and support of activists from the region became a fully registered organisation and goes under the name Collective Wave TIGV. With the united forces, the regional activists provided essential resources for creating a local organisation whose goal now is to build a strong, well organised, empowered, and inclusive trans and non-binary community in Serbia (Azdejković, 2021). It remains to be seen whether *Talas* will use artivism to raise visibility and to connect, agitate, and empower fragmented trans and non-binary community throughout the country.

Notes

[1] The term artivism was coined in 2005 by the Slovenian art theorist Aldo Milohnić and is a portmanteau of two different concepts – art and activism. Making socially engaged artwork whose primary purpose is activist intervention is certainly older than the term artivism and the development of artivism as a theoretical concept. In fact, the introduction of this term only encompasses various artistic–activist practices and actions whose common intention is to fight for a better and more just world.

[2] The Serbian community is the oldest, while Croatian, Bosnia and Herzegovina, Kosovar, and Montenegrin communities have existed for ten years or less.

References

Aladro-Vico, E., Jivkova-Semova D., and Bailey, K. (2018) Artivism: A new educative language for transformative social action. *Comunicar: Media Education Research Journal, 57*(26), 9–18.

Azdejković, P. (2021) Talas: nova organizacija za trans, interseks i rodno varijantne osobe. *Optimist: vodič kroz gej Srbiju, 60*, 26–31.

Duncombe, S. (2016) Does it work?: The Æffect of activist art. *Social Research: An International Quarterly, 83*(1), 115–34.

Gayten-LGBT. (2016) *Stilsko-jezičke preporuke za medije o izvještavanju o trans osobama.* Belgrade: Gayten–LGBT.

Gossett, R., Stanley, E.A., and Burton, J. (2017) *Trap door: Trans cultural production and the politics of visibility.* Cambridge: MIT University Press.

Hodžić, A., Poštić, J., and Kajtezović, A. (2016) The (in)visible T: Trans activism in Croatia (2004–2014). In B. Bilić and S. Kajinić (eds) *Intersectionality and LGBT activist politics: Multiple Others in Croatia and Serbia* (pp 33–54). London: Palgrave Macmillan.

Lippard, L.R. (1984) Activating activist art. *Circa, 17,* 11–17.

Milanović, A. (2017) Public space and a knot of visibility: Genders and sexualities exposed. *AM Journal, 14,* 113–122.

Milanović, A. (2020a) *Analiza izvještavanja o transrodnim osobama u onlajn i elektronskim medijima u Crnoj Gori za 2019. godinu.* Podgorica: Asocijacija Spektra & Kvir Montenegro.

Milanović, A. (2020b) Trans community (self)organizing in Serbia. In A. Milanović (ed) *Community (self)organizing of transgender movement in Western Balkans region* (pp 41–8). Podgorica: Asocijacija Spektra.

Milikj, L. (2020) Trans community (self)organizing in North Macedonia. In A. Milanović (ed) *Community (self)organizing of transgender movement in Western Balkans region* (pp 7–12). Podgorica: Asocijacija Spektra.

Novović, A. (2021) Intervju sa Jovanom Ulićevićem: Queer je biti svoj i imati kičmu. Portal Kombinat. Retrieved on 25 March 2021 from https://portalkombinat.me/queer-je-biti-svoj-i-imati-kicmu/

PR Centar. (2018) Perfomans Maske bunt protiv sistema koji ne prepoznaje postojanje trans osoba. Retrieved on 25 January 2021 from http://prcentar.me/clanak/perfomans-maske-bunt-protiv-sistema-koji-ne-prepozn aje-postojanje-trans-osoba/541

PR Centar. (2019) Montenegro Prajd karavan krenuo Crnom Gorom: Prvo javno okupljanje trans osoba održano danas u Kolašinu. Retrieved on 25 January 2021 from http://prcentar.me/clanak/montenegro-prajd-kara van-krenuo-crnom-gorom-prvo-javno-okupljanje-trans-osoba-odrano-danas-u-kolainu/912

Trans Aid (2019) *Osnovne smjernice za izvještavanje o interspolnosti.* Zagreb: Trans Aid.

Ulićević, J. (2020) Trans community (self)organizing in Montenegro. In A. Milanović (ed) *Community (self)organizing of transgender movement in Western Balkans region* (pp 23–40). Podgorica: Asocijacija Spektra.

Uzel, O. (2014) Tragic tropes: Transgender representation in contemporary culture. Geek Melange. Retrieved on 25 January 2021 from http://www.geekmelange.com/2014/03/tragic-tropes-transgender-representation/

Zulević, J. (2012) Istraživanje problema transeksualnih osoba u sferama školstva, rada i zapošljavanja, zdravstvene zaštite i državne administracije. In S. Gajin (ed) Model zakona o priznavanju pravnih posledica promene pola i utvrđivanja transeksualizma: prava trans osoba – od nepostojanja do stvaranja zakonskog okvira (pp 27–49). Belgrade: Centar za unapređivanje pravnih studija.

8

'The truth is what is in the body': an interview with Aleks Zain

Slađana Branković

Aleks Zain is a dancer/performer and an author in the fields of performance art, contemporary dance choreography, video, and sound work, who centres his conceptual framework and artistic practice in and on the body as the primary physical and sensory tool of creation, perception, and source of potential. He has exhibited and/or performed in his home country, Serbia, and throughout Europe, including the Netherlands, Italy, Finland, Austria, Bosnia and Herzegovina, and Croatia, as well as in Washington DC, USA. Apart from his artistic endeavours, Zain has also created a movement therapy system aimed to empower trans people and help them create positive relation with their body, which led to cooperation with human rights organisations across the post-Yugoslav space, such as Equal Rights Assembly (ERA), XY Spectrum, Udruga Domino, Trans Network Balkan, and others.

In terms of trans representation Zain's work goes far beyond the dominant discourse on trans bodies as inherently and exclusively tied to suffering and impossibility of self-actualisation. Not only is the body the tool of his craft, through which he emphasises its strength, capacities, and potentials, but a body which, through his art, becomes a place of potential identification for everyone, however sexed/gendered they are, avoiding the often imposed clustering of artists on the point of difference, which leads to segregation and devaluation of art and work produced by minoritised people. Unlike artivism or political art, Zain's work is not just a tool of political action, nor does it stop at the level of analysis and criticism (Milanović, this volume; Lippard, 1984), but takes a distinct course and potentially enacts a different kind of intervention into the societal and cultural spheres in the post-Yugoslav spaces in which he performs. Navigating the rough terrain of trans (in)visibility, by refusing to follow prescribed trajectories for marginalised artists often pressured to choose between being reduced to their difference, having it erased, or embedded into romanticised exceptionalism narratives, Zain manages to avoid all, thus changing the landscape of possibilities for artistic production in the post-Yugoslav space and trans and differently marginalised artists to come, without imposing specific socio-political pathways.

Zain's extensive body of work aims to question and deconstruct socio-political and cultural concepts such as home, family (*... and then I realized I barely even speak about you, Homebarrier, Apartments We Wrongly Called Home*), death (*Ecliptic*), and the binary of public and private (*An Installation for One Memory, Intimate Depressions, Body Confessions*). Through exploration of the most intimate and raw experiences and introspections, basing them in the body, movement, and uncensored streams of thought, Zain creates works that put the intimate and personal in stark contrast to the social and political concepts that function as regulators and disciplinarians of the body and thought, thus exercising critique, without falling into the trap of imposing his process or thoughts onto the viewer. Instead, his art tends to open the viewer for their own (self-)reflection, motivate them to think outside of existing conceptual boundaries, and explore their own potentials. In the process Zain challenges himself and expands his physical, mental, and sensory capabilities and durability, building his own performative and choreographic language through body and movement. Zain also appears as a co-author and collaborator on multiple artistic projects such as *Cut Off Point*, *Spiral of Silence*, *After the Fear*, and others. He has also participated in the retrospective exhibition of Marina Abramović, *The Cleaner*, by re-performing some of her pieces including *Imponderabilia*, *Relation in Time*, and *Artist's Life Manifesto*. Outside of getting a glimpse into the artist's background and creative process, in this conversation we discuss some of the artwork Zain created in more detail, reflecting on his motivations and intentions regarding some of the societal boundaries and concepts the artist addresses in his work.

Slađana:	You create body–sound installations, choreographies, performance art, and video and sound work. Why did you choose these media over painting in which you were trained from early childhood?
Aleks:	I needed something more direct. For me having canvas in front of me, at that time, was like I'm hiding behind something. I went first into the physical theatre (that I'm looking forward to letting go now also haha), and then into performance art and contemporary dance. I think performance art is what people know me the best for, but the dance is the 'love of my life'. I'm currently trying to 're-brand' myself as a dancer, as that is what I truly want to do till the rest of my life (not possible as there is a certain age limit to what your body can physically do, but still ...) I recently started getting back to canvas, more for myself rather than public display or work, but who knows ...

Slađana: In your work you discuss concepts such as body, home, family, and death, which stand for relations that are very intimate and personal but are at the same time regulated through society and politics, and from this personal and intimate position you question the socio-political aspects and their repressive function. What do you think is the role of art in discussing socio-political issues? Can it offer different approaches or solution perspectives to them, and is that an important aspect of your work?

Aleks: Huh, this answer really depends on my mood, however that sounds. I tend to lose the belief that anything we or I do makes any impact or sense. On the other hand, I guess you can, when you look into the history of art, see how the society changed together with it. I know I'm not going to change the world. However, I do want to be able to spark something in the viewer, like a need to think and re-think certain concepts (not necessary the ones I propose, but the ones that are important to them). I think that the structure of society is made so the people think less and produce/ work/consume more, so they notice less what is 'served' to them. Maybe the role of art is to open the space for more understanding and less just consuming. Once again, I really don't like the pieces that tell you openly 'you need to think that'. I think the role of giving a firm solution falls on the back of the activists, philosophers, thinkers, etc, more than on mine. Artist is like a first battle row – you open their minds up to be able to think or become willing to take action, and something that comes after has to give 'the final blow'. I really love the quote by Jan Fabre about his 24-hour theatre piece *Mount Olympus*, that each person who comes to see the piece is doing a political action. And it is a political action because they decide to stop their usual lives that we're all so very used to, and take themselves out of that constructed society for 24 hours. I think people can come out changed after that kind of experience (not necessarily Jan Fabre if that's not your cup of tea, but generally, after seeing a performing body or a piece of art that leaves an impression on them). When it comes to repression or any socio-political issue whatsoever, in order for the piece to work I need to have some relation to the subject I want to work on – it can be just really deep interest, it can be full on traumatizing experience, but I need to add something of myself to the stage for the story to 'work'.

Sladana: 'Adding something of myself to the stage' leads me to 'the personal is political', which originated as a motto of the second wave feminist movement in the 1960s, yet Western societies still tend to cling on the concept of personal and private as apolitical. In several of your works (*Body Confessions*, *An Installation for One Memory*, *Intimate Depressions*) you address the problems of personal/political, private/public binaries, and in a way, as does performance art in general, collapse them by exposing yourself and your intimate thoughts and struggles in a public space. What about this subject do you find important? What about it have you learned from those experiences of collapse?

Aleks: Referring to the last line in my previous answer – I do believe that personal is political. And political to me doesn't mean standing with a certain party for example, but being part of this society and working/creating in it necessarily makes the things you do political actions – that stands for daily decisions, not just art pieces. I really love the word 'collapse', so thank you for that. As I said – unless I give something of myself – the piece is not going to work, it will be bland. When you give part of yourself people have something to relate to, or respond to. I think that particular personal/public relation always exists when it comes to working in this field, it's especially maybe visible in performing arts and performance art. Even video, like *Intimate Depressions*. That was, for example, a really tough process. Close to mental torture to be honest. When the collapse happens, when all is finally out, not even on the screening in the Museum, but when the last render ends, I did have a sense of relief. I mean, you do have it sometimes at the end of the process, but this one was particularly strong. A lot of time I realize how much the process was consuming, and only then when I reflect upon the time during which the piece was in development/ creation process I understand how much it changed me mentally. What can be a good observation in that is how things we obsess or overthink about, or just go really deep into, can change our behaviour, thoughts, mental states, actions ...

On the note of exposure of the personal, I think one moment of relation with the audience can be created through it in the sense of when you see someone on stage with the same issue as yours – for example depression, as we've mentioned *Intimate Depressions* – it can give a sense of 'hey, I'm not alone in this world', or give some sense of empowerment, which is a part of the solution to the problem, right? I think being able to give something like that to my audience is also a big deal for me.

Slađana: One of the dichotomies that you address in your work is that of public and private. In the choreography *Body Confessions* you work through the binary of the body as public and private, and our relation to it in those two contexts. You are exposing the ways in which body is socially treated and through your dance you also offer mechanisms for coping with that societal pressure. If I understood it correctly, your performance also questions the dominant discourse on trans bodies as cause and source of suffering and problems, and suffering as inherent to transness, by framing it as a problem caused by societal norms which affect everybody, not just trans people, and body not as a shell we are trapped in, but as a tool, as strength, and inalienable possession, body as our potential. Would you agree with this reading of your work, and could you elaborate more on what you tried to accomplish with this piece?

Aleks: I think that the final and clearest point of the piece lies in the last line I say in the video that ends the piece, and which states that the body is the only true private property that you have, and to which no one but yourself has the right.

I believe that all other material properties can be in a way shared or communal, but the body is the only thing that can't, and that only belongs to you (or itself if we follow the question of only one matter existing).

The piece itself is structured in three parts. The first part is dedicated to that public image using the state of a dancer in the class repeating the 'combination' (when you do contemporary dance class/floor work out, you usually get a combination of movements to practice in line). The combination repetition is followed by the video of my own mouth telling me that basically I need to do better cuz I'm shit. The situation is partially a social pressure of 'you need to do this like that', and personal pressure of 'I need to be better in order for others to see me as a dancer' etc. Don't get me wrong, I also want to be better for myself, this is just a use of a familiar situation. The anger of not doing completely perfect builds up, the body loses the clothing and transfers to more meditative scenery of the second part of the piece. This part starts really slow and in a pretty darkened scenery and describes the body only with itself meeting itself. I did get a comment from a colleague once that it looks like I'm dancing both male, female, and non-gender part of each person. I didn't perceive it like that, but it's an interesting comment that kinda proves that this more meditative dance is more there to offer the space for people to see some deep relation they can create with their body rather than just the one I'm going through with mine. The meditative state goes from slow to fast, turning into drumming and hectic strong dance, which to me represents both freedom and power, but also fighting the struggles (whichever they are for you, I know my own). The last, third part is the video that is projected partially on the wall and partially on my naked back. In the video I say how I feel with my body on that day, and I finish off with the line I already mentioned at the beginning of this answer. So, it's more of a progressive visual presentation of different stages of body-relation, that I'd say serve as a 'gentle nudge' to the audience that we all have our own material that belongs only to us.

I do like your reading of what you could perceive just from the written concept you had in front of you, and I have to say that I'd be really interested to see your reaction to it live.

Slađana: I do hope that I will have the chance to see you perform live someday. You once stated that you are very non-spiritual and that you respond through your body and movement rather than spoken language, which to me sounds again like a type of collapse, this time of the body/mind dichotomy. Would you agree with this?

Aleks: On the contrary. Body is an object or a tool I'm more capable of using rather than my tongue-brain connection. We can understand it as a collapse in a vague term in the sense of me not believing in the dualist substance, rather going for contemporary monism, but tbh[1], I'm not that deep. I think brain and body are the same. It's just one organism. Some parts of each organism function better than others, etc.

Slađana: Staying on the same subject of body and its strength and potential, when you refer to the body's strength what do you mean by it? Pure physicality of it, or something else? When you write 'I believe that every border body faces is movable' what kind of borders do you have in mind? Is an image or the presence of a body which is different able to 'open the minds' of the viewers, 'spark something' in them, and make them re-think certain concepts, as you said previously?

Aleks: This is something I could talk for hours about. What I'm fascinated with is how we are convinced that we have a limit to what we can physically do and endure, but actually our body can do much more than that. The borders I speak about are mostly physical in that sense. I love long-durational performance art for this reason. You have that a lot in the work of, for example, Marina Abramović. A physical action, no matter how static it is, that is pushing the border of your own capabilities. I think there is a moment when the piece truly starts to 'work', and I believe that moment happens when the border of physical capabilities we have in our mind of what we can and can't do is crossed. So yes, I am interested in the borders of the body in the sense of how far I can go, and how far I can push the body to endure and continue 'working/functioning'. If I can connect my own need for pushing the physical border to something social it would be my irritation actually with that kind of collective delusion of physical body limits. I believe our organism can do much more than we believe it can. We just have to learn how to use it and to push further. When it comes to performance art, or even dance, or well any kind of work, non-related to the form – if it doesn't challenge you, it's just probably not going to be something spectacular.

Slađana: In this regard, and coming back to your comment on the process of creating *Intimate Depressions* which, as you said, felt close to mental torture, are you ever worried about possible negative consequences or pushing the body too far?

Aleks: I think that when you work with the body one of the things you practice, learn, and generally have to know is how you facilitate your body. You have to have a good understanding of where your body is, what you are doing, what is happening … Injury is something that is always possible and that happens, especially when you dance or do physically challenging performances, but it's the part of the job and is something that you learn through working daily on how to prevent and understand. It's like athleticism, basically. You hear about professional athletes having injuries sometimes, and how they go through it. It's the same with us who perform physically in any sense. Some recoveries

Slađana:	How does this choreography (*Body Confessions*) relate to your work in movement therapy, which you created specifically for trans folks experiencing distress and discomfort with their bodies? Has it in any way been informed by it, or are those two completely different projects?

are more tough than others, but I wouldn't say I have actual deep fears about it. It's better to navigate your body so there is the least possible damage, of course.

Slađana: How does this choreography (*Body Confessions*) relate to your work in movement therapy, which you created specifically for trans folks experiencing distress and discomfort with their bodies? Has it in any way been informed by it, or are those two completely different projects?

Aleks: It hasn't. I don't believe what people call art therapy is actually art. I don't make pieces so that I can feel better. *Use, Empower and Accept*, which is my movement therapy system for people with dysphoria is something I created by collecting exercises from my own experience that helped me lower my dysphoria so that I become able to perform. Given that it was created as a therapeutic and creative workshop, it doesn't have as a goal to create performers, but it focuses rather on finding ways to lower dysphoria and establish a safe space to have fun. So yeah, completely different projects.

Slađana: Can you tell me more about *Use, Empower and Accept*? How did you come up with it?

Aleks: As I started saying in the previous question, I realized that there are certain exercises in different systems that I learned from different mentors, related to performing, physical theatre, dance, performance art etc, that helped me become more capable to use my body. By collecting, transforming where needed, and arranging them into a progressive work alignment I developed a system of my own. I think this realization that there are things that helped me kinda pushed the thought of 'hey, there are people in my community, with the same problem as me, who are currently having it worse, let's try and do something for them'. It's not just what I want. For me it's also part of an obligation to help if I can. At least I see it like that. Not every person is going to have it awesome ofc[2]. Different systems and types of therapy or creative work in general work for different people and I'm aware of that. I also try to adjust the sessions to suit the needs that I sense people have when we start working. So, it can end in different and unexpected ways, the sense of going a bit out of the initial structure, but I think that is the beauty of collective work.

Slađana: That is very kind of you. I feel that your statements: 'The truth is what is in the body. Everything else is just a mental masturbation' from the concept of your work

GreškaGreškaGreška i/ili Freedom is when there is none can in a way summarise and connect a lot of your works. It is also one of the pieces I found most intriguing. Can you say more about the intention of this work?

Aleks: Hahaha, thanks! I still have ambiguous feelings about that one. It's basically a collection of scrapes of footage I had from streets, studio, etc. I often carry my small camcorder around or film something with the phone. I've put it together in the period while I was recovering from gender reassignment surgery. In a way it can be understood also as my longing to come back to the studio now when I look at it from the outside perspective of basically a year after it was made. The thing with freedom and emptiness comes from my belief that I truly felt and understood freedom after performing pieces by Marina Abramović, *Freeing the body* and *Freeing the voice*. When there is nothing left in you, when you reach over the end (both pieces are performed until the collapse), and you're again in the greenroom laying on the pillow everything starts to feel like all the things around you are less important than they were before … the sense like you're a *tabula rasa* for a second. When there is nothing left to worry about or when you're able to progress into another life (or, I guess, a stage of life) to me that feels closest to freedom that I can imagine. So, what's the point of everything? I have no answer. And I often don't know what I want to say or how to say it. So, the piece, as it's said in the description, is somewhat of a dubious entanglement of all these things.

Slađana: Since you mentioned Marina Abramović, you have been a part of the *Cleaner* exhibition at the Museum of Contemporary Art Belgrade, during which young artists re-performed Abramović's works. How was this experience for you and has it been challenging to perform pieces somebody else created, regarding your statement from the beginning of our conversation in which you said that it is important to add something of yourself to the stage for the story to 'work'?

Aleks: Well, as someone who also does performance art in that initial form, and was born in Belgrade, Marina means a lot to me, as my first meeting with this form was through her work years ago. I'm one of those people who went alone to theatre to cry in the last row watching *The Artist Is Present*. So, it is an honour in a way to perform something by her (and Ulay too, cuz I also love him), and especially as I got quite a number if pieces to perform during the exhibition. I think her work in general is challenging. What you see in her a lot of times is crossing that border I speak about. That's why I love her. I'd love to achieve that 'going to the end' in my work as I mentioned in the previous answer, that happens with her *Freeing Series* for example. There is also a lot of discipline and 'cleanliness' (specific term we use in arts, not sure how to describe it in English other than action being 'clear') in her work, which I love and which resonates with me. So yes, those pieces are sometimes tough, but again, that is what interests me and pushes me forward.

When it comes to investing something yours I thought more about authorship work. It's different when you create something and when you perform for someone else. Different instances. Marina invested her stories and thoughts and life, ideas, trauma etc in her pieces. I invest my skills and strength into reperforming what she already invested. Actually, as I'm turning to contemporary dance more and more, sometimes I prefer to perform for someone else rather than being an author.

Slađana: The *Cleaner* gave you the opportunity to connect and collaborate with other artists and together you performed in a collective event called *Fali ti 1 papir* (*You're missing one paper*). Within this project you created another intimate piece, questioning the concept of the biological family. How important are these kinds of collaborations for your own work and development as an artist?

Aleks: Oh, they're very important. I believe that artists shouldn't live in one place during their whole life, but that we need to move in order to learn from each other and understand and experience different perspectives. In the end, you also gain new collab/work/exposure opportunities and connections, but even more, you can also gain friendships :).

I understand that this sounds like a basic answer, but it is what it is xD.

Slađana: What are the biggest challenges you face as a young artist in Serbia, and how do you manage to overcome them?

Aleks: Money, mobility, and the psychology of a small surrounding. Idk,[3] I get frustrated a lot of times, especially with the last one. I always get puzzled when I get the question like this, cuz I'm not sure if I actually have a proven mechanism or a strategy for navigating in the art world. I guess you go from a project to project, you sometimes accept the work that you can get and other times you manage to pull your own project. But it's definitely not easy. I sometimes have to take also work that is outside of my preferred career, like remote freelancing and stuff like that. I'm currently, I feel, on a certain milestone, as in these months I like to have a lot of work and I'm transferring to fully be able to live just from being an artist/performer. One of my biggest dreams is to be part of an international dance/performance company, and when my body gets older to make my own. But that is a goal that surpasses the border of living in Serbia, in the sense that I am searching for the opportunity to move abroad. The issue here is that unless (and even sometimes if you are) you're fully employed in the state theatre or have a really good and devoted curator, you're barely making ends meet.

Slađana: Are you still interested in the concepts you dealt with in your work, some of which are recurring, such as home, family, the binary of public and private, or are you moving to something else? What can we expect from you in the future?

Aleks: Definitely. I think my inability to understand the concept of nuclear family is never going to be solved hahaha. However, three terms that I'm also currently interested in are depression, sleep (as in performing for the audience that is sleeping, I'm obsessed with Max Richter's album and concert *Sleep* that is made and performed for the people who are basically sleeping), and conflict. There are concepts that I'm currently working on, related to all of the mentioned, so I hope in the upcoming years you'll be able to see all. In the short run, I'm currently looking for ways to properly tour *Body Confessions*, and hope that would happen in the second part of the season. There is also a really heavy performance art piece that I want to do, and I hope that happens soon. I'm also working with two organizations, one in Montenegro and one in Slovenia on directing and choreographing two activist performances/plays in which the participants will be people from the community. And besides that, my dream of finding a constant company (basically a new home) still stands :).

Notes

1   Abbreviation for 'to be honest'.
2   Abbreviation for 'of course'.
3   Abbreviation for 'I don't know'.

Reference

Lippard, L.R. (1984) Activating activist art. *Circa*, *17*, 11–17.

9

Queering sevdah: gender-nonconformity in the traditional music of Bosnia and Herzegovina

Tea Hadžiristić

Since his 2014 album, *Moj Sevdah*, singer Božo Vrećo has become arguably one of the most popular singers in Bosnia and Herzegovina (BiH). Having launched a solo career after his success as the lead singer of the (no longer active) band Halka, Vrećo has released three albums, toured the region, and played sold-out shows from Stockholm to Belgrade, garnering glowing reviews and an adoring fan base. He sings sevdah, traditional folk music which is widely considered to be one of the country's main cultural exports – and 'quintessentially Bosnian'. Vrećo is as well known for his creative music videos and on-stage performances as he is for his daring gender non-conforming aesthetic. Assigned male at birth and self-described as both a man and woman, Vrećo is one of very few publicly 'out' LGBT celebrities in BiH and the region. He also breaks taboos about ethnicity and religion by dealing with religious themes and mourning wartime victims of 'other' ethnic groups.

His 2015 music video 'Aladža' is a poignant example of the apparent contradictions and novelty embodied by Vrećo. Shot on the famed Zelengora mountain, Vrećo appears in a series of gowns, with long black hair, a beard, and dark eye makeup, wearing replicas of Bosnian medieval jewellery. Some scenes show him amid a cluster of *stećci*, medieval tombstones scattered across Bosnian mountain ranges and often symbolic of the country's past. This imagery evokes the medieval Bosnia state, often imagined as a utopic time unpolluted by ethnoreligious differences, a pre-colonial period of Bosnian unity and even power. The song itself mourns the wartime destruction of the Aladža mosque in Vreco's hometown of Foča and celebrates its rebuilding, completed in 2019. The weaving in of gender non-conformity and cross-ethnic mourning and solidarity with the symbolism of national belonging is in many ways transgressive and unexpected.

Perhaps equally unexpected is the song's reception. In a country we are told is ridden with macho culture (Cerkez, 2015), inhospitable to gender and sexual diversity, hopelessly ethnically divided, and still healing from the wounds of war, one would not expect a queer singer like Vreće to be as popular as he is. Traditional music also seems an unlikely genre in which to push the boundaries of gender and sexual norms. Though predictably targeted by right-wing religious conservative leaders and associated press outlets, and the usual vitriol of anonymous online commentary, Vreće is warmly written of and welcomed by the majority of the country's media, who have dubbed him the 'Prince of Sevdah.' His sold out concerts, regional following, and the breathless online commentary of his fans are testament to his popularity. This may be aided by the fact that Vreće expresses his queerness outside of a Western idiom, delving into local traditions and histories and belying the notion of queerness as a threat coming from 'outside' (that is, the West).

This chapter seeks to interrogate the paradoxes and dualities embodied by Vreće as well as situate the 'Vreće phenomenon' in the broader context of the sevdah genre as well as LGBT activism. Is a queer singer of traditional sevdah music indeed as shocking as he may appear? Is his popularity unexpected? What political potential is generated by 'queering' sevdah, and how is it linked to activism for the rights and dignity of queer and trans people in BiH? In order to explore these questions, I provide a brief overview of the sevdah genre, and discuss Vreće's music and performances in this context, as well as reflecting on LGBT rights in BiH. I then turn to a thematic analysis of comments on Vreće's music videos and analyse the findings in an attempt to understand the significance and political potential of Vreće's popularity. My discussion explores these findings, situating the affective bonds between Vreće and his audience in the socio-political and historical context, and ties the articulation of a 'local' queer identity within BiH to other contemporary movements that seek to mine local histories and practices in order to imagine new, more liveable political futures for Bosnia and Herzegovina.

Sevdah: national tradition, zone of freedom

One of the surprising aspects of Vreće's popularity is his genre of choice – one might assume that a traditional folk music form is more conservative than 'liberal paradigm of pop music' (Kapetanović, 2014). However, sevdah's role as BiH's 'national' art form, its function as an archive of social history, and its significance as a realm of affect destabilises the idea that the genre is necessarily associated with a socially conservative tradition. Indeed, as Kapetanović (2014) points out, there are old sevdalinkas[1] that deal explicitly with same-sex desire and love or gender-bending social roles. Many more are ambiguous about sex and gender, reflect fairly open sexual mores, and messages about the importance of consent[2] or the perils of workplace sexual harassment.[3] In their contemporary interpretations of the living archive of sevdah music, musicians such as Vreće, Amira Medunjanin, Merima Ključo,

209

and notably Damir Imamović, redefine the meaning of 'tradition' by drawing on the openness, freedom, and diversity implicit in the sevdah canon.

Sevdah is a form of secular urban folk song from the Balkans, etymologically stemming from the Arabic word sawda, meaning black bile or melancholy (Buturović, 2007). Many sevdalinkas are indeed melancholy and touch on themes of doomed love or loss, though others are comic, playful, and erotic. The topos of the genre animates a picture of Bosnian life for the past 500 years – particularly under Ottoman rule – and as such is a valuable social history of norms and customs (Durić, 2018). The genre is 'mainly associated with the Muslim city elite and their life, aspirations, customs, and social and aesthetic norms' (Buturović, 2007, p 80) but has in the last century come to be seen as Bosnian national music. Customarily considered to be women's song by virtue of its lyrical subject matter, as opposed to the 'heroic' thematics of male song (Hajdarpašić, 2015), the genre historically allowed for the 'transgression of gender codes' by enabling singers to sing in the voice of the opposite gender, allowing men to express the emotional and lyric suffering associated with femininity (Buturović, 2007, p 79). Due to its provenance during the Ottoman era, sevdah has always been an arena where questions of East and West, national feeling, imperial pasts, modernity, and self and other are explored.

Sevdah's place as Bosnian 'national' music was defined over two centuries. In the 19th-century period of burgeoning European nationalisms, there was unease about cultural artefacts linked to the Ottoman Empire and scholars of music sought to deny the Ottoman influence on Bosnian music, attempting to 'purify national folk music' (Pennanen, 2008, p 132). The search for a 'pure' local source of sevdah was complicated by its heterogeneous origin, though struggle to prove the 'authenticity' of sevdah as Bosnian/Slavic music corresponded to attempts to articulate nationhood in the late 19th and early 20th centuries. As such, these scholarly attempts to define sevdah often drew on classic Orientalist tropes, which contrasted the decadent, emotive, carnal, Muslim East with a rational, modern, Christian West. The sevdalinka was seen by some as the hybrid product of a dignified, melancholic Slavic soul mixed with Ottoman eroticism – an 'eroticized convergence' of East and West (Hajdarpašić, 2008) that was somehow simultaneously a 'mixture of many elements' and 'absolutely original and authentic' (Kadragić in Pennanen, 2010, p 84). The hybridity of BiH's national song reflects how the country itself is seen in the Western imagination – as a crossroads between the 'civilised' West and the eroticised East – and its place on the periphery of Europe.

The 'golden age' of sevdah came in the post-WWII era of building a 'national' identity in the new federal republic of BiH in an effort to promote cultural and ethnic diversity in socialist Yugoslavia. This period cemented its popularity (Janković, 2006) and institutionalised the modern canon of sevdah, with many musicians doubling as collectors and archivists of folk songs and recording them for radio. After the violent breakup of Yugoslavia, there were attempts to define sevdah as specifically Bosnian Muslim (Bosniak) music and an overall conservative and increasingly religious turn in its interpretation[4] (Kozorog and Bartulović 2017). The most recent trend in sevdah is a post-nationalist, post-structuralist reading of the genre, which embraces its inherent hybridity and multitude of overlapping cultural histories that left their marks on it (Kožul, 2016). This has come on the heels of sevdah's popularity in the world music genre (Nenić, 2015).

This turn is perhaps most characterised by Damir Imamović, an award-winning sevdah singer and researcher who approaches sevdah as an alternative archive of social history (Dukić, 2015). In Imamović's interpretation, sevdah is a genre 'of emancipation of the socially marginalized' (Kozorog and Bartulović 2017, p 176) and many sevdalinkas he sings (and rescues from the archives) highlight female sexual agency, same-sex desire, and fluid gender identities. By rereading tradition in a 'non-canonical manner' (Nenić, 2015), Imamović makes the point that there is nothing inherently conservative about Bosnian tradition or that openness to difference and an emphasis on freedom are themselves traditional. With his interpretations of sevdah and queer gender representation, as well as signing both 'male' and 'female' texts, Vrećo is part of this non-canonical approach to sevdah which draws on tradition but seeks to expand understandings of it.

Vrećo's queer Bosnia

Though unusual in folk music, there is precedence for Vrećo's gender-bending aesthetic in Yugoslav music, particularly of the 1980s, a time of the first waves of gay activism as well as what would today be read as queer experimentation in music (Čulić, 2019). This period was in some ways personified by Oliver Mandić, a pop singer who wore drag in his music videos and stage performances until abandoning this persona during the 1990s Yugoslav wars and becoming an advocate of paramilitary Serb forces (Ramet, 2002). Yet unlike Mandić, Vrećo's gender duality is not just a feature of his artistry – he adopts the same queer aesthetic in daily life. Vrećo is often dubbed Bosnia's Conchita Wurst, the Austrian genderbending singer who was famously blamed by Serbian religious leaders for the 2014 flooding in the region (Gander, 2014). But unlike Conchita, Vrećo does not have a stage name or persona, nor does he wear drag (his gender presentation rarely resembles drag's exaggerated femininity). His social media communication to his fan base has done much to normalise gender non-conformity, for example his frank accounts of his childhood fascination with makeup and dresses (Đokić, 2017). By referring to Vrećo as 'queer' in this text, I have in mind the ways in which his self-described sexual orientation and public presentation of his gender defy heteronormativity and gender conformity.

I ascribe to Maljković's (2014, p 364) definition of queer as 'the identity which negates identity', not a fixed identity marker but a broad signifier of all things which challenge heteronormativity, challenging even the 'essentialised' identities under the LGBT umbrella, as well as the idea that such identities are stable over time and place. Vrećo does not use the word queer, or transgender, to describe himself. He describes his gender identity as 'dual' and has said that he has no desire to change his sex (Telegraf, 2015). Vrećo often describes sevdah itself as an outlet for his gender expression, a 'zone of freedom' that allows him to live as both a man and a woman, in part through singing both male and female sevdah songs (Gvozdenović, n.d.).

Moreover, Vrećo's openness is rightfully seen as brave by many, given the overall lack of social acceptance for LGBT people in BiH and discrimination faced by queer people in nearly all of spheres of life (Wakefield, 2020). Trans people in particular face violence at home and in public (Banović et al, 2015) and the majority of queer people in BiH worry for their safety (Wakefield, 2020). The risks involved in being 'out' means there is an overall lack of visibility for queer people, which reinforces negative opinions among those in the general public, who may not know many out LGBT people first hand (Gaillard, 2015). Trans issues are even less visible, and transphobia within LGBT groups poses added barriers. The medicalised focus on transition may obscure the existence of other trans identities and gender non-conforming people who have no desire to transition – who arguably may 'trouble' binary understandings of gender even more by straddling multiple identities. Vrećo is one such example, who does not describe himself as transgender but as 'both a man and a woman'.[5]

Socially conservative views tend to be propagated by prominent religious leaders and political parties. The three major religious communities in Bosnia (Roman Catholic, Serbian Orthodox, and Islamic) have been unusually united when it comes to condemning queer-friendly events (Gavrić, 2017) and claiming to defend 'traditional family values' (CBC, 2019). Given the role of religion in how ethnic identity is defined in the country, anti-LGBT attitudes are also entrenched in the ethnocratic system.

Vrećo is not, however, a spokesperson for the country's LGBT/queer movement. In interviews, Vrećo rarely speaks of his identity on a political level. He speaks about his attraction to and relationships with men, his dual gender, and emphasises themes of love, freedom, emotion, honesty, sincerity, and courage. He rarely uses the LGBT terminology, nor does he seem eager to label his gender identity:

> I see myself as a fighter for the freedom to be who you are, and for love, but not necessarily as part of any framework. My favourite definition is what the *New York Times* said after first encountering my music: that I am a synonym for freedom. That is the best definition. When you live as a man and as woman, you have no barriers. Your music and

your identity have no barriers. You are simply fighting to be who you are, which is the most important thing. (Story, 2020)[6]

The reliance on the somewhat depoliticised notion of 'love' and a lack of engagement with contemporary discourses on gender identity is occasionally at odds with rights-seeking activism. In 2017, an interview with Vrećo on a regional television show elicited disappointment from the LGBT community. After being arguably goaded by the interviewer's homophobic questions (and comments such as 'you don't have that irritating quality of effeminate men'), Vrećo disparaged the 'effeminate' mannerisms of gay men as 'an act', and contrasted his own 'authentic' gender duality against other, purportedly inauthentic, gender identities. The Sarajevo Open Centre, an LGBT rights organisation, published a response that called attention to the homophobic and transphobic character of his statements and underlined his responsibility as a celebrity to do better and avoid harmful stereotypes in the future (Sarajevo Open Center, 2017). Though sometimes frustrating for the LGBT population, Vrećo enjoys popularity among the general population, perhaps precisely due to side-stepping political discourse. His 'apolitical' approach to political themes might ring true given the almost complete dysfunction at the level of formal politics in BiH due to the post-war ethnocratic stalemate.

Fan comments on Vrećo's music videos

One of the more surprising aspects of Vrećo's popularity is the ardour and adoration of his fans, seen both at his sold out concerts and online. The marked enthusiasm and emotional pitch of many of the comments online (on his music and his personal social media) inevitably give rise to questions about their political potential. Namely, can the 'queer turn' in sevdah lead to changed attitudes about gender and sexuality? In particular, what kind political potential (despite his apolitical stance) is embedded in Vrećo's homegrown expression of gender duality through the genre of sevdah? Vrećo's music videos garner much online commentary, and what is striking is the effusive nature of the comments, as well as the marked absence of nationalist, homophobic, or transphobic content that one often finds in comment sections on Balkan music (which have been referred to as 'fertile ground for hate speech' [Lakić, 2019]). An analysis of comments on videos hosted by other channels (not just Vrećo's, which may delete hateful messages) found that negative comments were also by far in the minority.

To explore these questions, I conducted an analysis on the comments on his music videos and recording of live performances, using a qualitative thematic analysis approach (Nowell et al, 2017), which allowed me to consider the meaning of this online commentary in its full context, in conjunction with a Python script that made the data analysis more rigorous. Using the YouTube

Data Tool (Rieder, 2019), I extracted the entire comment sections for 15 videos, including ten music videos hosted on Vrećo's channel, and five videos of live performances, hosted by various other channels.[7] As the majority of 4,515 comments analysed were in Bosnian-Croatian-Serbian (BCS), I used the Serbian Stemmer tool (Milosevic, 2012) to lemmatise the words in the comments and generate a list with the frequency of each word stem. After deleting prepositions and pronouns, a word cloud was generated, which revealed the most common words used in comments. Based on this word cloud and by sorting comments by the most likes they had received from other users, several themes began to emerge. I used an inductive approach to identify the main patterns in the commentary while reflecting on the historical and social context, and familiarising myself with the raw data.

Several key themes were identified based on keywords that were frequent in the text, as well as others I hypothesised would be relevant (LGBT, for example), and generated a list of keywords that would correspond to each theme, including various possible spellings in BCS, with and without diacritics, and in English. These were run through a script that grouped these keywords by theme and generated a count of their frequency. These themes were also ranked by their popularity – taken to be the average number of likes comments received from other YouTube users – to judge their resonance with other users. The most frequent comments were accolades and congratulations, which were not further analysed.

On the basis of this empirical investigation, I identified four themes arising from the most frequent and most popular comments that can inform the research question: metaphysical themes (the sense that Vrećo is outside of time), place and nation (being out of place and questions of national belonging), queerness by any other name (the words used to describe and relate to Vrećo's gender fluidity), and affective experiences.

Out of time: metaphysical themes

The theme of the metaphysical came up 628 times. Vrećo is seen as 'sent from God' and his voice is often described as divine or angelic: 'God Himself is in his voice, may he be protected and full of love and happiness ... blessings';[8] 'Božo, you are an angel.'

These themes also resonated in many comments that referred to Vrećo as otherworldly, transcendental, and magical. This discourse spoke of Vrećo's music as being cosmic and a portal to another dimension, as well as Vrećo himself somehow not belonging to the mortal plane: 'You are an alien!'; 'Total hypnosis and journey to another dimension ... Everything is out of this world, Božo and the orchestra, and text and music, their synergy. Everything ...'

The image painted of Vrećo is of someone who is supra-human, divine, alien, and otherworldly, on the basis of both his talented singing as well as his gender fluidity. His queerness, in conjunction with his talent, is seen as not only 'out of this world' but also outside of time – or ahead of it. The way Vrećo weaves history with a queer futurity was remarked upon often: 'This is not from this world … The song seems to have been written 300 years ago, and he seems to have come from the distant future'; 'Božo is guiding us into the future, through the past'; 'Božo is a pioneer of a new era. After everything that has happened and everything that will happen, there will be a drastic shift in our values. People will judge each other differently, other people's lives will be precious, and the community will take care of each other knowing that we are all interdependent. Lovely! Onward, don't look back …'

The theme of Vrećo as a representative of the future was one of the most common themes, mentioned 97 times, but it was also by far the most popular among other users, suggesting particular significance.

Out of place: place and nation

Another theme that emerges from the comments is the sense of 'location' and ethnoreligious identity. These places do not appear fixed, with 'Bosnian' spilling over into 'Balkan' or 'Slavic' identity, and the overall impression that he engages with all of the ethnoreligious groups in Bosnia and the Balkans. Many comments express a sense of pride that Vrećo is Bosnian, or explain that 'even though' they are of a particular religious faith or ethnic identity, they are a fan of his: 'I am Serbian and proudly say that I enjoy his emotion and voice, I don't care who he is or what he is, his voice takes me to a special emotion and dimension'; 'I am a Muslim and your song moved me to tears. Keep it up, Vrećo.'

This theme of regional unity came up numerous times: 'Balkan brothers of all religions, nations, etc, whether we want to admit it or not, Božo represents us, and it is beautiful.'

There was a common reiteration of the trope that the Balkans (and Bosnia in particular) are a 'backward' and conservative place where someone like Vrećo would have trouble being accepted, and that he is brave to dress the way he does and be openly queer. This positions Vrećo as ahead of his time particularly in relation to where he is, and his detractors are referred to as 'immature', narrow-minded, and provincial: 'Božo, you really rise above Balkan provincialism'; 'Bosnia still needs to mature to tolerate the amount of energy and originality in Bozo, not to mention his clothing and gender plurality.'

Some comments suggest that Vrećo was born in the wrong place at the wrong time, but that this fuels his artistic abilities as well as potential to 'change minds' in Bosnia: 'Impressive. Božo may seem a little strange to our people. We should not judge anyone due to ignorance. Božo, you live sevdah, painful and melancholy. People of different genders live in you. This secret comes out when we hear and see you sing.'

Queerness by any other name

LGBT terminology was not frequently addressed by name. Instead, Vrećo's queerness is referred to in an almost euphemistic way – Vrećo is described as unique, different, brave, authentic, and free, all of which ostensibly refer to his gender presentation in his music videos and overall. Interestingly, this language mirrors the way he describes himself.

Many comments emphasise Vrećo's authenticity and honesty, which deviates from the common transphobic belief that gender fluidity is inauthentic or unnatural: 'Dear Bozo, this is so honest and pure. Excellent video, and real art. Thank you endlessly.'

The sense of Vrećo's daring queer aesthetic is interwoven with the evident respect fans have for his talent. Another common theme is artistry, with commenters expressing that Vrećo's is 'real art', not just 'ordinary' popular music, but something superlative, transcendent, and unique: 'You, sir Božo, are an artist. Not only do you sing remarkably, but in every song you tell old and mainly forgotten folk tales, and save them from oblivion.'

Some commenters speak in particular about how his talent, in conjunction with the courage he shows in embracing gender non-conformity, endeared Vrećo to them: 'The first thing I thought when the video started was "he's in a dress". After the first minute, every possible negative thought or prejudice disappeared'; 'I don't know, maybe you think you're a woman, but whatever you are, you're incredibly brave to present yourself this way in the Balkans!'

Though not spoken of in the language of LGBT rights, these comments demonstrate an acceptance of Vrećo's gender fluidity in other terms: the right to be different, the right to love, the freedom to be oneself, the importance of authenticity. There is also a sense that Vrećo is an emissary of this message of acceptance, but with little reference to LGBT 'buzzwords'. This mirrors Vrećo's own apolitical stance about LGBT rights and his reluctance to use labels for his gender: 'Božo is freedom, Božo is his own person and he does it wonderfully, wonderfully like this beautiful Bosnia of ours'; 'He may not be a priest, but it seems he was sent by God to spread love, peace, and freedom, with his angelic voice and attitude'; 'Božo. Your strength, love, and beauty are more powerful than their hatred and narrowmindedness. They can't do anything to you, no matter how much they bark.'

Affective experiences

Some of the most frequent themes discussed in the comments were the listeners' vivid, embodied affective experiences when engaging with the music and videos. References to emotion, love, and the soul were most common: 'If everyone had as much emotion and love as dear Božo, this world would be paradise'; 'I've never heard a stronger voice. This touches the soul'; 'This tears apart the soul, burrows into the heart, and awakens an explosion of emotions.'

Many commenters described crying, getting goosebumps, as well as feelings of sadness and pain: 'I cry every time I hear this song. It's so beautiful it hurts'; 'Goosebumps from head to toe!'

There was also a strong current of the notion that Vrećo's music is healing or medicinal – 'balm for the soul' or psychologically restorative and meditative: 'Božo heals and nurtures our souls with his voice and appearance.'

There was a clear sense that Vrećo's music was therapeutic on a personal level as well as a societal one. For example, his song 'Elma', about a childhood friend killed during the Bosnian War, featured very poignant comments empathising with his experience and sharing wartime stories. One commenter, from his hometown of Foča, said that Vrećo 'corrects all the injustices done here, and connects and heals people with love'.

Articulating liveable futures

Two key findings from the comment analysis stand out. One is that his fans see Vrećo as someone who transcends time, place, ethnicity, and gender binarism through his talent and queer aesthetic. The second finding is that his listeners have a deeply embodied affective relationship to Vrećo, and I argue, this is linked to the way in which he represents a future for Bosnia as a space of tolerance, diversity, and peace (or creates this future in the present tense of his music videos). This future is reimagined with reference to a shared past, as well as the healing of the traumas of division and war. These findings lend credence to the idea that Vrećo's popularity may have broader political potential, though not necessarily pointing to the existence of a yet-untapped wellspring of tolerance for sexual difference and gender diversity in BiH. Indeed, given the emphasis on Vrećo as an 'alien' who is exceptional and unique, there may be a sense that it is his sheer talent that gives him permission to subvert heteronormativity and gender binarism. It is not entirely clear how much this would translate into tolerance of gender non-conformity more broadly.

In Bosnia and Herzegovina, sevdah is often described as an affective and experiential realm of intense emotion: one *falls into* the state of sevdah, propelled by the music. The values and norms explored by Vrećo's music take place within this artistic zone, where they arguably have greater emotional valence. Investigations of affect in online interactions have explored the 'affective investments' that fans and audiences can experience in engaging with media (Barnes, 2013). The methodological toolkit offered by Chatterje-Doody and Crilley for considering the affective investments of online audiences through comments on images of war, is instructive in investigating the meanings created by audience reactions to media. They argue that 'online videos act as discursive nodes; points of reference for emotive engagement with the reported topic' and this emotive engagement has political and social significance and helps 'shape discourses, values and norms' (2019, p 169) about the topics at hand.

If the queer body can be 'object of affective transfer' (Liu, 2020) through which feelings of discomfort, belonging, fear, and shame are produced, the affective experiences of his audience can scarcely be divorced from Vrećo's dual-gendered, trans, queer body, voice, and aesthetic. The mystical and artistic elements picked up on by his fans seem inextricably tied to his gender fluidity, as do the ways in which Vrećo represents a futurity for the region as a whole ('it's as if he came from the distant future'). This future could be described as a time when gender fluidity and sexual difference is accepted and region is at peace. It is precisely through Vrećo's queer aesthetics that this promise for a future is articulated – as Muñoz wrote, the queer aesthetic 'frequently contains the blueprints and schemata of a forward-dawning futurity ... queer aesthetics map future social relations' (2009, p 1). This future is grounded in understandings of the past which focus on openness and unity.

Vrećo's music offers healing to a deeply traumatised country through an artistic realm that is inherently the domain of strong emotion, as well as a sense of national identity. Pride in Vrećo can be read as a sort of affective nationalism (Militz, 2019) for a united and inclusive BiH that contrasts sharply with the exclusive patriotisms of the country's ethnically defined constituents. In his videos, with his symbolism and tattoos[9] representing the diverse ethnoreligious history (and present) of the country (Vrećo, 2016), he performatively embodies the nation. A socially fractured and physically divided country is put back together through a queer body that straddles two genders at once; he at once embodies that mythologised, harmonious past, and a future in which difference is accepted. Like his gender identity, there is no transition – he embodies both 'before' and 'after', now.

If queer is what challenges normativity, essentialism, and the idea that identities are immobile in time and space, by queering sevdah, Vrećo queers the nation and offers an imaginary of BiH that is united, heterogeneous, and accepting of sexual difference and gender diversity. Simultaneously, by linking sevdah to queerness, Vrećo inscribes queerness with the local and national, challenging the common view that queerness itself is foreign to BiH. Perhaps his fans have an 'affective investment' precisely in this political and social futurity, which is enacted in his videos and songs. This promise may be far more meaningful than what is on offer from the mainstream political actors of the country, and it may be different from what is offered by EU accession and liberal LGBT policies. In some ways, this runs parallel to other political imaginaries in BiH which seek to recover the country's future from the loss of socialism and the arguable failure of the transition to capitalism, and challenge the nationalist hegemony of the present (Kurtović and Hromadžić, 2017).

Indeed, the fact that Vrećo eschews LGBT terminology for himself may make Bosnian audiences more comfortable with this gender non-conformity. With LGBT rights as a key part of the conditionality 'package' placed on BiH in its accession process to the EU (Slootmaeckers, 2019a), LGBT activism – and terminology – are sometimes seen as intrinsically 'foreign' to the country. This view is trumpeted by nationalist and conservative politicians who instrumentalise homophobia to champion their 'traditional' values in opposition to the West, and is held by a large part of the Bosnian population – almost half of respondents in one survey stated that LGBT issues overall were something imposed by the West (Gavrić, 2017). Given the mutually constitutive processes of nationalism and masculinity (Slootmaeckers, 2019b), it is no surprise that a masculine anxiety about blurred gender roles and same-sex desire is so intricately interwoven with a fear of incursion on national sovereignty by outside forces.

Indeed, norms about gender and sexuality in BiH have historically been shaped by encounters with hegemonic cultures, imperial actors, nationalist movements, and economic shifts. In particular, the position of BiH on the shifting periphery of Europe and under Ottoman and Austro-Hungarian rule has had a direct influence on ideas about gender and sexuality – and how they interact with questions of nationhood and modernity. A backlash to EU-backed LGBT rights has been seen in other Eastern European countries where politicians consider it 'a threat to the nation and local culture' (Slootmaeckers, 2019b, p 8). In some ways, queerphobic attitudes in BiH can at least partially be ascribed to this backlash to homonationalist discourses that pin LGBT-friendliness as a marker of modernity (Puar, 2007), as well as to conservative ethnonationalist views. In this context, Vrećo's silence on LGBT terminology may help him elide the sense of being 'yet another external imposition' (Selmić, 2016, p 225) as does his use of sevdah to explore what it means to be 'Bosnian' and articulate a sort of shared national identity.

Conclusion

Vrećo's pioneering sevdah can be situated in a broader trend of discovering 'the abundance of local traditions' (Nenić, 2015) and articulating a future that builds on emancipatory struggles of the past, including anti-fascism, socialism, and feminism. Alongside a new interest in archival work and revival of socialist organising forms (Kurtović and Hromadžić, 2017), sevdah has also been a tool in mining local cultural resources for emancipatory potential. For example, the Sarajevo Open Center, a feminist NGO that advocates for LGBT rights, launched two campaigns that used popular sevdah songs as slogans to combat homophobia and transphobia – '*Neka ljubi ko god koga hoće* [let anyone kiss whomever they want]' in 2013, from the popular song '*Snijeg pade na behar, na voće*', and '*Ah, što ćemo ljubav kriti* [Ah, why should we hide love]' in 2016. These uses playfully drew on local cultural traditions to articulate the tolerance embedded in these traditions, challenging the notion that Bosnian society is necessarily conservative. Indeed, 'Neka ljubi ko god koga hoće' is now something of an LGBT slogan. '*Snijeg pade ...*' was sung by musician Damir Imamović during BiH's first pride march, held in Sarajevo in September 2019,[10] with the sizeable crowd singing along to the chorus: let anyone kiss whomever they want. This was followed by an enthusiastic rendition of the anti-fascist anthem *Bella Ciao*.

The turn to the local in defining a new post-socialist politics comes on the heels of the failure of the post-Yugoslav 'transition' to capitalism to provide meaningful socio-economic change for BiH, the failure of the ethnically divided and politically captured state to articulate a common vision for a better future, and the inability of local and foreign institutional actors to draw on local progressivism to push for positive social changes (Kalezić and Brković, 2016). The failure of external actors has inspired calls for a 'local first strategy' which aims to focus on concrete needs of Bosnians while countering the 'dual hegemony' of the ruling ethnonationalist classes and the international liberal order (Puljek-Shank and Fritsch, 2019). Puljek-Shank and Fritsch deem this approach a 'third way' that allows activists to try to dismantle the 'co-dependent, uneasy stalemate' between local and international actors, which perpetuates the frozen conflict (2019). LGBT activist groups in BiH[11] are all too aware of this dual hegemony – caught, as Selmić (2016, pp 205–6) writes, 'in the fissure between the dysfunctional and ... impoverished state burdened by the legacy of ethnically motivated violence, on the one hand, and the Western European narratives of LGBT rights, liberation, and democracy, on the other'.

While many non-profits rely on international funding for their activities, many activists are aware that this fuels the perception that LGBT advocacy comes from the West, and that this funding does not always reflect the immediate needs of LGBT people (Selmić, 2016). LGBT activists tend to (though not uniformly) reject the aforementioned ethnonationalist order, and are more likely to 'position themselves away from nationalist discourses and argue that it is their right as citizens of the Bosnian state to be protected, not as members of one of the ethnic groups, or nations' (Cooper, 2014). This anti-nationalism can also be expressed through queer regional solidarity with other Yugoslav successor states, a legacy of feminist anti-war activism in the 1990s (Binnie, 2016; Bilić, 2020).

More recently, LGBT activism has recovered class as a poignant element of political struggle – as Selmić (2016) points out, this also has a practical advantage: LGBT activists acting in solidarity with other discriminated groups to address the most pressing societal issues upends the perception that LGBT rights are 'merely' a vehicle for EU norms. This was demonstrated strongly in BiH's first pride march in 2019, whose theme was 'general solidarity'. The event organisers spoke of the need to address the socio-economic situation in the country as a core element of LGBT rights more broadly (Povorka Ponosa, 2019), and signs at the march made a distinct link with local histories of anti-fascism, solidarity with refugees and migrants, feminism, worker's rights, and the rights of disabled people. These 'intersectional' positions reflect recent trends in Western LGBT activism (with many Western activists present in Sarajevo for the march) but 'translated' into more local understandings and histories of the struggle for justice.

Contemporary interpretations of sevdah are aligned with local queer activism in their attempts to elide both nationalist hegemonies and Western 'imposition' of values by redefining what is local and traditional. It seems that Vrećo's surprising popularity is at least partially due to his representation of the heterogeneous Bosnian past, as well as the fact that he explores gender fluidity and non-conformity through art rather than political activism. By taking up tradition in a fairly avant-garde musical project, Vrećo unhinges the teleology embedded in the idea that BiH must catch up to the inherently modern and sexually liberated West. In addition, by specifically engaging with religious themes, including Islam, he problematises the notion of 'queer secularity' in which queerness and Islam are positioned as incompatible, and where queer emancipation hinges on secularism (Khan, 2020). As seen from his fans' comments, appreciation for Vrećo's music is very much wrapped up in themes of the religious or transcendent, which is not uncommon given numerous global traditions where gender non-conforming people are considered 'divine' (Williams, 2010; Barry, 2016).

Queer, feminist, and post-colonial literature has questioned the civilisational discourses that have bound Western hegemony to the idea of progress. Rexhepi's (2016) critique of the homonationalism embedded in Europeanisation argues that positioning the EU as the 'container of progress and modernity to be aspired to by all' (p 33), queer people outside of Western Europe are cast as passive and in need of salvation. LGBT advocacy by the EU privileges Western forms of identity and models of coming out, which may prove counterproductive if the aim is social acceptance (Thiel, 2018). Instead, turns to local traditions such as sevdah can revive a form of cultural memory for tolerance and openness to difference with regards to sexual and gender norms, especially when they are treated as a form of social archive instead of a stable canon. This 'potentially reparative' turn towards the past (Rao, 2020, p 18) brings both queerness and tolerance of difference 'home', challenging the supposed imposition of such ideas by external forces as well the notion that LGBT rights can only be achieved through a liberal paradigm of progress. These projects do not merely romanticise the past but seek to create 'something new, remediated, capable of responding to the challenges of the present' (Kurtović, 2019, p 24), unearthing the political potential of what is 'already here' and what can be imagined for the future.

Notes

1 *Sevdah* is the word for the genre (or state), while *sevdalinka* is a single sevdah song. They date from the medieval era onward.

2 *Snijeg pade na behar na voće.*

3 *Vino piju age Sarajlije.*

4 Characterised by Omer Pobrić's Institute of Sevdah, founded in 2000.

5 One could describe Vrećo as bigender, which is a term for someone who has two genders and falls under the broader 'trans umbrella' – see Holleb (2019). Vrećo himself does not use this term, however.

6 Translation by the author.

7 This sample is not representative of the entire Bosnian population, of course, and it is not possible to know which country the comments come from. The majority of comments are in BCS and thus clearly stem from the post-Yugoslav region and/or diaspora.

8 All comments translated by the author.

9 Vrećo's numerous tattoos, arguably a central feature of his image, evoke a modern Bosnian mythos. His tattoos reflect the various religious and mythological beliefs that are all a part of Bosnian cultural heritage, such as traditional Catholic hand tattoos, ancient Slavic symbols, Jewish phylacteries and amulets, the hand of Fatima, and the 99 names of God in Islam.

10 The planning of the march is documented by the film *We Walk for Love, Baby*, produced by the Kriva collective, 2020.

11 Activist groups in the country include the Sarajevo Open Center (SOC), CURE foundation, Okvir Association, Queer Sport Sarajevo, Banja Luka Association of Queer Activists, Liberta Mo, Tuzla Open Center (TOC), and others.

References

Banović, D., Čaušević, J., Dekić, S., and Ryan F. (2015) *Život van zadatih normi: Transrodnost u Bosni i Hercegovini*. Sarajevo: Sarajevski otvoreni centar.

Barnes, R. (2013) Understanding the affective investment produced through commenting on Australian alternative journalism website New Matilda. *New Media & Society*, 17(5), 810–26.

Barry, A. (2016) Mortal to divine and back: India's transgender goddesses. *New York Times*. Retrieved 29 September 2021 from https://www.nyti mes.com/2016/07/25/world/asia/india-transgender.html

Bilić, B. (2020) *Trauma, violence, and lesbian agency in Croatia and Serbia: Building better times*. London: Palgrave Macmillan.

Binnie, J. (2016) Critical queer regionality and LGBTQ politics in Europe. *Gender, Place & Culture*, 23(11), 1631–42.

Božo Vrećo: Mržnja je jača od korone! (2020) *Story*. Retrieved 29 September 2021 from https://www.story.rs/celebrity-news/vesti/Božo-Vrećo-mrznja-je-jaca-od-korone/

Buturović, A. (2007) Love and/or death? Women and conflict resolution in the traditional Bosnian ballad. In A. Buturović and I.C. Schick (eds) *Women in the Ottoman Balkans: Gender, culture and history*. London, New York: I.B. Tauris.

CBC/Radio Canada (2019) Hundreds march against Bosnia-Herzegovina's 1st LGBTQ pride parade. *CBC News*. Retrieved 29 September 2021 from https://www.cbc.ca/news/world/bosnia-s-1st-lgbtq-pride-parade-1.5272937

Cerkez, A. (2015) Cross-dressing singer wins hearts in macho Bosnia. *CTV News*. Retrieved 29 September 2021 from https://www.ctvnews.ca/entertainment/cross-dressing-singer-wins-hearts-in-macho-bosnia-1.2320421

Chatterje-Doody, N.P. and Crilley, R. (2019) Making sense of emotions and affective investments in war: RT and the Syrian conflict on YouTube. *Media and Communication*, 7(3), 167–78.

Cooper, A. (2014) Living with Prajd: LGBTQ activism in Bosnia and Herzegovina. *Reviews & Critical Commentary CritCom, Council for European Studies*. Retrieved 29 September 2021 from http://critcom.councilforeuropeanstudies.org/living-with-prajd-lgbtq-activism-in-bosnia-and-herzegovina/

Čulić, I. (2019) Balkan music fights for LGBT rights: Forty years on the frontline. *Europa Vox*. Retrieved 29 September 2021 from https://www.europavox.com/news/balkan-music-fights-lgbt-right-40-years-frontline/

Đokić, D. (2017) BOŽO VREĆO Bezmjeran u svijetu mjera. *Gracija, 102*. Retrieved 29 September 2021 from https://gracija.me/Božo-bezmjeran-u-svijetu-mjera/

Dukić, P. (2015) Razumijevanje Sevdaha U Kontekstu Queer Romantike. *Ziher*. Retrieved 29 September 2021 from https://www.ziher.hr/razumijevanje-sevdaha-u-kontekstu-queer-romantike/?fbclid=IwAR2OTGKfq9HfPPQzW97PFclaeT-GLn9I5ui5BD7Mb2HmYfG5UOIElhQzPGw

Durić, R. (2018) The traditional Bosnian song Sevdalinka as an aesthetical, musical and philological phenomenon. *Spirit of Bosnia*, 13(1).

Gaillard, C. (2015) Fighting for visibility: A Bosnian coming out story. *LGBT.ba*. Retrieved 29 September 2021 from http://lgbt.ba/fighting-for-visibility-a-bosnian-coming-out-story/

Gander, K. (2014) Conchita Wurst's Eurovision 2014 win caused Balkan floods, says Serbian Church leader. *Independent*. Retrieved 29 September 2021 from https://www.independent.co.uk/arts-entertainment/music/news/god-punished-balkans-floods-conchita-wurst-s-eurovision-2014-win-says-serbian-church-leader-9419300.html

Gavrić, S. (2017) Bosnia and Herzegovina national LGBTI report. *UNDP.* Retrieved 29 September 2021 from https://www.ecoi.net/en/file/local/1421144/1226_1515406178_undp-rbec-blee-bosnia-and-herzegovina.pdf

Gvozdenović, N. (n.d.) Božo Vrećo: Sevdalinkama sam se otvorio jer bude u meni nemir i smiraj, kao kada se zaljubljuješ ... *Elle.* Retrieved 29 September 2021 from https://www.elle.rs/lifestyle/elle-licnosti/17258-bozo-vreco-sevdalinkama-sam-se-otvorio-jer-bude-u-meni-nemir-i-smiraj-kao-kada-se-zaljubljujes.html?p=1

Hajdarpašić, E. (2008) Out of the ruins of the Ottoman Empire: Reflections on the Ottoman legacy in south-eastern Europe. *Middle Eastern Studies, 44*(5), 715–34.

Hajdarpašić, E. (2015) *Whose Bosnia?: Nationalism and political imagination in the Balkans, 1840–1914.* Ithaca: Cornell University Press.

Holleb, M.L.E. (2019) *The A–Z of gender and sexuality.* London: Jessica Kingsley Publishers.

Janković, I. (2006) Geologija pesme. *Vreme, 831.* Retrieved 29 September 2021 from https://www.vreme.com/cms/view.php?id=473636

Kalezić, D. and Brković, Č. (2016) Queering as Europeanisation, Europeanisation as queering: Challenging homophobia in everyday life in Montenegro. In B. Bilić (ed) *LGBT activism and Europeanisation in the post-Yugoslav space: On the rainbow way to Europe* (pp 155–78). London: Palgrave Macmillan.

Kapetanović, M. (2014) A sto cemo ljubav kriti: Jugoslovensko muzicko naslijedje i postjugoslovenski kvir. In J. Blagojević and O. Dimitrijevic (eds) *Među nama.* Belgrade: Heartefact.

Khan, A. (2020) Queer secularity. *Lambda Nordica, 25,* 1.

Kozorog, M. and Bartulović, A. (2017) Sevdah celebrities narrate sevdalinka: Political (self-)contextualization of sevdalinka performers in Bosnia-Herzegovina. *Traditiones, 45,* 1.

Kožul, D. (2016) Damir Imamović: Sevdah je umjetnost slobode. *Novosti.* Retrieved 29 September 2021 from https://www.portalnovosti.com/damir-Imamović-sevdah-je-umjetnost-slobode

Kriva Collective. (2020) Dokumentarni film – Šetamo za ljubav, bebo/documentary film – We walk for love, baby. *YouTube.* Retrieved on 29 September 2021 from https://www.youtube.com/watch?v=t_cKY8zCS74

Kurtović, L. (2019) An archive to build a future: The recovery and rediscovery of the history of socialist associations in contemporary Bosnia-Herzegovina. *History and Anthropology, 30*(1), 20–46.

Kurtović, L. and Hromadžić, A. (2017) Cannibal states, empty bellies: Protest, history and political imagination in post-Dayton Bosnia. *Critique of Anthropology, 37*(3), 262–96.

Lakic, M. (2019) Reader comments: Fertile ground for hate speech in Bosnia. *Balkan Investigative Reporting Network/Balkan Insight.* Retrieved 29 September 2021 from https://balkaninsight.com/2019/01/29/reader-comments-fertile-ground-for-hate-speech-in-bosnia/

Liu, W. (2020) Feeling down, backward, and machinic: Queer theory and the affective turn. *Athenea Digital, 20*(2), 1–19.

Maljković, D. (2014) To Radi u Teoriji, Ali Ne u Praksi – Identitetski (LGBT) Aktivizam Protiv Kvir Aktivizma. In J. Blagojević and O. Dimitrijevic (eds) *Među nama.* Belgrade: Heartefact.

Militz, E. (2019) Towards affective nationalism. *Gender, Place & Culture, 26*(2), 296–300.

Milosevic, N. (2012) Stemmer for Serbian language. *GitHub.* Retrieved 29 September 2021 from https://github.com/nikolamilosevic86/Serbian Stemmer

Muñoz, J. (2009) *Cruising Utopia: The then and there of queer futurity.* New York: New York University Press.

Nenić, I. (2015) World music in the Balkans and the politics of (un)belonging. In I. Medić and K. Tomaš ević (eds) *Beyond the East–West divide: Balkan music and its poles of attraction.* Belgrade: Institute of Musicology.

Nowell, L., Norris, J.M., White, D.E., and Moules, N.J. (2017) Thematic analysis: Striving to meet the trustworthiness criteria. *International Journal of Qualitative Methods, 16*, 1.

Pennanen, R.P. (2008) Lost in scales: Balkan folk music research and the Ottoman legacy. *Muzikologija, 8*, 127–47.

Pennanen, R.P. (2010) Melancholic airs of the Orient: Bosnian sevdalinka music as an orientalist and national symbol. *Music and Emotions, 9*, 76–90. Helsinki: Helsinki Collegium for Advanced Studies.

Povorka Ponosa (2019) Solidarno za slobodu – slobodu okupljanja, slobodu identiteta i slobodu ljubavi!. *Povorka Ponosa.* Retrieved 29 September 2021 from https://povorkaponosa.ba/2019/09/07/solidarno-za-slobodu-slobodu-okupljanja-slobodu-identiteta-i-slobodu-ljubavi/

Puar, J. (2007) *Terrorist assemblages: Homonationalism in queer times.* Durham, London: Duke University Press.

Puljek-Shank, R. and Fritsch, F. (2019) Activism in Bosnia-Herzegovina: Struggles against dual hegemony and the emergence of 'local first'. *East European Politics and Societies and Cultures, 33*(1), 135–56.

Ramet, S.P. (2002) *Balkan babel: The disintegration of Yugoslavia from the death of Tito to the fall of Milošević.* Boulder, CO: Westview Press.

Rao, R. (2020) *Out of time: The queer politics of postcoloniality.* New York: Oxford University Press.

Rexhepi, P. (2016) From orientalism to homonationalism: Queer politics, Islamophobia and Europeanization in Kosovo. *Southeastern Europe, 40*, 32–53.

Rieder, B. (2019) YouTube Data Tools. Retrieved 29 September 2021 from https://tools.digitalmethods.net/netvizz/youtube/index.php

Sarajevo Open Center. (2017) Reakcija na mizogine, homofobne i transfobne stavove bh. izvođača sevdalinki Bože Vreće. *Sarajevo Open Center.* Retrieved 29 September 2021 from https://soc.ba/reakcija-na-mizogine-homofo bne-i-transfobne-stavove-bh-izvodaca-sevdalinki-boze-vrece/

Selmić, A. (2016) On the other side of an ethnocratic state? LGBT activism in post-Dayton Bosnia and Herzegovina. In B. Bilić (ed) *LGBT activism and Europeanisation in the post-Yugoslav space: On the rainbow way to Europe* (pp 205–30). London: Palgrave Macmillan.

Slootmaeckers, K. (2019a) Constructing European Union identity through LGBT equality promotion: Crises and shifting othering processes in the European Union enlargement. *Political Studies Review, 18,* 3, 346–61.

Slootmaeckers, K. (2019b) Nationalism as competing masculinities: Homophobia as a technology of othering for hetero- and homonationalism. *Theory and Society, 48,* 239–65.

Smajić, M. (2016) Božo Vrećo – virtuoz sevdaha koji širi ljubav i briše granice. *Deutsche Welle.* Retrieved 29 September 2021 from https://www.dw.com/bs/bo%C5%BEo-vre%C4%87o-virtuoz-sevdaha-koji-%C5%A1iri-ljubav-i-bri%C5%A1e-granice/a-19081065

Story (2020) Božo Vrećo: Mržnja je jača od korone! Retrieved 29 September 2021 from https://www.story.rs/celebrity-news/vesti/Božo-Vrećo-mrz nja-je-jaca-od-korone/

Telegraf (2015) Ovo je bosanska Končita! Retrieved 29 September 2021 from https://www.telegraf.rs/jetset/1415461-bosanska-koncita-nikadane-bih-promenio-pol-foto-video

Thiel, M. (2018) Introducing Queer Theory in international relations. *E-International Relations.* Retrieved 29 September 2021 from https://www.e-ir.info/2018/01/07/queer-theory-in-international-relations/

Vrećo, B. (2016) Moja nova tetovaža. *Facebook.* Retrieved 29 September 2021 from https://www.facebook.com/VrećoBožo/posts/1020915582 0039707:0

Wakefield, L. (2020) Bosnia takes first small step towards recognising same-sex relationships. *Pink News.* Retrieved 29 September 2021 from https://www.pinknews.co.uk/2020/04/15/bosnia-herzegovina-federation-same-sex-lgbt-couples-relationships-rights-sarajevo/

Williams, W.L. (2010) The 'two-spirit' people of indigenous North Americans. *The Guardian.* Retrieved 29 September 2021 from https://www.theguardian.com/music/2010/oct/11/two-spirit-people-north-america

Index

References to endnotes show both the page number and the note number (231n3).

A

activism 97–127
  art and 180–2
activist art 182
activist groups 222n11
activist organisations 35, 59, 74, 86, 87, 159, 163, 181, 188
activist work xii, xiii, 159, 183–5, 190, 191, 193
affective experiences 25–7, 214, 216, 218
affective investments 217, 218
Albanians 100, 101, 105–7, 110, 161
Alternative Montenegro 48–50, 54
American Psychological Association 86
Anglo-American bias 12
anti-academism 3
art xiii, 35, 180, 181, 190, 196–8, 203, 205
artistic practices 181, 182, 184, 196
artivism 180, 182, 183, 188, 191, 192, 193n1, 196
Ashkali 115, 127n15
Association Spektra 45, 185, 186, 188–90, 193

B

Balkans 6, 7, 44, 99, 162, 188, 210, 215, 216
banners 54, 103, 179, 180, 186–91
Belgrade 42, 43, 45, 49, 65, 66, 68, 101, 104, 156, 160, 189, 190
Beyond the Rainbow (film) 126n4
bigender 60
binary sexual difference 5
biological mistake 43
biotechnologies 30, 32
  unequal access to 30–3
Blagojević, M. 6
Body Confessions 206
Bojanić, Marko 41–4
  newspaper interview with 41–4
  pathologising compassion 41–4
Bosnia 208, 212, 215, 217
British feminism 1, 158, 159
brutal violence 29, 33

C

Center for Equality and Liberty (CEL) 101–3, 115, 120, 122

Center for Social and Group Development (CSGD) 102, 104, 118, 120
children ix, xi, xiii, 27, 50, 51, 108, 116, 137
cisgender men 35
cisgender women 32, 35
citizenship 23–37, 67
Civil Registration Agency (CRA) 123, 124
Civil Registry Office 31
Civil Rights Defenders 103
coloniality 10
communication 31, 33, 34, 71, 79, 182–4, 190, 192
community activities 102, 144, 185, 190
community building 139, 141, 142, 149, 151, 182, 184, 192
community media 136, 149
community members 182–4, 191
community-oriented goals 182
counterhegemonic process 5
Croatia 4, 9, 137, 138, 148, 179, 185, 189, 190, 192, 196
culture 1, 13, 54, 66, 101, 103, 109, 146, 150, xiv

D

dancers 101, 197, 200
De-Centring Western Sexualities (Kulpa and Mizielińska) 4
Detransition (Peters) 98
discipline 27–30
discrimination 24, 35, 36, 47, 48, 61, 62, 65–7, 69, 70, 122, 123, 157, 184
discriminatory attitudes 60
domestic violence 28
Draškić, Marija 14n6

E

economic hardship 43
emotions 121, 212, 215, 217
Enja 145
epistemological challenges 3
ethnic fragmentation 5
Eurocentrism 5
Europeanisation 49, 54, 221

F

Fanon, F. 7
fellow transgender activists 149
feminism 10, 12, 160, 163, 165, 219, 221

Filipčič, Pia 151n1
Foucault, M. 12, 41
Fraser, N. 53
freedom 26, 122, 188, 201, 204,
    209–12, 216
friendships 33–5, 42, 149, 150, 205

G

gay xi, xii, xiv, 98, 134–7, 141, 146,
    148–50
  movement 36, 137, 138
gender 5, 6, 26, 27, 45, 54, 59, 60, 62, 65,
    66, 73, 83, 100, 106, 136, 143, 158,
    170, 172
  administration 30–3
  bending 110
  change 63, 110
  confirmation process 33, 78, 124
  confirmation surgeries 32, 72, 105, 107,
    108, 111, 119, 172
  dichotomy xv, 8
  difference 12, 66
  diversity 4, 5, 9, 10, 84, 217, 218
  dysphoria 63, 81, 116
  equality 36, 123
  expression 31, 53, 65, 67, 110, 142, 212
  fluidity 215, 216, 218, 221
  hierarchies 157, 163
  identity 24, 29, 30, 35, 44, 60, 62–4, 69,
    72, 97, 114, 117, 123, 180, 212, 213
  ideology 137
  incongruence 62
  legal recognition of 65
  marker 97, 113, 122–4, 126n1
  non-normativity 13, xi, 13
  norms 27, 81, 82, 221
  police 27–30
  politics 5
  reaffirming treatments 50, 51
  stigma 69
  terminologies 2
  transnational cause of 3
gender-affirmative approach 68, 71
gender-affirming medical interventions 43
gender-affirming process 42
gender-affirming surgeries 42, 43, 63, 64,
    78, 81, 83, 84
gender binarism xiv, 59, 59–87, 217
  idea of 81, 83
gender binary categories 23
gender-changer 106
genderisation 54
gender-nonconformity 208, 216, 217, 219
  Bosnia and Herzegovina, traditional
    music 208–22
gender-reaffirming treatments 48, 52, 54
Gender Recognition Act 158
genealogical pairing 13
geopolitics 49

Germany 105, 112, 113, 116
Geten 65, 68, 70, 74, 86
global neoliberal capitalisms 6
Gramsci, A. 55
*Guidelines for Psychological Practice with
    Transgender and Gender Nonconforming
    People* 86

H

hate crimes 26
healthcare 42, 43, 48, 52, 54, 67, 70, 79,
    82, 84, 86, 119, 120
healthcare insurance law 48
health insurance 31, 32, 42, 45,
    48, 62
Health Insurance Fund 26, 32
Health Insurance Ordinance 65
Hill Collins, P. 150
historical narcissism 98
homonationalism 221
homosexuality xi, xii
hormonal therapy 63, 65, 107, 113, 114,
    119, 120
humanitarian actions 51
human rights 45, 49, 50, 53, 54, 101, 104,
    122, 124, 185, 188
hypertrophied patriarchal 'tradition' 2

I

imperial policies 158
inclusion strategies 179–93
Internal Macedonian Revolutionary
    Organization 37n1
intersectional standpoint 41, 47, 52,
    53, 55
intersectional trans activisms 35–7
intimacy 29
intractable oppression 138–40

K

knowledge 10–12, 34, 36, 37, 83, 86, 120,
    139, 141, 147, 150
  production 10, 11
Kosovar-German transgender 105
Kosovo 97–9, 101–5, 107, 115, 119, 121,
    122, 124, 125
  LGBTIQ+ movement 97–127
  tracing trans history in 97–127
Kosovo Family Law 123
Krasnić, Alexandra 104–14, 126n7

L

Law on Healthcare Insurance 48
Left Hand of Darkness (Le Guin) 87n2
legal gender recognition 60, 62, 63, 66,
    67, 71, 136, 142
Legebitra 135
legitimate gendered subject 133, 149
lesbian rights xii, 66

lesbians 34–6, 98, 101, 117, 136, 137, 141, 147, 150, 155, 158
Levizja 101
Lezbejska i gej solidarna mreža (LGSM) 155–6, 159, 169, 173n1
LGBT 4, 7, 33, 34, 40, 137, 138, 212, 214, 216, 220
  activisms 4
  community 34
LGBTI Equal Rights Association 3
LGBTIQ xii, 47, 49, 50, 71, 99–104, 115, 118, 119, 125
LGBTIQ+ xiii, 41, 49, 50, 53, 71, 98, 125
  activism 47
  movement 125
  rights 104, 115
LGBTI Support Center 35
LGBT movements
  tensions within 138–40
liberal standpoint 47
Lugones, M. 5, 139

M

marginalisation xi, 85, 139, 145, 169
Marks21 (M21) 156, 162, 171
marriage 123
  equality 137, 138
Masks 181
  in Croatia and Serbia 189–92
  in Montenegro 185–9
May, Theresa 158
media 83, 84, 138, 142, 180, 181, 183, 187–9, 191, 217, 218
medical transition 42, 67, 74, 136, 142
medical treatments 49–52, 74
mental health x, 28, 33, 59–89
mental health professionals 71, 85, 86
Metelkova 151n3
methodological considerations 27
Milošević, Slobodan 14n4
Mizielińska, J. 4
Montenegro 40–2, 44–5, 48, 51–3, 55, 184–90, 192
  Masks, performance 185–9
  solidarity in 40–56
Montenegro Pride 40
Morina, Sadri 104
Muñoz, E.J. 15n15, 138, 218

N

national identity 23
neocolonial peripheralisation 5
neoliberal capitalism 5, 11, 157
neoliberal transformation 51
networks
  of care 33–5
  of support 23–37

New York Daily News 98
non-binary persons 59–89
non-normative genders 3, 9, 172
North Macedonia
  LGBT activism 35
  transgender lives in 23–37

O

oppression x, xiii, 2, 139, 140, 142, 144, 145, 149, 156, 162, 163

P

pathologising compassion 41–6
(non)pathologising narratives 40–56
patriarchy 163–4
patriarco-neocolonial entanglements
  Yugoslav Marxist organising 159–62
performance art 196, 197, 199, 202–4
personal communication 76, 79, 81, 101, 102, 115, 118, 141–8, 164, 166–9
personal documentation 24, 31
physical violence 27–8, 65, 100
Plummer, K. 15n20
Podgorica 40, 42, 43, 45, 185, 186, 188, 189, 193
Polić, M. 14n9
police 30, 33, 69, 103
political action 181, 182, 196, 198, 199
political art 182, 196
(post)socialist gender troubles 155–74
post-war Kosovo
  transitioning in 114–20
post-Yugoslav trans worlds 1–15
  trans turn, challenges 4–7
power 25, 77, 81, 85, 139, 141–3, 145, 158, 159, 180, 181
praxis 12, 156, 157, 160, 161, 169–70, 172
Preciado, B.P. 26
Prenner, Ljuba 138
pride xiii, 40, 103, 104, 124, 139, 157, 165, 215, 218
Pride Parades 40, 50, 104
Prishtina 101–3, 115, 116, 118–20, 124
psychosocial support 71
public healthcare 48–53
  competition over moral deservingness 50–2
  healthcare insurance law 48
  intersectional standpoint 52–3
  misusing trans issues 50–2
  transphobic nationalism 48–50
public space 25–7, 29, 30, 67, 70, 179–81, 183, 184, 186, 187

Q

Queer Montenegro 41, 45
queerness 44, 99, 125, 126, 155, 209, 214–16, 218, 221

queers 8, ix, 8, 10, 209, 211, 212, 215,
  217, 218, 220, 221
  politics 149, 150
Quijano, A. 5, 15n11

R

race 5, 6, 41, 54, 114, 134, 144, 151, 159,
  161, 172
racial formations 48
reactionary anti-trans tsunami 2
real-life experience 61
recognition 11, 29, 41, 54, 142, 150
resilience
  of trans existence 40–56
resistance strategies 179–93
right trans person 144, 145
Rilindja 101, 104, 105, 108, 110–12, 114,
  125, 126n6

S

safe space 33, 75, 102, 135, 183, 185, 187,
  192, 203
self-fulfilling prophecies 29
self-help group 67, xiv, 67, 68, 74–83
  gender binarism 80–2
  information, support, and
    community 75–6
  medical/psychiatric system,
    navigating 76–80
self-support group 41, 44, 76, 184–6,
  190, 191
semi-structured interviews 140
Serbia 59–89, 171
  laws, health, and discrimination 62–5
  trans activism in 66–7
  transgender and gender non-binary
    (TGNB) persons in 62–5
Serbian leftist activism 155, 156
  transphobia in 155–74
Serbian trans community 179, 191
sevdah 208–13, 216, 217, 219, 221
  national tradition and zone of
    freedom 209–11
  queering 208–22
sevdalinkas 209
sex 27, 31, 32, 101, 103, 106–10, 158,
  165, 166, 209, 212
  change 48, 49, 52, 88n14, 108
  markers 31, 158
  work xi, xiii
  workers xiii, 27, 29, 36, 45
sexism 113, 138, 157, 163–4, 168
sexual diversity 3
sexuality 29
sexual liberation 10
Skopje Pride Weekend 23, 37n2
Sleep 206
Slovenia
  multi-ethnic character of 151

trans activism in 134
transgender movement in 133–51
Slovenian language 151n2
Slovenian transgender
  community 144
Slovenian transgender movement 133,
  134, 148, 151
Slovenian trans movement 134, 141, 149
  frictions 142–6
  locations 146–8
  motivations 141–2
social change 59, 181, 182
social history 209–11
socialisation 25–7
socialism 3, 6, 11
Socialist Federative Republic of Yugoslavia
  (SFRY) 51
socialist gender troubles 155, 157, 159,
  161, 163, 165, 167, 169, 171, 173
socialist modernity 8
social justice 12
social legitimisation 13
social media commenters 50, 51
social power 139, 143, 145, 146
Spektra 41, 44, 45, 53, 56n11, 186, 189
  founding of 44–8
Stryker, S. 8
Stubbs, P. 49
support groups 40, 76, 135, 147
survival 97–127
sworn virgins 44, 100, 125

T

TERFism 158, 163, 165–8
togetherness 2
tolerance 47, 217, 220, 221
tortuous paths 133–51
traditional gender roles 81, 171
trans, intersex, and gender-variant
  people (TIGV) 179, 181–5, 188,
  190, 192–3
trans activism 36–7, 40–1, 48, 59, 141,
  145, 149, 151, 184, 185, 190
  in Serbia 66–7
trans-affirming mental health services 82–7
Trans Aid 189
TransAkcija 135, 142–4, 147
trans artivism 179–93
Trans Balkan, 189
trans community xiv, 13, 142–4, 179, 180,
  186, 188–90
trans-exclusionary politics
  colonial dimensions of 157–9
transexclusionary radical feminists
  (TERFs) xv, 55, 158, 159, 165–7
  war 1
TransForma 27, 35, 36
trans futures 133–51
transgender activism 146

transgender activists 97, 136–8, 140, 141, 143, 147–50
transgender and gender non-binary (TGNB) persons 59–89
  clinical work with 71–4
  and mental health 60–2
  in Serbia 62–5
  trans-affirming mental health services 82–7
transgender clients 59, 61, 72
Transgender Day of Remembrance (TDOR) 45
Transgender Equality Network Ireland 61, 148
transgender health 82, 86
transgender identity xiii, 29, 33, 35, 72, 74, 80, 145
transgender movement 133–8, 140–3, 146, 148–51
  and people 134–8
  in Slovenia 133–51
transgender organisations 146–8
transgender persons 32, 35, 42, 44, 65, 101, 104, 105, 135, 185, 190
transgender rights 36, 124
transgender self-help group 59
transgender sex workers xiii, 33, 36
transgender women 27, 29, 36, 112, 135
transgender youth 61, 146
Transgressing Gender: Two is not Enough for Gender (E)quality (conference) 4
trans groups 35, 142
trans-hostile conservative feminism 3
trans hostility 1
trans identities xv, 6, 37, 114, 158, 212
transition 42, 99–101, 105, 110, 114–16, 119–22, 124, 212
  legal battle and public campaign 120–4
  process 33, 42, 77, 78
TransMisija 133, 135, 136, 138
transnational gender 10
transnational mobilisations 11
Trans Network Balkan 148, 189, 192, 196
transnormativity 135, 143, 144
Transovci (Transians) 41, 44, 45, 55n8
trans persons 33, 36, 43, 46, 51, 75, 79, 83, 114, 116, 144, 145, 162

transphobia 81, 82, 85, 113, 134, 136, 138, 155, 157, 165, 166, 168, 170, 179, 183, 184
transphobic nationalism 41, 45, 48–51
Transpozijum 148, 151n5
trans rights 34, 48–50, 115, 120, 124, 179
trans self-support group 179
Transserbia 87n7
transsexuality 111, 112
transsexuals 29, 43, 107, 111–13
trans support group 37, 71
trans woman x, 28, 29, 45, 81, 107, 135, 143
trans women 32, 36, 37, 45, 65, 68, 158, 159, 163, 167, 169
trans Yugoslavias 7–10

V
Valiavicharska, Z. 161
Velikonja, N. 139
Vijesti 41, 45–7
violence x, xi, xii, xiv, xv, 23, 23–37, 65, 67, 69, 145, 188
Vrećo, Božo
  affective experiences 216–17
  liveable futures, articulating 217–19
  metaphysical themes, out of time 214–15
  music videos, fan comments 213–14
  place and nation, out of place 215–16
  queer Bosnia 211–13
  queerness 216, 219–22

W
Western Balkans 7
women 27, 29, 30, 35–7, 81, 105–14, 156–8, 160–4, 171, 173, 212
workshops 147, 184, 185
World Health Organization 45
world-systems analysis 6
The Wretched of the Earth (Fanon) 7
wrong body 43

Z
Zagreb 4, 45, 66, 160, 189
Zain, Aleks
  interview with 196–207
Zulević, J. 64, 87n6